We were taken under fire by the NVA at precisely the moment I reported on the intercom that all six Marines were aboard for liftoff. The pilot lifted quickly and began backing the helicopter away from enemy fire, trying to turn to a new heading before he began his run toward safety. As we lifted, the rear rotor was thrust into the trees where it made tremendous whacking sounds. From the NVA we took hits somewhere in the body of the aircraft and somewhere in the radio system; the intercom went dead. The noises were incredible.

Our wounded helicopter began to shudder and shake violently. We hit hard. Immediately after impact—while the air was filled with loud sounds and lots of debris and dust flew everywhere—everyone in the back of the helicopter shared the same thought. . . .

FORCE RECON COMMAND

3d Force Recon Company in
Vietnam, 1969–70

Lt. Col. Alex Lee, USMC (Ret.)

IVY BOOKS • NEW YORK

Copyright © 1995 by Alex Lee

All rights reserved under International and Pan-American Copyright Conventions. Published in the United States by Ballantine Books, a division of Random House, Inc., New York, and distributed in Canada by Random House of Canada Limited, Toronto. Originally published by Naval Institute Press in 1995.

http://www.randomhouse.com

Library of Congress Catalog Card Number: 96-94466

ISBN 0-8041-1023-9

Manufactured in the United States of America

First Ballantine Books Edition: November 1996

10 9 8 7 6 5 4 3 2 1

This book is respectfully dedicated to the men of Third Force Reconnaissance Company, Fleet Marine Force, Pacific, who served in combat in the Republic of Vietnam during 1969 and 1970. These men served with honor, unreported to their countrymen. They did great things because they were willing to dare greatly. Their nation should be proud to have such sons.

Unquiet soul, why be aggrieved in private?
Our troops are dying out there where they fight.

Homer
The *Iliad*, VI

CONTENTS

COMMANDING GENERAL'S COMMENTS

The Third Force Reconnaissance Company had the unique mission of providing direct intelligence to the staff of the commanding general, III Marine Amphibious Force (MAF), and we considered it important that this collection effort not be sifted and studied en route. Let us not draw lines or build fences around the mission of gaining intelligence concerning the enemy. The leader on the battlefield needs to know the latest fragile intelligence upon which to make his decision, as the lives of his troops and the success of his mission depend upon it. The information must be as fresh as possible since conditions change quickly and action must be taken rapidly.

As commanding general, III MAF, in Vietnam, I had special trust and confidence in Alex Lee and sought his services to command the Third Force Reconnaissance Company. The men of the company operated under severe hardship and went into the utmost danger daily, risking their lives each time. These operations were costly in men and matériel, but the expense was more than offset by the timely and reliable intelligence Alex Lee and his warriors provided, and in the long run, lives were saved and battles were shortened. Vietnam is many years behind us, yet we should not forget that the man with the rifle must operate on timely intelligence. Computers and other instruments certainly have their place, but there are no substitutes for the eyeballs attached to the brain of the trained observer.

Long-range patrolling in our Corps had its origin years before Vietnam. Generals Jim Masters, Ray Davis, myself, and others produced and arranged funding for the equipment needed for this type of intelligence operation. To make a long story short, the training and outfitting of and the acceptance gained by these Marines with highly specialized skills culminated with the employment of Third Force Reconnaissance Company in this unique role.

As the commanding general, I used the Third Force Recon to gain the upper hand on the enemy and to verify any questionable intelligence. One example comes to mind. General Abrams, my boss, expressed concern that the North Vietnamese Army (NVA) had heavy artillery in the Ashau Valley, as evidenced by a then-recent intelligence photo showing several heavy artillery shell casings. If the NVA did have heavy artillery in the Ashau, something had to be done about it. I phoned Third Force Recon to check, since I was certain these casings had been left behind by our own 175mm artillery that had recently returned from that area. First Lt. Buck Coffman, boarding a light observation helicopter, flew to the area, quickly hopped out, and picked up several of the shell casings that had been in the photograph. Buck tells of this exploit in more picturesque language than I can use here.

Third Force Recon then presented me with those casings, which proved to be ours. I informed General Abrams. Case closed! This was typical action by a great team. Their intelligence inputs provided me with the firm ground upon which to make informed decisions.

Third Force Recon has written a superlative chapter into U.S. Marine Corps history. I salute the accomplishments of these dedicated and heroic Marines and corpsmen. I am proud to bear the title "Godfather of Long-Range Patrolling," along with others who can also claim the honor. We say that the Marine Corps needs a few good men. I can add only that the Marines got the best of the good ones with Alex Lee and his company. His book should be required reading for all true professionals.

Semper Fidelis
Lt. Gen. Herman Nickerson, Jr.
USMC (Ret.)

FOREWORD

In my view, you have to be a special person to be a Marine or a sailor that serves with us. This book tells the courageous story of a special breed of warriors: the dedicated Marines and sailors of the Third Force Reconnaissance Company who indeed "dared greatly" while serving in the Republic of Vietnam during the complex 1969–1970 era.

Our author, Lt. Col. Alex Lee, USMC (Ret.), is a brilliant and courageous warrior who served his nation and his Corps of Marines with great distinction in both peace and war. We are indeed blessed that he takes us from start to finish as he leads us through the enormous challenges his command overcame in developing a truly long-range penetration and deep reconnaissance capability under grueling combat conditions in the extreme northern provinces of South Vietnam. As their commander, A. Lee, as his warrior friends affectionately call him, was responsible for organizing, training, molding unit cohesion during a time of great uncertainty, and arranging for that special support required to conduct long-range penetration operations for reconnaissance and other special missions against a dangerous and determined enemy.

The rugged mountain terrain in the west and northwestern region of I Corps, with its double- and triple-covered jungle canopy, favored the enemy as it helped conceal supply bases and facilitated infiltration of NVA forces, including replacement troops. The weather, always unpredictable in the northwestern high country because of the violent Laotian monsoon storms—coupled with Vietnam rainy seasons—was at times horrendous and also favored the enemy. Operating at great distances from our forward combat and fire support bases and well beyond the protective firing fan of even long-range artillery, these special operation missions were generally not conducted in Vietnam prior to 1969.

A brief review of the overall situation leading into 1969, along with some background information, may be useful in understanding the events that A. Lee describes and in learning from these experiences.

U.S./Allied military strategy again began to shift its focus from large-unit operations against North Vietnamese and Vietcong main force units of battalion through division size to a more balanced approach. In this new approach, the pacification effort to protect villages, hamlets, and the population was greatly expanded concurrently with a continuation of the assault on main force units that supported guerrilla operations and threatened pacification and the security of the Vietnamese people. This approach had long been favored by senior Marine commanders and was welcomed by the CG III Marine Amphibious Force (CG III MAF), which was responsible for the defense of the First Corps Tactical Zone (ICTZ). It should be noted that the Republic of Vietnam was divided into four corps tactical zones. The ICTZ was the northernmost zone of more than ten thousand square miles and included, south to north, the provinces of Quang Ngai, Quang Tin, Quang Nam, Thua Thien, and Quang Tri, which bordered the Demilitarized Zone (DMZ) and Laos. The ICTZ was of utmost strategic importance as its defense was crucial to all of South Vietnam.

The enemy in the ICTZ was not simply guerrilla forces, although about twelve thousand Vietcong guerrillas were operating in the region along with about eleven thousand logistics and administrative troops. Rather, the enemy forces were North Vietnamese Army regulars: some forty-nine thousand of them backed up by six thousand main force Vietcong. In Northern I Corps, where the Third Force Reconnaissance Company operated and fought, the North Vietnamese were capable of launching heavy attacks against the U.S./Allied forces and threatened the civilian population.

The NVA forces enjoyed relative safety in their logistics base situated just north of the DMZ and in Laos, where they were afforded sanctuary for political reasons. It was from these sanctuaries that the NVA controlled and established the complex infiltration and logistics network in the terrain of the northwestern frontier leading into and overlooking the Ashau Valley.

The planned withdrawal of major U.S. combat forces from Vietnam included redeployment of the entire 3d Marine Division out of the ICTZ and created a serious gap in overall operational capability for CG III MAF. It set the stage for increased intelligence, surveillance, and reconnaissance requirements to include a new and independent role for the Third Force Reconnaissance Company.

The premature withdrawal of U.S. forces from Vietnam was already under way in 1969 when Lt. Gen. Herman Nickerson, Jr., was alerted to the fact that he would take command of the III MAF in March of that year. He knew the situation well, having served as both the commmanding general, 1st Marine Division and as the deputy commander, III MAF, during the 1966/67 time period. The withdrawal of the 3rd Marine Division from Vietnam, along with other combat and combat support capability, would be well under way by the summer. Facing a situation at the operational level of war wherein larger forces had only partially destroyed the NVA in the region, his command must now defend the ICTZ with fewer forces at his disposal.

General "Nick," or "Herman the German," as we affectionately called him, knew well the value of intelligence, and he was a staunch supporter of all efforts to improve Marine capabilities in that arena. He is truly one of the pioneers who brought us to the level we enjoy in today's Corps of Marines, and Alex Lee has captured the thoughts of many as he calls General Nickerson the "Godfather of Long-Range Patrolling." As he prepared to depart for Vietnam, the general wasted no time putting his concepts for better intelligence into action.

General Nick first summoned Major Lee from Quantico, asked him to go with him, take command of the Third Force Reconnaissance Company, and put them in the deep reconnaissance business! A few days later, we were called in by General Nick for our "mission-type orders." In essence, CG III MAF (designate) considered a dynamic, integrated intelligence/surveillance and reconnaissance capability throughout the ICTZ to be a vital part of any future force posture. He knew that there were a number of diverse and complex capabilities within the Marine, Army, and Free

World Military Assistance Forces operating in the ICTZ. With respect to ground reconnaissance, General Nick wanted First and Third Force to do deep operations, and he wanted it all to be wired together. "Make a plan for my approval in Vietnam, and then make it happen."

This mission was accomplished during the April–August 1969 time frame, and the Surveillance and Reconnaissance Center (SRC) became a reality. The SRC was implemented and led by a consummate professional, Lt. Col. Gerry Polakoff, a brilliant and innovative warrior. Gerry is gone now, but his significant contributions to our Corps live on.

Properly organized trained and equipped force reconnaissance units not only collect vital combat intelligence information on enemy capabilities, terrain obstacles, hydrographic data, and a host of other items that assist in "knowing the enemy," they also have a superb capability to conduct a wide variety of special operations, including amphibious and other limited-objective raids, tactical recovery of downed aircraft personnel, and other direct-action missions. Today, Marine Expeditionary Forces have fully integrated force reconnaissance units with other specialized capabilities inherent in Marine Air Ground Task Forces to make them special operations capable. Combined with naval amphibious capability to include U.S. Navy Special Warfare (SEAL) teams, we routinely deploy amphibious ready group/Marine expeditionary units (special operations capable) as part of naval doctrine. This was not the case in 1969, however, when very few senior commanders and staff officers had a full appreciation for deep reconnaissance or special mission activities.

Early on in our small Marine Warfighting Manual, which contains our philosophy, we talk about friction and the countless factors that make war or conflict a difficult enterprise. Often the friction is self-induced, and we see this lesson over and over as Major Lee and his people prepare to execute their assigned mission. Professional military people must strive to eliminate or at least minimize these frictions and, in any event, overcome them. A. Lee and company did just that! Today's Marine will see immediately how important it is to understand the commanders' intent.

This splendid book should be read by all military professionals for a better understanding of how difficult it is to do something new or different. Anyone who has pioneered new concepts will relate immediately to the author's frustrations. ·

For Marines, the book also contains excellent history on the development of force reconnaissance as we know it. Further, concepts such as Sting Ray and, even more important, Small Independent Action Forces (SIAF), have enormous potential today as we seek to influence larger areas of operations with smaller forces, capitalizing on the right technologies.

Finally, let me thank the author for the chance to provide a foreword for this inspiring book. Alex Lee, you have written accurate history with intellectual integrity and in language that warriors understand. Above all, you have kept faith with your splendid Marines and sailors of Third Force Recon. Their heroic deeds are now properly recorded for all who care about our nation's warriors. I have been privileged to serve with and know well many of the people discussed herein. I also got to see Third Force Recon in action. To all those splendid warriors—thanks for your professionalism. You helped make our Marine Special Operations Capable Forces a great weapon in the nation's arsenal. Take care of yourselves, take care of each other, God bless, and *Semper Fidelis*.

Gen. Alfred M. Gray
USMC (Ret.), 29th Commandant

ACKNOWLEDGMENTS

Great statesmen and victorious generals must find writing the books in which they set out the details of their wartime lives, decisions, and feelings an effort that is, perhaps, less difficult than I found in writing this book. When I finally set out to pen the story of a particularly challenging and painful year in my life, I found that getting it down on paper was not easy. Great and important men are allowed to paint word pictures in sweeping terms of strategy and national priority. Their very position in life permits them to use wide brushes to sketch big blue arrows across the maps depicting all the campaigns—military and political—that were waged. Yet, they rarely need deal with the names and faces of individuals who died executing their orders. Generals and politicians may care for those who do the actual fighting—some care to a degree that is far greater than seems possible—but the pain engendered by that caring is cushioned by layer upon layer of subordinate decision makers who are far from those who struggle through the jungle with living Marines, Marines who die when mistakes are made.

Writing about something you lived through, something as personal as combat, is hard work! But, so was living anywhere in the world as a Marine officer in 1969 and 1970. It is that particularly hard and demanding form of life that I try to describe in this book. The events that took place so long ago in a country whose importance many Americans have chosen to deny or to ignore or to simply forget were serious, life-and-death events for us, though they may not have been important in the greater scheme of world history. Some of those events were rewarding, some were bitterly painful, and still others were accompanied by humor that helped ease the stress of combat in the sad, dark days of 1969/70.

In sitting down to expend the emotional and physical effort needed to write this book about my experiences, I was acutely aware of the debt I owe to other people for their part in shaping those experiences. I cannot ignore their impact on the development of my views, opinions, attitudes, and knowledge.

The people I want to acknowledge here were not part of Third Force Reconnaissance company in the Republic of Vietnam; they will not otherwise appear in this book. They have, however, had a significant effect on me, one that cannot be ignored as I present the story of Third Force Reconnaissance Company to the reader. Some were part of my life before the events of 1969 and 1970; others came into my life during that time; and still others touched on, and altered forever, my later life—some long after the events I set forth here.

These people have had an important effect on how I have come to view my life and the profession of arms to which I dedicated so many years of service. Knowing these people caused me to review and revise my vision of myself and to constantly reexamine my concept of who and what I became as a Marine and as a man. From these people I also came to see it as my duty to tell the story of Third Force Reconnaissance Company. After all, as the commanding officer, it came to pass that my decisions, made daily, hourly, or minute-by-minute, altered the equations of fate for every man in the company as they lived out the days and nights of their combat tour of duty.

First, and before all others, I must credit my wife, Bronwyn. In her view it was essential that I make the effort to set down for posterity the story of what happened in Third Force Recon during my time as commanding officer and to explain as much of *why* it happened as I honestly could. She pressed me constantly, from shortly after our first meeting to the day I sat down and typed the first word into the computer, to commit the story to writing. She had never before known anyone who had fought in Vietnam, meeting Marines for the first time through me, and she often suggested to those she met that they assist her in urging me to write it down before my viewpoint on the events of that year was lost forever.

Second, I wish to acknowledge my mother, Isabel Chamberlain Lee, who instilled in me a love of words and a thirst for knowledge that remains unquenchable to this day. Curiosity developed in my soul as she read to me from the classics. She taught me to do my best at whatever I attempted, and when I chose to follow the soldier's trade, she understood that I would return either bearing my shield—or upon it. Her admonitions guided all I did as a Marine, in peacetime and in war.

The individuals mentioned next have all had an impact on who and what I have become over the past forty-two years since first I swore an oath to the United States of America. I include them to permit the reader to learn something about me and to pay homage to these men.

Staff Sgt. Armando C. Araque

The world's meanest drill instructor, Araque proved to me, many long years ago—long before the era of restraint against the laying on of hands—the true value of high-stress training. His lessons remain with me today. Araque hated what he called half-steppers—defined as whiners and any other type of weaklings. His leadership was so powerful that he was able to instill in me, while trying to break me into my component parts, the knowledge that there really are reasons why your heart should hurt and your eyes should tear when you hear "From the halls of Montezuma to the shores of Tripoli." He taught me the value of being a true believer in the philosophy that underlies being a Marine.

My staff platoon commander, The Basic School, Quantico, Virginia

In just a few short months, this officer was able to demonstrate by personal example every single known obnoxious trait that a senior can employ to totally alienate those who have the misfortune of being junior to him. He was petty, mean spirited, self-centered, subject to playing favorites, personally demeaning, snide, obsequious to seniors, and, worst of all, condescending in the most infuriating manner to anyone junior to him. We all learned from his negative leadership how not to deal with Marines placed in our charge. He accidentally taught more than forty angry lieutenants how to be better leaders, even though we did not appreciate the value of the lesson until we had acquired some additional experiences in the Corps with true leaders.

Staff Sgt. Pearly J. Pelletier

As platoon sergeant, Third Platoon, Company E, 2d Battalion, 4th Marines, Pelletier took the time to teach me how to be a real officer. He instilled in me an appreciation for the proper interaction between Marine officers and staff noncommissioned officers. Pelletier made it clear to me that effective leadership is personal in nature, requiring that the officer get out front, get involved, and get dirty as hell while leading from the front.

Capt. Sammy T. Adams

As company commander, Company H, 2d Battalion, 4th Marines, Captain Adams was the finest rifle company commander I ever saw in the flesh. He was inspirational, energetic, and so damn professional that everyone worked beyond capacity to do whatever he wanted done. His innate professional gift was that of total belief in the value of those who worked for him. He gave freedom of action to his officers and troops, demanding competent performance without oversupervision from above. Captain Sam once risked his career to ensure that I had the chance to run Company H during the most important field test of 1958. He did it to show me that he had confidence in his Marines. I took the lesson to heart.

Staff Sgt. Howard E. Wallace

Wallace was of the old school, using at all times, in all the years I knew him, such oblique terms of reference as, "If the lieutenant wishes," and "Begging the lieutenant's pardon." Yet, despite his gruff nature and his rigid adherence to Old Corps speech that emphasized rank barriers, Wallace was both a subordinate and a friend. He taught me that *no* real barriers exist between those of unequal rank if both parties are actually professionals dedicated to getting the job done. We shared peacetime service with the Seventh Marine Regiment in California and combat service with the regiment when it deployed to Vietnam.

PFC Gary A. Rood

As an infantryman in Company F, 2d Battalion, 7th Marines, Private First Class Rood demonstrated the amazingly heroic conduct that can be expected of young Marines under fire. In a bitter firefight—for our lives, as the North Vietnamese were positioned to kill most of us—Rood moved forward as casualties mounted in his machine-gun team: from ammunition carrier to assistant gunner to gunner. Out of ammunition and surrounded by his dead and wounded comrades, he leaped up and headed to the rear of the company to get some grenades. Returning quickly, Rood attacked and overwhelmed the enemy machine gunners, killing them all. With no more machine gunners to throw grenades at, he turned the Russian-made 12.7mm heavy machine gun around and used it to hose down the NVA riflemen. This forced them to pull back enough to permit us to evacuate wounded and reorganize the unit. Rood was unimpressed by what he had done, viewing it simply as his job.

Col. Edward Snelling

Tough as an elephant tusk, Colonel Snelling was one of the finest men I ever served. His concept of leadership was always mission-style orders and sufficient leeway to see the job through to the logical conclusion *without* interference from above. A proven hero from the Korean War, Colonel Snelling brought a dignity to his command that added immeasurably to my understanding of just how one should treat one's subordinates. He was also, at all times, a gentleman who carried his rank and responsibilities in a way that defined the word Marine.

Maj. Jean P. Cole

Major Cole, who served as an enlisted Marine in Korea, epitomized for me the concept of honorable service. Being older than most of the other majors because of his enlisted service, and lacking the pretty papers and schoolbook trappings of the boy wonders with whom he competed, Jean was often shunted aside and given less than desirable duty. He took no visible notice, performing any and all tasks with every bit of energy and competence that anyone could ask. In the 1970s, a time of rampant careerism and self-interest among many of those around us in the

Marine Corps, with future generals pushing and shoving for the limelight, Jean Cole stood out as an example of what it means to place the good of the Corps before personal goals or desires. It is the largely unsung men like Major Cole who take to heart and personally live by the concept of serving this great land with one's strength, one's effort, and, if need be, one's life.

The Good Marines

Thousands of good Marines touched my life and for that I am grateful. In peacetime or wartime, it is the good, dependable young men of the Corps who often go unnoticed and unrecognized. Yet, it is their honorable performance that makes serving—at any rank one happens to have attained—worth all of the time and all of the emotional capital that one must expend to do the job right. God bless the good Marines!

INTRODUCTION

During 1969 and 1970 I was in the middle of the wartime power structure; my rear-rank days were long past, and I was only part-way up the officer ladder. I was privileged to be placed in command of a small, specialized, and heavily committed unit in the I Corps area of the Republic of Vietnam. The Marines of Third Force Reconnaissance Company were the northernmost combat unit deployed against the North Vietnamese Army (NVA) by Lt. Gen. Herman Nickerson, Jr., the commanding general, III Marine Amphibious Force. General Nickerson was the commander of all Marine combat forces assigned to fight in Vietnam.

As General Nickerson's long-range reconnaissance asset, we carried out his policies and those of other general officers who held command authority at various higher levels in the convoluted power structure that controlled U.S. participation in the battle for Vietnam. By the nature of our location, we also carried out missions and policies that were mandated from far, far away by civilian political masters. As the commanding officer of Third Force Reconnaissance Company, it fell to me to make the everyday decisions and to issue the orders that caused individual Marines to take great risks in the execution of the desires of those generals and politicians.

I had no formula with which to write this book, and I could not escape the fact that throughout the period I describe, I was fully aware that the United States of America was quitting in Vietnam and that whatever we did in combat would be lost in the mists as the withdrawal plans were executed. Therefore, lacking an easy "war book" formula to write by, I endeavored to explain some of what took place during that year in the life of Third Force Reconnaissance Company. I have tried to illustrate the complexities faced by myself, the commander, and how those difficulties affected the lives of the Marines and the assigned Navy corpsmen who manned the company.

I have also tried to provide an overview and background explanations of some of the accomplishments of Third Force Reconnaissance Company. At the time we were fighting in the war it was often impossible to provide background reasons for all of the tasks that the Marines and corpsmen in that company were asked to do. Regardless, they willingly accepted the most dangerous and challenging missions. For a superb description of Third Force Reconnaissance operations at the team level by a man who was there, I urge the reader to pick up *Force Recon Diary, 1969* and *Force Recon Diary, 1970* by Maj. Bruce H. Norton, U.S. Marine Corps.

While I constantly speak of myself and describe events from my perspective, this book was not written to be about me, nor is it intended to be a compilation of my exploits. Everything favorable that happened in the company happened because the men of Third Force Recon were superior professional fighting men who overcame great difficulties and performed superbly—no matter what was asked of them, no matter the level of danger involved, no matter the utter lack of appreciation from their countrymen for their efforts. They were amazing.

As is the case with most authors, I do have some axes to grind, and I have taken the liberty of grinding them here. I grew bitter during the Vietnam War years as I saw those who used the war as a ticket-punching exercise prosper. There were even jokes at the time about the battalion commander's package: namely, a Silver Star, a Legion of Merit, a Purple Heart for a cut from a C-ration can, and a soft job in Da Nang for seven months of the twelve-month tour. Somehow the young men—most just eighteen or nineteen years old—who did the dying did not get mentioned when that joke was told. In fact, in some circles the troops who lived in the bush—dirty, bone weary, terrified, and hungry—were either ignored or openly disdained.

We all saw the waste in men, matériel, and energy, and we hated it because we wanted to win the fight and go home without sacrificing any more of those commodities. Somehow the provision of air conditioning, ice cream, and movies to the rear areas where the staffs, the sedan drivers, and the radio/TV folks lived never seemed important to Marines who spent their tour in the jungle doing their best to stay alive. The anger and the animosity expressed in this book really stem from my opinion that, by my rough estimate, only about 9 percent of those who went to Vietnam actually took an active part in the war. The rest may have worked hard, sweated, and worried, but they did not fight the NVA regulars or the Vietcong guerrillas, with their three levels of strength: local, provincial, and interprovincial (the toughest of them all).

In order to understand this book, the reader must understand, to a certain degree, just what a Marine force reconnaissance company is and what it is not. Throughout history, kings, khans, emperors, chieftains, generals, and other commanders have created special units to perform a wide variety of missions under their direct control. For example, around the close of the twelfth century, Genghis Khan created a unit called the Mangudai (those who did great things while daring greatly) to do his personal bidding. This unit may well be the true antecedent of the force reconnaissance companies that have become part of the Marine Corps structure. Led by a Mongol warrior known as Yessutai, the Mangudai horsemen traveled as far west as modern-day Hungary. They performed their fighting tasks in small units, against great odds, and often they died in the execution of the Khan's will. Contemporary force reconnaissance Marines who served in the war in Vietnam can relate to that.

But however much we might enjoy tracing a continuous lineage back to Genghis Khan's forces, the specific wellspring from which force reconnaissance came forth as a unit is found in World War II. In 1942 Maj. Gen. H. M. Smith sent for Sgt. Charles "Pat" Patrick and told him to create a really top-notch reconnaissance squad for a special mission. That squad was to be composed of eight Marines who would be tested and accepted by Sergeant Patrick after an arduous weeding-out process.

While the mission was later scrubbed—the unit was to have been integrated with an Army element for insertion by submarine into North Africa with Gen. Mark Clark—the unit lived on. Soon it was expanded to platoon strength, and by the end of the war it had further expanded to become a special battalion operating directly under the control of the commanding general, Fleet Marine Forces, Pacific. As an arm of the highest commander, it was based in Hawaii and made forays into all of the operational areas of the Pacific War.

Typical of special missions entrusted to this battalion was their assignment during the amphibious assault on Tinian in the Marianas. One company, commanded by then-First Lieutenant Patrick, swam at night across the Saipan-Tinian channel prior to D day, marked and cleared obstacles on the landing beaches for the assault waves, and swam to sea to board a destroyer that had been modified as a special assault transport. Once aboard, the company dressed and returned ashore, under the leadership of Lieutenant Patrick, to fight as infantry.

During the many battles in the Pacific, this Amphibious Reconnaissance Battalion reportedly conducted more than 180 separate pre-assault and post-assault reconnaissance operations. These efforts were both effective and useful, but the battalion's activities were kept secret for most of the war. In fact, the existence of this battalion was so well concealed that when they were awarded a Presidential Unit Citation, it had to be a classified document.

In addition to leading the way into the battles for Saipan and Tinian, Patrick, as a platoon leader—and later company commander—also made reconnaissance landings in such diverse places as the icy Aleutians and the bitterly contested fight for Iwo Jima. Patrick went on to serve with great distinction as a captain in Korea and during the peacetime years that followed.

After World War II the Marine Corps suffered the same manpower shortages that faced all of the services. Slogans like "Only one hundred thousand may serve," rang hollow, as the Corps muster roles showed less than seventy-seven thousand on active duty. In the post-war reduction in force, the specialized elements were the first ones cut, and the Amphibious Reconnaissance Battalion disappeared from the Corps. It is logical to assume that higher commanders of the time were aware of the need for such units, but they just could not afford to field them.

By 1950 every aspect of the Marine Corps worked shorthanded—all of the time. In fact, it is well documented that the Marine brigade that entered the Korean War in August 1950 was far short of the manpower mandated by the formal Tables of

Organization. The early days of the war saw the Fifth Marine Regiment operating with one "phantom" rifle company of zero strength in each of its infantry battalions, giving them, roughly, a 30 percent shortfall in combat power. That meant that the regiment was sent to fight a war lacking about 660 frontline Marines.

Fortunately for the Marine generals fighting in Korea, a small reconnaissance capability had been retained at the division level. This unit, a company in strength, was able to provide the senior Marine commander an entity that was responsive to his needs for information gathering and various other missions. A famous *Life* magazine cover from 1950 shows two members of that unit, Capt. Kenneth J. Houghton and Gunnery Sgt. Ernest DeFazio, after they had been in a firefight at the conclusion of an intelligence-gathering mission on the enemy-held bank of the Han River. Houghton, later promoted to major general, and DeFazio, eventually a colonel, were both important in gathering support for development of a force reconnaissance capability for use by commanders above the division level in the Marine Corps.

After 1953 the Marine Corps returned to a peacetime footing, and the need for specialized units was put on the back burner. Some platoon-size (that is, roughly thirty-five men) elements were created and fielded at both the Atlantic and Pacific Fleet Marine Force levels. A test unit was established to evaluate doctrine, tactics, techniques, and equipment. Many capable Marines served with honor in the Fleet Marine Force platoons and the test unit, adding their views and opinions to the body of thought that related to these specialized types of operational units. The proposed organization became a reality in August 1957 when First Force Reconnaissance Company was activated under the command of Maj. Bruce Meyers. That unit—together with Second Force Reconnaissance Company, created two years later and commanded by Maj. Joe Taylor—continued to test and evaluate organizational and operational concepts.

But it takes power to move ideas, and power equals rank. The working Marines were too far down the chain to move all the mountains that would have to be moved. The Marine Corps, like most bureaucratic organizations, did not react energetically to ideas that came up from those with more enthusiasm than rank.

What was really needed was a champion, a driving force who would bring to bear enough energy, in the form of rank and position, to force the issue to final decision. Such a man was already in place in the Washington headquarters of the Corps. That champion was then-Colonel Nickerson, who worked both overtly and behind the scenes to see that a force reconnaissance capability came to pass. By 1959 Nickerson was a brigadier general, responsible to the commandant for the fiscal policy of the Marine Corps. He was in the right place at the right time. Nickerson and a few other forward-thinking officers, some of whom—like Nickerson and James Masters—were the great, heroic figures of the time, found ways to obtain the needed funding within austere budgets. (Solving the financial puzzle and securing the necessary manpower, equipment, and support for the new companies earned Nickerson the nickname "Godfather of Long-Range Patrolling.")

To stimulate discussion General Nickerson published an article in the Marine Corps Gazette that set forth his recommendations for the organization and operational employment of a force reconnaissance company for both pre-assault and long-range post-assault reconnaissance. This company could operate independently, if necessary, and would be the eyes and ears of the amphibious force commander, responding to his desires and freeing the reconnaissance elements of division subordinate units from force-level requirements. For the very first time since World War II, the force commanders would have units that were clearly theirs to employ as they deemed necessary for the efficient collection of ground intelligence data.

The idea was strongly opposed by large segments of the Marine Corps, but the resolute General Nickerson pressed on, and the appropriate staffing decisions were finally reached in the Washington headquarters. The units were no longer held to be provisional in nature; they were established formally as components of the Marine Corps structure. Operational concepts were prepared substantially in the manner that General Nickerson had envisioned them, Tables of Equipment were written, and Tables of Organization were rewritten and published. Force reconnaissance was more than an idea; it was now a reality.

Early Developments

While the concept for the force reconnaissance companies was still under development in the 1960s, a conflict between disparate factions within the reconnaissance community arose, and it has not been healed to this day. On one side are those who hold the view that force teams must avoid all contact with enemy forces, no matter what the situation. "Data collection only!" is their cry. They tolerate no kind of offensive or aggressive combat effort of any kind during reconnaissance operations. Their motto is "Survival by avoidance."

In 1965 one adherent of this data-collection-only faction taught his Marines "Quail Tactics," a dubious maneuver in which the four-man teams were to scatter if fired upon (like quail bounced from their bush by a hunting dog) and to reassemble at a rally point. Obviously, the Marines who practiced acting like quail would very likely be destroyed, one at a time. Tactics like this are an invitation to disaster, and they are contrary to the philosophy of caring for our brother-Marines that I thought we all learned early in our service to the Corps.

The other faction, which had a number of powerful supporters within the Marine Corps during the early 1960s, proposed strongly that the newly created force reconnaissance companies should become some sort of supercommandos. They saw the companies ranging far and wide in the enemy rear areas, blowing up bridges and shooting up trains in a manner reminiscent of the movies made about the resistance forces who operated in occupied France during World War II.

Neither side of this argument became a clear winner, but at the time the First Force Reconnaissance Company was initially committed to the war in Vietnam, the data-collection-only faction was well ahead on points, having produced the four-man team as the Table of Organization and specified in the Table of Equipment that the company was to have no individual weapons more powerful than the sub-machine gun.

During the course of the war in the Republic of Vietnam, enormous energy was expended to improve the force reconnaissance doctrine, tactics, techniques, and equipment. Marines from the Landing Force Development Center at Quantico, Virginia, studied the special-mission elements of other nations and sought ways to improve the effectiveness of force reconnaissance teams. Civilian and military research and development entities were urged to find innovative solutions to reconnaissance problems. Equipment was tested, tested, tested, and retested—to destruction.

For nearly three years I had the good fortune of being the reconnaissance officer in the Ground Combat Division of that Landing Force Development Center, overseeing all of that effort. It was directly from that duty that I returned to the war in Vietnam to command Third Force Reconnaissance Company. It had also been my good fortune to bring to that duty in Quantico operational combat experience as a commanding officer of two different rifle companies in infantry combat in Vietnam and more than four years of special operations experience with an operational organization outside the Marine Corps.

The unit that I had been loaned to was rather unusual in that it was a multidisciplinary, multiservice group that worked directly for the highest echelon of our government. A couple of our members had engineering backgrounds, one was an expert in detonation physics, another a chemical engineer, two or three were operations analysts, and some were operational field types, like myself. Known as Weapons Planning Group, Code 121, it is best described as a combined operational analysis team and operational force that could respond either as a think tank or as a small, immediately deployable operational unit. At all times, some of us were ready for instant departure at the whim of the president or one of his minions to some out-of-the-way portion of the globe.

In the Landing Force Development Center it was clearly understood that new technology must be harnessed to make the reconnaissance teams more effective, either at data collection or the application of combat power or, with luck, both. Additionally, it was clear that these force-level units needed to be part of a full-blown control system that integrated *all* intelligence information. Once the work of collecting data is done, someone must have the ability to make sense of it *all*. Key to this was the creation of the Surveillance/Reconnaissance Center by then-Lt. Col. Alfred M. Gray and Lt. Col. Gerry H. Polakoff.

This organization, known in military shorthand as the SRC, would consolidate and organize the entire intelligence effort for the amphibious force commander. This would allow the force commander to employ all of "his" reconnaissance and other intelligence-collection assets effectively. The SRC would work directly for the commanding general and would assign tasks to any and all intelligence-gathering units available in the operational theater. For the first time there would be a single entity that would coordinate ground reconnaissance, aerial reconnaissance, photography, electronic warfare (including radio interception), agents, and the intelligence-collection efforts of frontline units. Not only would the SRC make data collection assignments, it would also be the controlling site for all forms of compilation and analysis of information received, as well as the central source providing intelligence information to the commanding general and all of his subordinate commanders.

The SRC was a ground commander's rudimentary version of the Tactical Warfare Center concept used by the U.S. Navy to amass in one place on the flagship—for the use of decision makers—all of the needed information. Obviously, Colonel Polakoff's SRC was the distant antecedent of the control center of the Surveillance, Reconnaissance, Intelligence Group (SRIG) found in the Marine Corps, as it was reorganized in the 1980s prior to the deployment of Marine combat forces to the Gulf War. (As a minor aside, let me note that it was a force reconnaissance team from Second Force Reconnaissance Company, operating under control of the SRIG, that recaptured the U.S. Embassy during the retaking of Kuwait City.)

Combat-Driven Developments

As the war in Vietnam progressed, it became obvious that some form of the commando idea for force reconnaissance companies had merit. Because of improved technology, however, a middle ground between the two competitive factions opened up. Development of laser range finders, offset bombing beacons, and other sophisticated matériel items made it clear that it was both possible and imperative that force reconnaissance teams be ordered to take an active role in the delivery of firepower against the enemy. A philosophy known by the code name Sting Ray was developed to take advantage of the fact that a force reconnaissance team, with the right equipment, training, and direction, could inflict far more damage and pain upon the enemy than would be expected from so small a unit.

For example, tests of the laser ranger finders proved that a Marine on an observation post could call artillery on an enemy unit without the need for ranging rounds to get the guns on target. Laser accuracy, being measured in tenths of a meter, would combine with artillery computers to ensure that the initial rounds would be on target. Hence, an utterly surprised enemy would be subjected to "fire for effect" without warning. Similar increases in accuracy of firepower delivery would be possible, with smart bombs being guided precisely to the target by reconnaissance Marines using laser illuminators.

All in all, Sting Ray made sense because it employed the skills of reconnaissance teams who were already operating in the enemy's backyard to inflict casualties on that enemy, whenever and wherever he was encountered. Bits and pieces of this concept were already in use by the units operating in the Republic of Vietnam, and it worked. The doctrine and other formal expositions of official policy, however, lagged far behind both developing concepts and real world events.

Meanwhile, the rest of the military establishment was also pressing for improvement of the capabilities of small units. Each service had broken into the elite-unit game during the time of President John Kennedy, who had loudly proclaimed his enthusiasm for the U.S. Army Special Forces. Starting in 1961/62, the Navy expanded the mission of the Underwater Demolitions Teams (UDT) and created new units known as Sea-Air-Land teams, or SEALs. Because the mission of the SEALs included combat operations above the high-water mark (the traditional demarcation between UDT's responsibility and that of the Marines of the landing force), many Marines felt that the Navy's SEALs were a bad idea.

Regardless, there was no opportunity to quibble because everyone was going to be involved in the political, high-visibility special warfare game. Doing their best to keep up, the Air Force entered this field of endeavor with its Air Commandos. They too wanted a piece of the action. By 1965, in the civilian world of think tanks and operational analysis, probably five hundred studies of special warfare tactics, techniques, and equipment were going on at the behest of the various services. Not to be left behind, the Department of Defense's Advanced Research Projects Agency began an analysis effort known as the Small Independent Action Force study, or SIAF.

Everyone was getting involved with activities that were seen by Marines to be force reconnaissance–type missions, yet it was obvious at the time that the other services were getting more money, more matériel, and more command emphasis on special operations than was the Marine Corps. It was a most challenging and frustrating period, and I found myself in the middle of it all.

Overview

Throughout the 1960s one key facet of the formally established force reconnaissance doctrine that did not change was assigning the units the specific task of serving the needs of the force commander. The primary mission remained one of providing pre-assault and long-range post-assault reconnaissance operations in support of the landing force. While the precise definition of what constituted a long-range post-assault mission was never clearly established, this phrasing provided virtually unlimited flexibility in mission assignments. In training exercises the force reconnaissance company would begin operations ashore in the objective area three to five days before the landing, and after the forces came ashore they would be given missions requiring surveillance outside the force beachhead line of road networks and other routes over which the enemy might reinforce his units in the beachhead area.

Fortunately, none of the arguments between the warring reconnaissance factions centered around taking the force-level units away from the overall amphibious force commander. What did happen in practice, though, was a steady blurring of the roles and missions between the force reconnaissance companies and the reconnaissance battalions of the Marine divisions. In theory, the division unit was supposed to be involved in reconnaissance work within the area assigned to the division commander—that is, within his artillery fan, which was considered the outside limit of his ability to influence the action. It supposedly fell to the force reconnaissance elements to protect the entire objective area, hence the vague use of the term long-range post-assault missions.

In fact, by 1969—the fourth year of the war—there was little or no evident difference in the assigned missions of the force companies and the division reconnaissance battalions. The force reconnaissance companies never became commando elements, nor were they ever forced to be absolutely nothing but noncombative data-collection agencies.

What happened, though, in response to General Nickerson's instruction, was that one of the units—Third Force Reconnaissance Company—was directed to actually separate from attachment to the Third Division and to begin operating independently in the manner it had been designed to do. Independent operations would require direct submission to the commanding general all of the information that was collected. Independent operations would include establishment of separate camps, mess halls, repair facilities, ammunition storage sites, landing pads, truck parks, etc., etc.

While the documents that created the force recon companies provided the men and equipment to do these things, they had never been tried in combat before. The company was to do so as the direct reconnaissance arm of the commanding general, III Marine Amphibious Force, not a lower-level commander or intermediate staff section. It is the story of that time—filled with so many trials and tribulations—that makes up the bulk of this book.

This story is worth telling because it illustrates important truths about the war in Southeast Asia that were never allowed to reach the great mass of the American public. Literally hundreds of effective and skillful American fighting units participated in that war, and thousands upon thousands of hardworking, decent, responsible, and militarily competent young men served in those units. In 1969/70 those two facts were carefully hidden from most of the people who should have learned about it when it was taking place. Instead, the men who fought the war were pilloried, personally, by a nation that had had a steady diet of bad information foisted upon it. Military men were depicted as fools, boobs, sadists, drug-maddened monsters, and victims of some great plot. The absolute nonsense presented to the American people completely overshadowed any notice of the hard and dangerous work performed by decent men doing the very best that they could under the circumstances that prevailed.

Sadly since the war, revisionist history has come to be the standard of the nation, and the truths I deem to be important about the units that performed well, and the men who fought and died in Vietnam, have been buried by polemics and outright, intentional politically correct distortions—read lies—to a degree that should disgust anyone capable of independent thought.

In presenting to the reader the story of the men of Third Force Reconnaissance Company, two quotations from the past come to my mind. The first was made about the Marines who fought and died on Iwo Jima during World War II, and I am not ashamed to reapply it to the men of Third Force. The words are engraved deeply into the dark stone of the Marine Memorial in Washington, D.C., where they can be read by every Marine as he or she makes the pilgrimage to pay respect to those who have gone before. "Uncommon valor was a common virtue."

The second quotation is contained in a history book, written by Richard S. Collum and published in 1890, entitled *The History of the United States Marine Corps*. The dedication Mr. Collum chose 105 years ago was: "To the citizens of the United States, this work is respectfully dedicated; with a desire that the services of the United States Marine Corps may be intelligently appreciated, and that the nation may recognize the debt that it owes to the Officers and Enlisted Men, who in all the trying times in our country's history have nobly done their duty."

It is my hope that whoever reads *Force Recon Command* will understand fully just how proud they should be of the men who served in Third Force Reconnaissance Company, men who daily faced death while the war in the dying Republic of Vietnam wound down around them. They too were Marines who *nobly* did their duty.

Lt. Col. Alex Lee
USMC (Ret.)

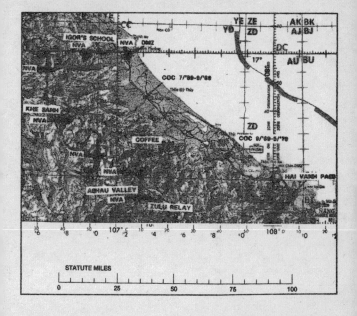

Area of Operations—Northern I Corps—
Assigned to Third Force Reconnaissance Company

Third Force Reconnaissance Company conducted reconnaissance and surveillance missions throughout Northern I Corps, from the Hai Vanh Pass to the DMZ. Occasionally, operations would occur outside the area designated on the map.

In 1969 the emphasis was to the north, with operations along the DMZ, and to the west, along the Laotian border. After the departure of the 3d Marine Division, Third Force Reconnaissance Company moved to Phu Bai and expanded its operations. Missions took place, for the most part, within the borders of the Republic of Vietnam, north of the Hai Vanh Pass, and south of the 17th parallel, which demarcated the boundary between the two Vietnams.

1

THE SUMMONS

Janice Williams, the youngest, brightest, and hardest-working secretary in our office, was calling me over the loudspeaker. "Major Lee! Mrs. Brown is on line three. She says it's very, very important." That cryptic sentence, and the phone call that followed, altered the course of my military career, my personal life, and my view of my personal worth as a man and as a Marine. It also changed the lives of many who were drawn into the chain of events it foreshadowed. The call was important because Mrs. Brown was General Nickerson's secretary at Marine Corps headquarters, and anything the general might have to say to me would surely matter greatly.

"Herman the German" was beloved by those who performed honorably and professionally, feared by petty-minded half-steppers and tea-sippers who were unable to meet his standards. He was a hard, yet fair, officer who clearly had the power to influence our lives. No thinking Marine would ignore anything that he might say.

Arrival at a point in my life where General Nickerson might call me was the result of a convoluted set of circumstances. Planning never entered into it. Assignment in early 1960 to a dismal tour as guard officer in the California desert at a Marine barracks placed me in close proximity to some of the best scientific minds ever assembled to address military problems. The Marines in that barracks provided security at the U.S. Naval Ordnance Test Station, China Lake, where the Navy undertook to meld science with operational know-how. When I agreed one day to a request that I look at some scientific ideas and comment on them from an operational viewpoint, a surprising thing happened. I was stolen from the daily grind of guard duty and assigned to a top-secret organization with a most enigmatic name—Weapons Planning Group, Code 121.

This interesting assignment would never have been possible if both of the officers senior to me in the Marine barracks had not been Marine tankers instead of infantrymen. I was an infantry officer, and the brains behind Weapons Planning Group needed a mud Marine, someone they could send out in the dark and the rain, into someone else's country, to find out the answer to questions posed by the big bosses above them. They opened technology's door to me, asked that I do some analytical work, and carefully examined my responses. Shortly after that, I was dropped from the muster roll at the Marine barracks, and my records for the next few years did not, in any way, accurately reflect either my whereabouts or my activities.

In 1965, after four years of seeing things from the supposed big picture level, I was fortunate enough to return to the Marine Corps to an operational Fleet Marine Force assignment in the 7th Marine Regiment. Assigned to duty in the 2d Battalion of the regiment, known as 2/7 in the shorthand of the day, I found myself taking part in a full-scale pre-deployment workup for movement of the battalion to duty in Okinawa as part of the unit-for-unit exchange known in the early 1960s as transplacement. The workup at Camp Pendleton included long days in the field and long hours on the weapons ranges. All of the training served to resharpen my infantry skills in the world of regular forces.

In the spring of 1965, 2/7 took part in a huge amphibious operation, and the rumors flew through the command that we would not land at Camp Pendleton but would steam west, instead, to Vietnam. We did not take part in a surprise deployment then, but the exercise was followed by the not-unexpected deployment, in May, of our Regimental Landing Team, RLT-7, to the Republic of Vietnam. RLT-7 sailed from San Diego with 8,008 Marines and attached naval personnel. For many standing at the rails of the gray amphibious transport ships it was their last look at the United States forever.

I learned how to be an effective combat commander from Lt. Col. Leon Utter, who led 2/7 through the long months of combat with great dignity and a devotion to teaching his subordinates everything he had learned in thirty years of service. Successful service in combat with Utter's battalion added greatly to my already strong sense of self-confidence. The only drawback was that, in the view of many, my confidence level and my naturally aggressive nature made me a rather difficult person to deal with.

As an infantry officer, known in Marine Corps parlance as an 03, command of a rifle company, which consists of six officers and about two hundred fighting men, is a highly valued assignment. I commanded Company E—one of the four letter-designated rifle companies in infantry battalion 2/7—during combat operations for part of 1965 and took command of Company F in March 1966 during a major engagement with the NVA.

Combat command at the company level was an extremely rare opportunity for my particular age group, as we were very senior captains in 1965, and few from my year group got a combat assignment in Vietnam until after they had been promoted to major in the fall of 1966. I had, by good fortune and the blind chance of timing, been able to serve in those two combat commands, with a short interval as a battalion operations officer in the middle of my tour. This provided me with a great deal more hands-on experience and was a surefire winner when it came to bragging rights at the club bar. (My contemporaries from our year group were, in 1966, of similar age and experience but they reached the promotion zone for major before being sent to the war and served their tours in the Republic of Vietnam, in the main, as staff officers.)

Getting to be the recon guy at the Landing Force Development Center, beginning in August 1966, was not easy. I was not specially selected, nor did my orders to the Quantico complex tab me for anything in particular. I was simply to report for duty. Receiving those orders was a great disappointment, one that dashed hope of an assignment to what we called in the 1960s Junior School, a course for the professional education of captains and majors. Since school was not in my future, I was expecting the worst. It came to pass immediately.

Taking my records and orders in to the headquarters building two days early, I spoke with the adjutant, Maj. Gene Bratt, an outstanding officer I had known in Hawaii in 1957/58 while I served in the 2d Battalion of the 4th Marine Regiment, which was, prior to the Vietnam War, the ground element of the 1st Marine

Brigade. Major Bratt had extremely bad news for me. He examined his desk and avoided making eye contact as he said, "A. Lee, you won't like your assignment, but you are the first 03 captain to come in without a tag on him and I have been ordered to take the first 03 I can find and assign him as commanding officer, Casual Company."

While the words *commanding officer* sound acceptable to the uninitiated, any professional knows that a casual company is a dumping ground, serving mainly as a holding tank for those who are heading out of the Marine Corps—either by their own choice or as the result of courts-martial. Appealing to Major Bratt on the basis of effective personnel assignment, I pressed my luck and quite forcefully pointed out that I had recently—it had been only twenty-six days since I was last under fire—had combat experience. I suggested an assignment to The Basic School, where second lieutenants are prepared for duty in the Fleet Marine Force.

Major Bratt laughed and told me that I was "too senior," and that a number of officers from my year group, albeit none who had been to Vietnam, were already teaching at that school. The crowning blow was leveled on me when the major admitted that the next job open was athletic officer for the base. Not being in any mood either to counsel short-timers leaving the Corps or count jocks in the gymnasium, I took my papers and orders and left Major Bratt's office. I decided to use up the last two days of my leave seeking employment.

Quantico is a huge facility that offers many challenging assignments for officers of any rank. What I needed was a real job for a brand-new major, which the promotion board said I was going to be in a matter of three or four weeks. Behind me I had four years of classified work, much of it devoted to the application of modern technology to military requirements, so I felt qualified to hunt for a home in the Landing Force Development Center.

I went to visit that center and sought an appointment with the chief of the Ground Combat Division. That gentleman turned out to be Col. Milton Hull, a Navy Cross recipient for his heroism in Korea at the Chosin Reservoir. More important, I had known him in Hawaii with the 1st Marine Brigade in 1958. He greeted me cordially and asked how he could help. I laid out my tale of woe and asked if he could find me a place in his outfit. Colonel Hull was a big, imposingly strong, and bulky man, and he began to roar with laughter at the thought of my being in charge of the brig-rats and short-timers in Casual Company.

Once he had settled down he told me that he had slots for more than twenty officers, only eleven of which were filled. He asked if I had any reconnaissance experience, and I outlined briefly the diverse assignments I had survived during my time with the Weapons Planning Group. That real-world operational experience—combined with the fact that I had attended the Army's Ranger course and Special Forces School, the Marine Corps Amphibious Reconnaissance School, the Navy's Test Parachute School, a portion of the British SAS training, and several classified courses of instruction provided by civilian agencies of the government—gave me a strong case.

After considering the matter for a few minutes, Colonel Hull decided to offer me the reconnaissance desk in the intelligence branch. It was a great feeling; I was going to get a real job. I was going to be the development center's recon guy.

The deal was far from being closed, though. Colonel Hull and I had to accomplish my reassignment from "For Duty," which would land me in Casual Company, to the specific billet that he had offered. This took horsepower, and that meant a trip to the office of Col. Stanley Pratt, the development center's chief of staff—a hard, cold-blooded, tough-minded, zero-nonsense, mean-as-hell colonel of Marines who had been one of the few para-Marines in World War II. He grilled me without mercy for an hour or so, then without so much as a wink to let me know his decision, he grabbed the telephone and began berating the chief of staff of the base for failing to keep him up to snuff on who was coming to Quantico from the Republic of Vietnam. He then demanded, in the most profane terms, that the colonel on the other end of the telephone get his ass in gear and get his personnel people to effect, immediately, the assignment for duty of one Capt. Alex Lee to the development center, whenever that officer finally happened to arrive at Quantico.

I enjoyed every minute of the call, and once he was finished, attempted to thank him. He waved me out of the office as if I was some tramp who had wandered in off the street. As we left, he roared at Colonel Hull, "Okay, you bastard, I pulled it off, and you owe me another one. Now go away and try to get some work out of that sawed-off captain!"

Two days later, now anticipating a better outcome when I turned in my orders to the base adjutant at the headquarters, I checked in officially with Major Bratt's office. He was very polite. Shortly thereafter, his clerks handed me my orders and sent me off to move into my office at the development center.

The next few days were a blur. I concentrated on learning from the departing incumbent in the reconnaissance billet, Major Charon, all the things he was working on, what he expected in the future, and where all the troubles were likely to appear. Major Charon felt that I might be hampered in dealing with the Fleet Marine Force elements, as I had come into reconnaissance from the classified side—working with other agencies of the government—rather than the workaday Marine units.

I pointed out, however, that my operational time encompassed everything they did plus a large number of things they did not do as part of their mission. I felt that getting along with field Marines would not be my problem. The obstacle, as I predicted, was the vast amounts of energy wasted in responding to powerful people who had never been outdoors in the rain. For some reason, staff officers and civilian managers who have had little or no field experience tend to oversupervise and overcontrol the actions and activities of the operational types who make their living in the field. Typical of such interventions was that of a retired admiral who had strong congressional ties and whose high level of interest was mostly devoted to the question of whether or not his manufacturing company made money.

Dealing with people like that was always difficult, but the Marines who actually went to the field and did reconnaissance work and I got on famously because it was clear to them that I was trying to help them, not trying to shove anything down their throats. It worked.

Once in the billet and partially settled in my job, I began to find some surprisingly unusual things coming my way. The recon guy was the development center's full-time jack-of-all-trades: all manner of things fell into his rather vaguely defined area of responsibility. It turned out that the job included such wildly diverse equipments as the AN/PSR-1 seismic detector and the AN/PPS-6 handheld radar. Neither of these items was intended for use by reconnaissance units, but there they were on the division chief's status board, with my name attached and due dates for reports marked in red. The seismic detectors had been dumped on Major Charon, and the small man-packed radars were assigned to him for examination of tactical usage while the electronics section did the physical testing of the equipment. No matter the source, the projects were now mine.

Most of the officers in Ground Combat carried three projects, some five; the recon guy had sixteen on the board. Some were fun: testing parachute timing devices from high altitude, working with steerable parachutes, and doing underwater communications tests with SCUBA gear. Others were fanciful, eccentric, and of little or no real value—despite interest in the outcome from certain members of the power structure.

One project that comes to mind was an underwing pod for delivering reconnaissance Marines to the beach by carrier-based A-6 aircraft. Much money was spent, many drawings were created, and a mock-up was fabricated. But the concept of sitting in an aluminum coffin attached to the wing bomb rack as the aircraft was catapult launched from a carrier operating at night off a hostile shore did not sit well with those who might find their rear ends encased in the pod. Possible, yes, but entirely unrealistic.

Other aspects of the job required the recon guy to take part in operations-analysis work devoted to new tactics and techniques. The Marine Corps owned equipment that looked useful, and it could also acquire potentially useful equipment from the other services. Someone, however, had to figure out appropriate tactical uses for those various items. Typical of the equipment was the electronic beacon that permitted ground units to vector the computer-equipped A-6 aircraft onto the proper track for blind bombing enemy targets. We were to analyze possible uses for the device by reconnaissance units.

Another example was the Patrol Seismic Intrusion Device (PSID) developed by the U.S. Army's Limited War Laboratory at Aberdeen Proving Ground. It was our job to test it for field performance, make recommendations for tactical use, and advise headquarters on how many to beg, borrow, or steal.

This was a thoroughly challenging job, one that pleased me completely. The late summer days of 1966 found me virtually buried in projects, glad as hell to be there, and enjoying the simple pleasure of working hard on things that would be of value to the Marine Corps. I was overworked and enjoyed that fact, but because of the workload, I began to search for an assistant.

As a newly promoted major in October 1966, getting anyone to care about what I wanted in an assistant was unlikely—if not utterly impossible. The power structure merely assigned me one out of the blue. One day, late in the afternoon, a fine, sturdy young captain arrived in the office and announced that he was my new assistant. He was big, had an open face, and wore an infectious grin that demonstrated an exemplary attitude of cheerful willingness, cooperation, and well-meant effort. Sadly, he was not the least bit interested in science, nor was he literate enough to write reports. He could not deal successfully with the confusion and hubbub of the research and development world. Worst of all, he was a slow learner and could not handle the jargon and acronyms that are part and parcel of that world.

His inability to write a simple declarative sentence was bad enough, but he could not keep up at meetings where we contacted other service and/or national representatives. He had to go, and a more qualified officer had to be located. Good fortune came to my rescue, and one of the best qualified reconnaissance officers in the entire Marine Corps accidentally fell into my hands.

Far down in the bowels of the Warrant Officer Training Course portion of Quantico's officer education component was a newly commissioned officer who fit the bill. Not just any "butterbar" second lieutenant, my new assistant, Clovis Clyde "Buck" Coffman, Jr., was a great barrel-chested bull-roarer of a man who jumped out of airplanes, swam with the sharks, and had just come back to the United States after twenty months of combat—as a reconnaissance Marine—in Vietnam.

The son of a Marine colonel and nephew of a general officer, Coffman had enlisted, as a teenager, and served in the Korean War. Decorations buried his left chest, and his Officer's Qualification Record reflected meritorious elevation to first sergeant, followed by promotion to officer rank on the field of battle. No boards or other extraneous bull, just promotion by the commanding general of the 1st Marine Division (then–Major General Nickerson) followed by staff officers frantically seeking a means of making it all legal. Not least amid the clutter of awards and decorations was the Navy Cross for extraordinary heroism, presented to Buck in a personal ceremony by President Lyndon Johnson.

As the days, weeks, months, and years passed, Coffman also became my friend, my alter ego, and my blood brother. We lived by the credo, "Here, there, and anywhere—any time, any place, anything, no questions asked."

Now that the question of an assistant was settled, we looked to see who would drop out of the sky as the new boss of the intelligence branch. In 1966 our branch chief was a calm and somewhat reserved officer who was constantly taken aback at the unscheduled and unapproved comings and goings of his reconnaissance staff, but we made our deadlines and he did not get his rear chewed to ribbons for what we did or failed to do. While he never understood us, he tolerated our free spirits nevertheless.

When that boss departed, we were assigned to work for a new leader, a most amazing officer, one who fit no known mold. But his arrival was rather unusual: he shuffled in, his complexion ashen. We were confused as to whether he would last the day. Our new leader had just left the Bethesda Naval Hospital after surviving a major heart attack. He had beaten back all the threats of being boarded out of the Corps and was deeply engaged in overturning the power structure's refusal to promote him to the rank of lieutenant colonel, for which he had been selected earlier in the year. A fighter, he eventually got his promotion approved, got in shape physically, got himself back into full-duty status, and was able to give another ten years of magnificent service to Corps and country.

Lt. Col. Gerald H. Polakoff became the new chief of the intelligence branch. A 1945 enlistee for World War II and a young officer in Korea, he was now a respected professional with an amazing dossier of experience behind him. Known respectfully as the Commissar because of his family's heritage as émigrés from Kiev, Polakoff spoke some Russian, Chinese, Spanish and fluent Farsi. He was brilliant! There had been no one like him, ever, in my previous experience, and it turned out that I would never know another officer who gave so much to those who worked for him.

The team that was to respond to the telephone call from Mrs. Brown was being assembled.

I encountered only one other man in the Marine Corps who

possessed an intellectual curiosity equal to that of the Commissar. That man, Lt. Col. Alfred M. Gray, sat across the room in the same office and presided over the special intelligence matters that came to the development center. Gray, who served magnificently as the commandant of the Marine Corps from 1987 to 1991, and I served as foils for Polakoff's wit, as sounding boards for his ideas, and as daily (and nightly) participants in professional give-and-take during which we hashed over everything from tiny tactical details to the broadest philosophical questions found in the profession of arms.

Working in the development center was serious business, and we knew it. Our mission was one of support, but we were expected to put in the same kind of hours in the stateside assignment that we would have in combat. We did that with great enthusiasm. Colonel Polakoff was as smart as a whip, and he kept our noses to the grindstone. He was dedicated to his subordinates, and we appreciated that for him, loyalty downward was paramount.

The Commissar taught you to question everything. He would propose a doctrinal change—perhaps assigning an artillery firing battery to a reconnaissance unit—argue that position in detail with all manner of solid and plausible rationale, then follow that by taking the contrary position and supporting that side equally well. What he wanted was a team of informed officers who did their research, formed their opinions, and delivered them in such a way as to refute all the solid and supportable aspects that the other side might bring to the table. More important, he constantly forced us to question things we were told, leading us to ask ourselves if the pronouncements from on high were sensible.

Illustrative of Polakoff's questioning mind was his analysis of a bulky 1965 operations study called MARCOR-85, in which it was stated that the Marine Corps of 1985 would execute its helicopter assaults from fifty nautical miles at sea. Combat Requirements Branch used that figure; the Aviation Division used it when they spoke of aircraft procurement; and the Navy bandied it about freely in various studies and proposed doctrinal publications. Colonel Polakoff thought there was something fishy in the whole idea, hammered it out with us in our internal discussions, and headed out to see the general. His questioning of the accepted figure and the search for the rationale behind it produced the fact that not one person at any level in the Marine Corps could be found who admitted placing that fifty-nautical-mile requirement into the text.

Polakoff asked why not forty, eighty, or a hundred nautical miles offshore. Was the figure driven by missile threat, air cover necessity, steaming room, etc., etc.? There was no answer, and with that parameter placed in a better context, everyone could look to the future with more flexibility. Arbitrary numbers must never dictate development of doctrine or equipment. Words have meanings, and those meanings must be applicable to the problem under study. From such mundane matters are battles won and careers jeopardized.

There are those who dislike anyone who goes about questioning the writ from above, and Polakoff and his henchmen—us—were often perceived by outsiders with considerable hostility.

In this stimulating environment, Buck Coffman and I were involved in both the great and the not-so-great aspects of research and development. We tried our best to find new and better equipment for the units in the Fleet Marine Forces. The Marine Corps was involved in a hot weather war, but it needed new diving gear for cold water work. A better parachute was needed, so we tested a series of Rogallo wings, parasails, and sport chutes for possible use by the field units. Free-fall parachute insertions required a dependable release timer, and a candidate cribbed from the Czechoslovaks was duly tested. Endless ideas on how to assist the troops in Vietnam came to us, were examined, and were either tested or discarded.

Doctrine was likewise reviewed and changes to formal publications suggested, along with the supporting rationale. Personnel equipment of other services and other nations was examined to find anything that was superior to the equipment then in use in the war. We did boats; we did cameras; we did radars; we did weapons; we did explosives; we did sensors; we did night-vision devices; we did underwater communications; we did biological warning devices (germs that gave off visible light in the presence of human effluvia in air passed across their petri dish); and we did anything else we were handed.

I continued an involvement with lasers that had begun seven years before at China Lake. We were pushing for development of a handheld laser device with which infantrymen could identify targets for the A-4M attack aircraft equipped with the Laser Spot

Tracker or for laser light-sensor-equipped projectiles launched from field artillery pieces. It was our job to expand Marine Corps reconnaissance capabilities as far as technology and the application of common sense would take us.

Outside commitments also took enormous slices of our time and a considerable amount of our energy. As part of my assignment I became a representative for the Marine Corps to quadripartite committees (the United States, Britain, Canada, and Australia) looking into the coordination of national research efforts in the areas of parachute delivery systems and night-vision equipment.

I was also a representative to the Joint DoD AeroSpace Recovery Committee that met from time to time to discuss the potential of various newly proposed recovery techniques for use by the pilots being shot down over North Vietnam. This committee seriously examined such diverse ideas as inflatable airplanes stowed in an ejection capsule and the use of wings and/or airfoils similar to those employed to recover satellites from orbit over the northern Pacific Ocean. The rubber airplanes had their champions and so did less complex designs such as Rogallo wings. I was the only member of the committee who had ever jumped a Rogallo and when I described, and later demonstrated, the rather depressing "fly-stall-fall" characteristics of that particular wing, its proponents decided that wounded, dazed, disoriented pilots should not die at the hands of their escape systems.

Into all this serious effort would come, from time to time, some rollicking good fun. One firm, for example, was intent on enhancing the ability of Marines to hear while in the field, and to that end had produced some dark green, eighteen-inch-long plastic replicas of human ears. Since no one knew who should examine this suggested solution to a combat problem, the recon guy got the green ears and the requirement to check out whether they amplified sounds and thus benefited the wearer. Not a lot of scholarly work went into the project, but we made an honest effort to test the idea. We were, of course, cut little or no slack by other officers in the development center, nor were we free from fault in the matter, as we took turns wearing the ears to the Officer's Club and to the PX.

It turned out that use of the plastic ears did provide a tiny, but measurable, increase in hearing ability. Wandering around in the bush in combat with huge green ears clamped to your head, however, was deemed both silly and dangerous. Not only that, no officer known to us had the slightest desire to introduce big plastic ears to the Marines in the field. The project was written up and shelved forever, but the test ears reappeared occasionally at social gatherings at Quantico—often at the oddest or most embarrassing moments.

Work assigned to the intelligence branch continued to expand, and we published many papers on topics other than equipment, ranging from a proposed doctrine for sensor use to the expansion of operational concepts such as Sting Ray, which posited that small units with firepower can seriously damage larger formations, then fade back into hiding. The sensor doctrine development was a huge undertaking, as it had to be created fresh from whole cloth, and it had to be delivered to headquarters against an incredibly short deadline. Doing this required that the team grow, and so our department welcomed Maj. Joe Flynn, an infantry officer with a postgraduate degree in electronics. He and I hammered out the project, outlining the proposed doctrine for sensor use, concepts of organizational management within the Marine Corps, and all the other bells and whistles needed to inaugurate sensor technology in reasonable order.

Some of that work, which was known as Project STEAM (Sensor Technology and Management), survives to this day in the names and duties of Marine Corps elements dealing with sensors. Major Flynn and I put forty-two consecutive eighteen- to twenty-hour days into meeting our deadline. We were proud of the seven-hundred-plus pages of work, but the deadline was met only because the secretaries were able to convert our stream-of-consciousness thoughts into legible and acceptable text for shipment to headquarters.

Sting Ray excited us more than anything else we were doing. It had begun with a vaguely worded idea in a concept paper devoted to operations in the undefined future. The authors postulated that the Marine Corps units fighting in the last decade of the century might employ search-and-attack teams to bring artillery fire, naval gunfire, and air strikes down on the enemy, versus attacking him head-on with infantry and armor in the classic manner. We believed in the ability of small units to make a positive contribution to winning battles, one that would be far greater than their cost in men and matériel.

Using Sting Ray techniques, reconnaissance teams could take advantage of the growing ability of the aviation and artillery arms to provide accurate and responsive fires, and by so doing directly account for the destruction of large numbers of the enemy. It was our view that laser-guided precision munitions and laser-target designators were items that should receive expedited development so that force reconnaissance units in the Republic of Vietnam could use them against the NVA.

While carefully considering Sting Ray, we concurrently studied combat operations of the Navy's SEAL teams, the operations of the Army's various long-range patrol/Ranger elements, and the Marine reconnaissance units in Vietnam. Coffman and I were firmly in the camp of those who sought to take advantage of the presence of reconnaissance units in areas nominally controlled by the enemy. Neither of us believed in the silent observation philosophy. We wanted to ensure that the teams would be prepared to inflict losses on the enemy—large losses!

Sting Ray, however, was just one of the multitude of missions that reconnaissance teams might be ordered to undertake. If ordered to employ this tactical concept, the teams would need the ability to call artillery fires and direct air strikes, thereby killing large numbers of the enemy quickly. For team survival, any offensive action of this type would be followed by immediate disengagement. Sting Ray was controversial because many Marines felt that reconnaissance should merely look and listen, leaving combat action to regular infantry units. Our view was that they could do either, or both, as the situation and the leader in tactical command might determine. We saw effective use of technology as a way for the small element to become a serious threat to larger formations.

We in the Marine Corps Landing Force Development Center were not the only ones looking at the abilities of small units to be more effective. The Army had an entire laboratory at Aberdeen Proving Ground devoted to both matériel and doctrinal matters affecting the small unit. At higher levels, the Department of Defense had the Advanced Research Projects Agency study known as Small Independent Action Forces, or SIAF. I became the SIAF officer for the Marine Corps and attended the DoD meetings and traveled, worldwide, with their representatives to examine the special operations equipment, training, personnel selection, and operational doctrine of many nations. SIAF was a serious business, examining everything from boot soles and head nets to laser-guided precision munitions that would be delivered to targets illuminated by the designators carried by small independent forces.

While we took all of this seriously, lighter moments came as well. One of these occurred just before Christmas in 1968, when Lieutenant Coffman and I found ourselves in London at the holiday party for both the active-duty and reserve elements of the British Special Air Service. These legendary SAS characters did their best to impress the Yanks, introducing us to bankers in thousand-dollar suits who took four months off each year to crawl around places like Somalia; London cabdrivers who were cold-weather specialists who spent each winter in northernmost Norway "watching" the Soviets on the ice fields; and their overall commander, Brigadier General Slim, the son of the famous Viscount Slim of Burma.

The SAS men are superior professionals who made serious work of trying to assist the SIAF committee in assessing equipment, manpower, and training. Similar professional exchanges took place with the special operations units of Canada, Germany, France, Italy, and Australia. In every case, we learned something we could apply.

When Mrs. Brown's call came in early 1969, our section was becoming well known for being virtually buried in projects. She told me that General Nickerson wanted Buck Coffman and me to come *immediately* to his office in headquarters. We left for Washington in the next five minutes, both of us wondering what we had done to be summoned on such short notice. I suggested to Buck that perhaps the general was going to have us shot, but he felt that if General Nickerson was really mad, he would have us drawn and quartered instead. Neither of us had the slightest idea why he wanted to see us.

When we finally arrived at Mrs. Brown's desk, she smiled broadly and seemed glad to see us, a fact that eased our tension a bit as we were quickly moved into the inner recesses of the general's office. Herman Nickerson was well known for his powerful manner and his personal charisma. We both stood stiffly at attention and waited his pleasure. To our surprise, the general was quick to put us at ease and quick to get to the point. We were the first, save some other generals and Mrs. Brown, of course, to be told that he was going back to the war in Vietnam. He was to receive his third star and would be assigned as the commanding general, III Marine Amphibious Force. That would give him total responsibility for every Marine committed to that war.

Buck and I made congratulatory noises, but the general was not finished. He asked both of us to submit letters to waive our overseas control dates—the dates before which we normally would not be returned to duty in Southeast Asia—and to request that we be returned to combat duty in the Republic of Vietnam. He was most complimentary about our reports and analyses and pointedly asked that we plan on being in Third Force Reconnaissance Company in Northern I Corps, where we would shift to independent operations—just as the doctrine based on his vision of the battlefield set forth. In his terms, he wanted to see us take over as the northernmost tip of his spear, providing reconnaissance cover for his command, working directly for him.

General Nickerson asked that we get the necessary papers signed and back to the staff weenies at headquarters by that afternoon. We were jubilant at the idea, but I was forced to ask the general to consider that we also owed a debt of loyalty to General Armstrong at Quantico, who had every right to expect that we would not leave a pile of unfinished projects on our desks. General Nickerson agreed that there should be sufficient cleanup time to pay our debt to General Armstrong, but he was firm on getting the papers moving—right then! Lieutenant Coffman and I were immediately out the door and on our way back to Quantico without further chitchat.

We arrived at Quantico and began hammering out the request forms. First, the administrative people said we could not get it done that quickly; then, the senior officers chimed in with the same story. Continued pressure got us through the lower levels, however, and soon we were dealing with the boss. General Armstrong was a true Marine Corps character as well as an honorable and dependable leader. He listened quietly to our request, then told us that he was sad to see us go, but he was pleased that we were going to go to a unit that would work directly for General Nickerson. He also expressed the hope that we would find the opportunity to continue to help him by testing some items of equipment in combat and sending him reports on our findings.

With General Armstrong's signature on the requests, we then needed only the agreement of the commanding general of the Marine Corps Development and Education Center, Lt. Gen. James Masters. Things were now much easier, as "Jungle Jim" Masters was a contemporary of General Nickerson, and he too had known Lieutenant Coffman since Buck had been a baby. General Masters signed, recommending approval of the request, and we headed back to Washington to carry our papers to the appropriate staff there. All told, a mere five hours had elapsed.

Once we delivered the requests for waiver of overseas control date, the rest was up to the bureaucrats who inhabited the personnel elements of the headquarters. Since *all* of those folks worked for General Nickerson, Buck Coffman and I were in no doubt that we were headed west. After a brief stop at Mrs. Brown's desk to report our mission completed, we headed south to Quantico for the second time that busy day.

We had been summoned, and it was time for us to pack up and head off again to war. This time it would be different: we would have all our experience, all our study, and all our preparation to back us up. More important, we would be going back to the war as a team. We had worked together in countries around the world during our time at the development center, and we felt ready. We believed in what we had accomplished at Quantico and felt that the return to combat would prove to be a fitting test of our ideas and of ourselves. Despite our considerable backgrounds, neither of us had any idea just how completely we would be tested during the passage of the coming year.

2

GETTING THERE IS HALF THE FUN

Every large organization contains a host of bureaucrats who take great pleasure in seeing to it that all things that can be made to fit routines are, in fact, made to fit those routines. The U.S. Marine Corps is no exception. As I began to make my way back toward the western Pacific and the war in Vietnam, I ran afoul of some routines that I had never encountered previously, probably because my orders were not the standard, run-of-the-mill paper-work, but were by "dispatch." I was, of course, not the first Marine to receive short-notice orders by message traffic; it definitely seemed like it, though. It turned out that the nature of my orders upset the Quantico paper-movers and made everything more difficult than it really should have been. The result was frustrating, and it wasted time for which I had better uses.

New times and new wars always require new tactics and techniques. Because Marines deployed to the war in Vietnam from many far-flung airports, our petty bureaucrats with power spread themselves wider and dug in deeper within the far reaches of the Corps. The first member of that group that I had to cross swords with worked right among us at Quantico. As a field-grade (major or above) officer who had waived his overseas control date, I had somehow wound up in an unusual and troublesome category. In some evil fashion the bureaucrats seemed to believe that I was threatening established routines, and that would never do! I had extreme difficulty getting the most mundane things accomplished as I closed down my tour at the development center. For some reason my request for a detachment date (the precise day that I would be released from duty at Quantico) was moved three times, my household effects could not be collected on the date requested, and on and on and on. The whole evolution of clearing the base was fraught with daily contact with those bureaucrats, but worse was yet to come.

In 1969, if one wanted to get to the Republic of Vietnam in any sort of speedy fashion, routing was everything. Bad routing could leave you in "temporary storage" for long days and weeks while transportation was arranged. When I set out on my trip I was routed via Camp Pendleton in California for two weeks of what we laughingly called Camp Punji. (This was an orientation program where the uninitiated learned that punji sticks are sharpened bamboo and that you should never point your foot at a Vietnamese or pat him on the head.)

Four years of classified involvement with this war, a full combat tour in 1965/66, and several trips to that country during my development center work should have allowed me to skip learning about the nature of punji stakes for the umpteenth time. But it was not to be. Routines were to be observed, with many more surprises to come. A call to General Nickerson, who was already in Da Nang, seemed a bit of overkill, so I accepted the inevitable with what might pass in some circles for good grace.

My personal habits were also nearly the cause of a sudden halt to my trip westward. I am aggressively—some say excessively—willing to get involved in whatever project is at hand. Forced to go to school, I participated fully. Having already been to the war, I offered my classmates information and advice as we went through the fieldwork and the demonstration Vietnamese village exercises. When the instruction was wrong—which was *not* often the case—I felt free to say so because the inexperienced Marines and the majority of officers assigned to that indoctrination course were going west to lay their lives on the line; they deserved the truth. All of this was so useful to those I was with that they tried to retain me as the school's executive officer. Since I had no desire to get out of my orders, it was an interesting time.

An officer, well senior to myself, sent for me and bade me sit down and be comfortable. He asked after my health and seemed sincere in his manner. At last he came to the point, advising me that he had enough power to actually get my overseas orders canceled if I wanted to be the executive officer of the indoctrination school. I courteously pointed out that I desired to carry out my orders. The bureaucrat was flabbergasted and said that he might act unilaterally to scratch my name from the outbound roster. I suggested in a quiet fashion that if he did so, it would be a gravely serious mistake in judgment—one that would have career-damaging results. Despite the not-so-thinly veiled threat, I tried to maintain the external signs of good humor, excused myself from further discussion of the matter, and went to finish packing.

Shortly thereafter our movement number came up, and we were all counted, counted, and counted again by junior members of the bureaucracy. After fitting ourselves to their routines for the zillionth time, we got on the buses.

There was nothing humorous or even humane about this movement. The somber and frightened young men who rode those buses were beginning their long journey toward war, with no flags flying and no trumpets to urge them on. They had no support from unit integrity; they had no coterie of friends who would share and ease the experience; they had nothing whatsoever to lean on as they looked directly at their worst fears—the unknown future, with death a distinct possibility. Each of us on those worn bus seats was utterly alone. We were merely a collection of individuals grouped in an odd lot for shipment west like cattle on the way to market.

Many who made that lonely trip to Norton Air Force Base that day, each wrapped in his own fears, were destined to return in gray-issue caskets stacked in C-141 aircraft. Going west, we Marines had no more unit cohesiveness than did the dead returning unknowingly eastward to open graves across America. This treatment of the troops as if they were ciphers began to build, in the transit process, a level of alienation that was often impossible to overcome in the operational units in Vietnam. The individual replacement system dehumanized and demoralized many thousands of those who served in that war.

Units moving to war together have the inner strength of the team, the oneness that grows in a group that has worked together, and the deep sense of comfort that comes from being with known and trusted comrades. (Luckily, that lesson has been well learned since Vietnam, and in the Gulf War deployments of 1990, the Marines went to war as units.)

Once we were out of the buses and on the ramp at the Air Force base, I felt that the bureaucrats were all behind me and that things were pretty much decided in the case of this one wandering Marine major. Aside from the Air Force colonel who wanted to borrow me from the movement roster for a temporary assignment handling the "casuals" being processed through Norton Air Force Base, all was now pretty much proceeding as it should. The chartered Continental Airlines 707 lifted from the runway, and all of my conflicts with the routines and other foolishness that the petty bureaucrats held dear were over. Or so I thought.

Long hours across the Pacific Ocean gave me much to think about at the time, and more to remember today. Only a few second-tour Marines were on board; the rest were fresh out of training. Everyone did his very best to hide what was happening inside, of course: they were sleeping, laughing, playing cards, hassling the stewardesses, reading—whatever.

Arrival in Da Nang was no surprise to those of us who had passed that way before. The first-timers, though, were visibly shocked by the heat, the humidity, the ugliness, the confusion, and, above all, the noise. The flight line was a place of chaos: vehicles roared up and down the access road, refuelers clustered around the aircraft, and the noise of F-4s and A-6s taking off from the main runway was deafening. Many of the young Marines were openly awed by the sight of men scarcely six months older than themselves sporting the infantryman's tan—back of neck and forearms—and the swagger of those who had "seen the elephant" (that is, faced the armed adversary and lived to tell the tale). These battle-hardened folks wandering around the flight line might have been no more than rear-area clerks, but they impressed the new arrivals.

Once we were clear of the aircraft, the troops were further bewildered by a lot of shouting and some unnecessary hassling. The enlisted Marines were lined up and counted, recounted, treated to too much guff, and finally marched off in one direction while the officers were herded in another, to be sorted and sent on to various locations. A short, square, ugly major kicked my overstuffed seabag and roared to me to "Get moving!" Because I really did not need any new enemies, I passed over the opportunity to punch him in the nose and walked on. It was clear that with all the hubbub around us, I was unlikely to impress anyone by requesting immediate transportation north to Dong Ha, where the 3d Marine Division was located, so I wandered along as part of the herd.

It was amazing. The petty bureaucrats had found another place where they could excel—the safe rear areas of the Vietnam War. It turned out that the only place where they did not appear at all was out in the jungle where we met the North Vietnamese.

When my turn came for orders processing, I was surprised to find out that my name appeared on the list of those slated for duty in an administrative slot on the First Division staff. I asked who had decided this and was given the officer's name. He was a full colonel, one whom I had happened to work for in years past. Our association had been brief, and no bond of mutual respect had been formed. By this time I was tired, sweaty, and thoroughly sick of the never-ending foolishness.

The senior noncommissioned officer in charge allowed me to use his phone to check out this change of plans. Several of the minions of this colonel told me that he could not be reached, but persistence paid off, and I was allowed to speak directly to the imperial personage without interpreters. His first comments sent me into a fury. He had seen my name as prospective commanding officer, Third Force Reconnaissance Company, and since he knew me, and since I was *just* an infantry officer, he had reassigned me.

Choking back my desire to shoot the bastard, I pointed out that there was no such thing as just an infantryman, for it was those who served in the infantry line units and went forward to the sound of the guns who made the Marine Corps tick. I pointed out that many years had intervened since he had last seen me; in that time I had been ordered to many special schools that he did not know about; I had taken part in many special combat operations that he would not learn about because he was not cleared for knowledge that highly classified; and I had a full tour in the infantry in combat in 1965/66 behind me. This was quite a heated and personally degrading confrontation, and as a means of closing the pointless harangue, I suggested, "Sir, why don't you just make a call to General Nickerson, and we can let him settle this whole thing, once and for all?"

He was deeply offended by my attitude and terminated the conversation by hanging up—without any clarification as to what was to happen next.

Waiting there in the area set aside for processing, I nearly suffered apoplexy. I felt totally at the mercy of men who belonged to no clan of mine. As the time passed, I realized that I mirrored the bitter anger that privates and privates first class are forced to hold within themselves after being treated shabbily by that certain kind of arrogant officer who looks down on all those who happen to be below him in the rank structure.

After an hour or two that seemed to be endless, the gunnery sergeant who pushed our papers from one pile to another called me back and handed me orders to the 3d Marine Division. I will never know if that colonel called the general; I never saw or heard of him again. Hoisting my gear, I began hunting a ride north to where the NVA was trying to destroy the 3d Marine Division before it was to be extracted as part of the planned withdrawal of U.S. forces from the Republic of Vietnam. A northbound C-130 was waiting on the ramp, with all four engines turning, so I hurried aboard and counted my good fortune. All of the red tape was behind me, and henceforth everything would proceed as it should.

At the command post of the 3d Marine Division things took on a much more workmanlike appearance. There was far less milling about in the replacement control areas, and you could sense an overall feeling of competence. This feeling was shattered for me by a violent shove from behind. I had been standing on a wooden-plank walkway that was laid down just outside the entrance to a large, general-purpose tent. In less than a second, I found myself flat on my face, stretched out on the ground outside that tent.

Evidently, I had been blocking movement on those wooden duckboards of those who wanted to stroll, arm-in-arm, three abreast. Three large Marines in flak jackets, with colored towels draped around their necks, had decided to move me out of the way. I was thus introduced to the effect in Vietnam of the worst aspects of the Black Power movement then in ascendancy in the United States. When I leaped up with a bellow, one of the men told me to "Fuck off, honky!" and they walked away.

We had all heard from friends and through references in reports that militants had a hold on a portion of the black Marines and that violence in Dong Ha and at the Quang Tri Combat Base was not unusual. That knowledge was not sufficient preparation, however. Later I was told that I had been lucky to avoid making them any angrier; the colored towels they wore indicated that the three were high-ranking individuals in the local power cell of the movement.

I was still a bit shocked and was bitterly mulling over my concern over this new condition as I checked into the 3d Marine Division. I wasn't sleepwalking, but my ability to spot petty bureaucrats with power had been impaired. Division adjutants are minor functionary staff officers; they do not make policy and they do not unilaterally assign officers with the rank of major. This one seemed to think he was an exception. He happily told me that I would be held in a pool of majors for a few days until it was decided just who would be assigned to staff duties and who would go out into the bush to work as either executive officers or operations officers of battalions. When I quietly suggested to him that I did not fit the normal pattern of arrivals and that if he looked, he might find my name among those who had already been slated for specific assignment, he appeared to be insulted by my uncooperative attitude.

He was not a big-deal colonel, just a major, so this time I wasn't even polite when I told him to get his boss on the phone— "Now!" After blinking back his surprise, he went to do just that. The colonel I met through these circumstances was a dull and uninspiring type who was unprepared for any sort of confrontation. What he wanted was to get his rear end out of the 3d Marine Division, where it could be damaged by incoming fire from the nearby NVA. He took an instant dislike to me and made that decidedly clear in short order when he insisted that I was going into the pool along with all the other majors and told me, "Get out of the office and comply with the orders that you have been given."

As I left, I cheerfully pondered assassinating the officers manning the roadblock that faced me. Moving smartly down to the operations area of the headquarters, however, I bummed a telephone and worked my way through the various links in the communications chain until I was speaking with Captain Anderson, General Nickerson's aide-de-camp. In as few sentences as possible I outlined my predicament. In response I received a hearty laugh, followed by the comment, "No sweat!"

Having done what I could, I then hauled my possessions down to the billeting area for the majors in the pool. Selecting a cot, I stretched out and took a nap. Within minutes, though, I was shaken awake by a sergeant who exclaimed, "Sir, sir. There was a screwup in the CP and you got sent to the wrong place. I have your orders, and the Jeep is waiting to take you to 3d Reconnaissance Battalion right now." Seeing the logic in getting out of the headquarters as quickly as possible, I did just what the sergeant asked me to do.

Third Reconnaissance Battalion had a reputation as a solidly competent organization that accomplished dangerous work. Some of that work was being done by Marines of Third Force Reconnaissance Company because that unit had been folded into the battalion, where it virtually lost its identity. My job would be to take the force company out of there, to operate it independently, and to reclaim the unit identity while doing the bidding of the commanding general. The commanding officer of the battalion, however, had a different idea: he wanted to make me the battalion executive officer while he retained his total control over the present commanding officer and men of Third Force Reconnaissance Company. As his executive officer, he opined, I could take part in the overview of operations, rather than becoming involved minute-by-minute as a company commander. And he wanted to put this into practice immediately.

Our discussion was rather heated and not resolved to his satisfaction. Because I was unwilling to give him a cheery "Aye, aye, sir," he ordered me to wait outside his office while he did some checking with higher headquarters. Evidently he spoke to the right people, because within a few minutes his views had taken a sharp turn, and I was now the "prospective commanding officer," Third Force Reconnaissance Company.

Finally, after twelve-thousand-plus miles of being pushed and shoved, I was where I was supposed to be! Success or failure were now the two options open to me, but it was going to be *my* responsibility, not that of any outsider, to see which of those two conditions was to describe my fate. The command billet that I had been asked to fill was mine.

3

FINDING THE CORNERS

No more important moment exists for the warrior than the instant when command of a unit is passed to him and he realizes that the responsibility for all that happens, good and bad, has settled on his shoulders. It may happen on a sunlit afternoon, with flags cracking in the breeze and drums echoing your pulse as you count your blessings and good luck at having received yet another opportunity to live out the most sought-after of all possible assignments—command! Or it may happen in a muddy paddy ditch, as it came to pass when I took command of Company F, 2d Battalion, 7th Marines—under fire, partially surrounded, and under no illusion that I was assured of living out the hour, much less the entire day.

It was quickly evident that my arrival in Third Force Reconnaissance Company generated a considerable amount of hostility and concern. Word of what was planned for the future of the company reached the departing commander, Maj. Rex Karchner, when Lieutenant Coffman checked in a few days prior to my arrival. Karchner was convinced that I was going to wreck the outfit if I tried to take it from beneath the sheltering armpit of 3d Reconnaissance Battalion.

Rex was a good and honorable man (an old friend as well), without the slightest prior contact with special operations activity of any kind. Sadly, his failure to understand the role planned for the Third Force and his loyalty to the 3d Recon Battalion commander wed him to an operational concept that subordinated force reconnaissance operations to those of the division-level reconnaissance battalions. That view clashed with mine and with the plans of General Nickerson. That clash destroyed our previous friendship, and the short, unceremonious change of command was fraught with personal tensions. The event was reduced to a stiff, uncomfortable moment of formality as Karchner angrily stepped aside and accepted my statement, "I relieve you, sir!" He replied with the expected, "I stand relieved, sir!" and grudgingly wished me luck.

Now I was in command, and I had to get busy to find the unit's corners—shorthand for an analysis of the personnel, equipment, and training status—solve any and all problems that that entailed, and move out smartly to fulfill my mission.

When I assumed command of Third Force Reconnaissance Company, it seemed that I had spent the preceding nine or ten years in continuous preparation for that moment. The excitement of seeing something that had seemed impossible come true was a thrilling once-in-a-lifetime experience. Command slots for majors are virtually nonexistent in the Marine Corps, in peacetime or war. Majors then were either shuffling papers in Vietnam or shuffling papers and writing letters to each other in the name of their bosses at Marine headquarters or in the Pentagon.

There was no hint of easy times ahead, no hint of great cooperation from others, no hint of anything other than the final culmination of something promised me by Capt. Jake Skavril, the officer who swore me into the U.S. Marine Corps so many years before. "Kid," he had growled, "a smartass like you can go into the army and be an engineer or some such shit, but if you decide to be a Marine, we'll give you a rifle and a hard time."

Taking command of Third Force seemed to fit that description 100 percent! Here I was, given the tools—the promised rifle—to do a job; all I had to do was assemble that rifle properly, aim it correctly, and fire it effectively. I was proud, properly and respectfully proud, to accept the challenge.

Just a cursory examination of the unit made it quite evident that an almost endless number of things needed to be done. Buck Coffman had already begun getting himself installed as the company operations officer (S-3), his trip from Quantico being less hassled than mine. He had taken the first few days to get his feet on the ground and to analyze the condition of the unit. When I took the command from Major Karchner, Coffman's first task was to immediately begin briefing me on all the things and stuff that needed sorting out. He had been careful in his analysis, and the enormity of the change needed became painfully evident.

I first learned that everything that belonged to Third Force—every weapon, every radio, every tool, every single item of military equipment—had been absorbed by the 3d Reconnaissance Battalion as community property. Things were not much better when it came to people. Many individual Marines who had come to Vietnam as force reconnaissance replacements had been deemed better employed elsewhere by the recon battalion commander and his staff. In truth, the force reconnaissance capability provided by the Marine Corps for use by the overall commander, in this case General Nickerson, had devolved to nothing more than a dependent of the recon battalion, one that was treated like a despised bastard stepchild.

Third Force was sneeringly called "F Troop" by officers and troops of the division reconnaissance battalion alike. This disrespectful comparison between Third Force and the bumbling incompetents in the TV series about a cavalry outpost in the old West was not used in jest; it was used in a hostile manner to demean everyone in the unit. Whether this disrespect was driven by pride in their own capabilities or envy of the Marines assigned to Third Force, the result was the same. Morale within the company was zero, or a little less.

Regardless of the situation within the company, combat operations were being conducted. Lieutenant Coffman had created, virtually from thin air, a functioning Combat Operations Center (COC). From that COC we began immediately to control the Third Force operating teams, taking our missions from those assigned to us by the 3d Marine Division or those that the recon battalion deemed logical. Actually, despite our initial difficulties, the commander of the 3d Reconnaissance Battalion, Lt. Col. R. R. Burritt, and I began to develop some rapport. He and I met on a cordial basis each day and divided up the missions. He would assign those within the artillery support fan to his elements and pass all the longer-range missions and those in the back country to Third Force.

All of this was a start, pending the arrival of Colonel Polakoff and his establishment of the Surveillance Reconnaissance Center in Da Nang. Once that was in place, Third Force would go independent, and we would finally be doing what we had been asked to do for the Marines of III MAF.

Change can be sudden or incremental. I chose to combine the two, fighting huge battles to solve some problems immediately and slipping up behind the petty paper people on some others. The first major battle involved the practice of sending Marines out to risk their lives without "allowing" them to test-fire their weapons. Lieutenant Coffman and I were of one mind on the matter. A Marine who might easily be killed because of a malfunctioning weapon (at the time the M-16 was famous for its faulty performance) was not going to go to that death on our orders. He was going to fire his weapon to prove to us that it worked—before leaving.

The corporate power structure at the Quang Tri Combat Base opined that test firing was impossible, and they trotted out various excuses: it had never been demanded by anyone else before; it was dangerous; it was noisy; it was not in the plans for the combat base; and it was not really needed. We were told that firing would upset the perimeter guard if it took place during darkness before the teams made their departure for the field—silly. We were told that firing would awaken sleeping watch officers from the division staff who manned the rear command post of the 3d Marine Division—so what?

"The Igor," Coffman's title for himself among the troops, had a deep, slanted pit dug, had it covered, had it equipped with an electric light so the target at the bottom could be seen, and had a nice table built at the top for the one firing to rest his elbows on as he proved to our satisfaction that bullets came out the end when he pulled the trigger. We were told that test-firing weapons within the perimeter could not be conducted safely—plainly not true.

Many staff luminaries demanded that the test-firing cease, but each one refused to explain to my Marines that rear-area sleep was more important than the life of a force reconnaissance Marine. No officer was willing to directly counter my argument that the previous situation was virtually a criminal dereliction. Of course, it was clear that many considered me a dangerous fanatic on the subject. I was, and remain today, devoted to the precept that Marines can be trusted to use their weapons properly, and they must be prepared to do so when in danger. I cannot begin to understand, nor can I ever condone the actions of, those who would separate fighting men who are looking death in the eye from their weapons or ammunition.

Shortly after word of our test-fire pit spread to other units in the combat base, we had recon battalion Marines, engineer battalion Marines, and Marines from all elements at the combat base sneaking into our area to use it before heading out on patrol, leaving to clear mines on a road, or departing on whatever mission might take them in harm's way. This small but telling triumph added to each Marine's understanding that he was important in his own right. Many of my Marines were proud of the pit—the first of several as we moved from place to place—and wanted the company to charge outsiders a test fee to earn funds for the unit beer ration.

Additionally, it was important to have something that was ours and was special to us all be our first step. It had also been my goal, of course, to use this as a way to bind the unit together as a living, breathing band of brothers who saw anyone who was from another unit as an outsider.

Next on my list of adventures was a two-pronged assault. One attack would be launched against the supply demons to get our major items of equipment out of the recon battalion stockpiles; the other would focus on slaying some of the dreaded personnel dragons.

We wanted our equipment back, and we wanted it back clean and serviceable for troops in combat. A force reconnaissance company rates a lot of gear: several million dollars' worth of trucks, weapons, rubber boats, parachutes, radios, and even a three-stove mess hall. Lieutenant Coffman or I would find out about a weapon, a vehicle, a piece of radio gear, or an electronics test item that was on the Third Force Table of Equipment but not present for duty. We would track it down to the offending party and offer sudden, perhaps terminal, violence if we did not obtain immediate return of the item. The battalion supply people became very cooperative—very quickly.

Actually, though, this collecting was an enormous, bone-wearying hassle. Worse, many of the items were unserviceable. Tentage was worn and torn; weapons were in need of major maintenance; vehicles had been run for months without oil changes; electronic test equipment was broken; radios were missing parts; and the diving gear had been badly damaged by rough usage. New equipment would have cost an enormous sum and was not available. We were forced to accept that we would be expected to continue to fight the war with equipment that was nearly junk. Because of the cooperation of those who had been keeping the gear, however, it was far easier to solve the equipment problem than to deal with the personnel field and the obstacles therein.

Our fierce adversaries in personnel had the power of the unit diary behind them. Transfers from unit to unit required heaps of what the British have always called "bumph." Bumph, in the forces of the queen, is actually toilet paper, but it has come to mean all of the forms and fluff that keep military bureaucrats happy. Third Force Reconnaissance Company was in woeful condition when it came to the Marines assigned to do the work. Roughly 65 percent of our assigned strength was *on hand*, ready to fight. The company had 110 men to fill 142 billets for fighting men and 7 officers to man the 12 company command and staff slots. Many key people were there on paper only. For example, the sergeant who was the equipment noncommissioned officer in Division Special Services was away from Third Force on temporary assignment.

Getting the assigned officers and staff noncommissioned officers back from other units was a tedious and bitterly contested battle. It took exorbitant amounts of time and energy to work with the appropriate clerks who controlled all of the bumph.

Replacements were essential, and none were clearly slated for Third Force Recon. Independent operations would require a company that was up to strength, not one that was limping along with 50 percent of the needed officers and few senior qualified noncommissioned ones. Of the seven officers present for duty, one, unfortunately, was a short-timer who was both snotty and stupid. I fired him the day after meeting him, suggesting that he spend the last few days of his war filling sandbags or performing some equally rewarding task for the 3d Marine Division. I needed another powerhouse like Buck Coffman, and as luck would have it, one was found.

The assistant division commander of the 3d Marine Division sent for me and suggested that I take his aide as my executive officer (XO). Normally I would have bristled at the idea, because aides are usually tall, pretty, political, and more interested in their promotion to higher rank than in the welfare of the troops. This aide, however, was just what I needed. A former infantry and reconnaissance master sergeant, Norman Hisler was made a captain thanks to the Enlisted Commissioning Program of 1966/67.

Captain Hisler was a godsend. As the operational tempo steadily increased and the level of stress on the company raised the tension around him, he stood in Third Force Reconnaissance Company like a rock, keeping all things in perspective and enforcing, utterly without question, my decisions as to policy. As a youth, Norman Hisler had the opportunity to choose between a football career at the University of Texas or the Marine Corps. He chose combat in Korea as a private, and never looked back on his decision. Had he not been assigned as my XO, I might never have lived to write this book.

With Captain Hisler and Lieutenant Coffman in place, the company began to take on some of the look I was seeking. Still, we desperately needed other officers to round out the unit and to replace a couple of the holdovers who were not going to measure up to my standards. Once we were allowed to go into independent operations, the company would constantly be placing young officers in liaison slots with higher commands and with other units, an assignment that would require the individuals to be calm, intelligent, resourceful people who could be counted on to use common sense. No braggarts or other hot dogs could do that type of work, and I was worried that enough officers might not be found in time.

This concern was quickly and efficiently squelched by Captain Hisler's immediate actions. He first stole 2d Lt. Wayne V. Morris, an adjutant from 3d Recon Battalion, and used that officer's knowledge and abilities in the personnel field to counter the bureaucrats and their ever-increasing demand for bumph. Having been a staff sergeant in the administrative world when commissioned, "Lobo" Morris could do it *all*! He had been in Vietnam on a prior combat tour where he was, for a time, the senior enlisted man—prima facie first sergeant—of a badly mauled rifle company in the 4th Regiment.

Wayne Morris was not a force recon Marine by dint of training, experience, or schools that handed out badges; he became one, forever, through personal professional performance. As fate would have it, he commanded a platoon and served as the administrative linchpin for the company, earning us an outstanding rating for compliance with all the fussy little directives and, at the same time, conducting himself as a leader of Marines. Who would have guessed in 1969/70 that Lieutenant Morris would one day be Colonel Morris, the last one of all those who served in Third Force Recon to remain on active duty, the last Marine permitted to wear the ribbon denoting combat service with the company during the period covered by the U.S. Army's Valorous Unit Award.

While Captain Hisler and Lieutenant Morris teamed up to scrounge people and gear for Third Force, I turned my attention to the intelligence officer (S-2) billet. From the officers present I selected Peter Robertson, who was a first lieutenant with prior combat experience in an infantry unit. Lieutenant Robertson was confident in the extreme, being, by his own evaluation, "about one-half step and two inches short of all-American" as a basketball player. He had the kind of calculating and inquiring mind that was needed to make the intelligence billet function. He was later instrumental in creating mission-related training for the recon teams that made them far better collectors of information, a skill that added much to the performance of the company.

Other officers were caught in Captain Hisler's net, considered, and either added to the team or thrown back to their units. The finest by far was another volunteer from the infantry, 1st Lt. Robert "Beak" Hensley, who had just come over from the 4th Marine Regiment. A well-qualified, combat-experienced infantry lieutenant, Hensley was the most self-effacing officer I ever met. He was from a small city in Oklahoma, which he always said as one word, "PoncaCityOklahoma."

Despite his lack of a reconnaissance-related operational background, Hensley fit in because he was an intelligent, capable, and loyal officer. He was chosen to combine command of a recon platoon with duty as operations assistant to the Igor. He worked untold hours for Lieutenant Coffman and took superb care of his Marines as well. No task was ever assigned to him that he did not accept with a quick, positive response and an immediate startup aimed at getting all the things needed and all the actions done to bring it to successful completion. His careful and steady work freed Lieutenant Coffman to focus on the larger scheme afoot as the company prepared to go independent.

Among the staff noncommissioned officers present for duty was one gem, Riley, the incumbent company first sergeant. He quickly earned my respect by identifying the good Marines and helping me weed out the nonperformers. As Riley's tour in Vietnam was coming to a close, he was quick to find another first sergeant, Lonnie Henderson, who came over to us from the 9th Regiment when Riley headed home. Sergeant Henderson was known as "Moose" for the obvious reason that, at "five feet, seventeen inches," he was huge. Moose was a recon Marine all the way, the only man I ever met who carried rock-climbing gear in his pockets in garrison. His footlockers were crammed with pitons, rock nuts, and coils of climbing line, all from his days as an instructor at the Mountain Leadership School in the high Sierras in California.

As the company staffing developed, Sergeant Henderson was backed up by a gunnery sergeant, David Billedoux, another rather large man who had had a great deal of prior reconnaissance and infantry experience. Gunnery Sgt. James F. Hamilton became our chief parachute rigger. While "Ham" was not as large as either Henderson or Bilodeau, he was no midget. These three imposing senior enlisted Marines occasionally called on the sergeants of other units to register their displeasure over some actual or perceived slight to Third Force Marines. When that happened, people listened!

With the passage of time, more and more of our personnel problems were settled. Marines volunteered from other units; Marines who looked promising were shanghaied from incoming replacement drafts; and Marines came in through the pipeline from Camp Lejeune, North Carolina, where Second Force Reconnaissance Company was training replacement force reconnaissance Marines for deployment to the war. Many of the latter, however, were grabbed to fill some slot in the rear in Da Nang or at 3d Marine Division.

While all of this reorganization and rebuilding of Third Force may sound easy, it was not. Resistance to what we had to do to support our mission was not always present, but it was there often enough to make things adversarial in the main. We were making enemies by the score as we assembled the required men and matériel to prepare the company for General Nickerson's orders. Time was short, as we had only August and a portion of

September 1969 to prepare for the departure of the 3d Marine Division and acceptance of independent tasking from III MAF

Meanwhile, the operational tempo was picking up. More surveillance was wanted in the demilitarized zone (DMZ), and more interest was being paid to the far reaches of Northern I Corps, where we were expected to patrol outside the artillery fire support fan. The force reconnaissance mission specifies "long-range postassault reconnaissance," and while we were not not part of an amphibious assault, we were ready to begin performing those longer-range missions. All during the hunts for personnel and matériel, the company operated its COC (controlled team missions) and generated intelligence reports for higher headquarters.

One of the first things that we did, as reorganization continued, was to increase the number of teams assigned to the operational platoons. In fact, to get ready for increased responsibility, we disregarded the Table of Organization published for a Marine force reconnaissance company and created, from the manpower available, more teams for deployment. We felt that the company would need to field more teams if we hoped to be successful.

Team size was also a matter for revision. The formal published organizational charts for the company reflected that the observe-only faction had been in power when the documents were published. Each team was to be made up of four men. Lieutenant Coffman and I considered a four-man team to be too small for any sort of credible fight and too small to defend itself while carrying anyone who might be wounded. Also, because of the amount of equipment, extra radios, and such that more sophisticated missions entailed, six men were needed. Thus, much shifting took place within the company to assign six men to a team.

Actually, this was, in part, an institutionalization of what was being done most of the time. The majority of patrols run by Third Force were already using six men: point man, team leader, primary radio, assistant team leader, secondary radio, and tail-end Charlie. Third Reconnaissance Battalion used patrols of varying sizes, some as large as fifteen men, but it was our goal to standardize in order to make training and operations more efficient.

In addition to reorganizing, we moved, an action that had a significant bearing on the success of Third Force Reconnaissance Company. Initially we moved less than five hundred meters away, but it placed the company in a separate, lockable compound with improved living conditions for the troops and our own helicopter landing pad. Third Force remained in the Quang Tri Combat Base, but we did not have to share any facility with any other unit. At last we were out of the area controlled by 3d Recon Battalion, where hostility was the order of the day.

Once the company was relocated, new policies were immediately implemented. *First*, no Vietnamese civilians were allowed into the compound, which cut the potential for drug involvement. We enforced the policy by placing sergeants and staff sergeants at the gate to handle any washing and sewing of uniforms that was needed. *Second*, visitors were banned, both for security reasons and to cut the ties with other units where many good Marines were suffering the pain and stress that had drifted across the Pacific Ocean from the United States. That pain and stress revolved around the Watts riots of 1965, the disasters of Chicago's riots in 1968, and the virtual destruction of the nation's capital in 1968/69.

Tensions were also being fueled by organized Black Power elements within the Marine Corps units in Vietnam. These men were hostile to the established military rank structure, and they were dangerous. Members of those elements swaggered openly in the Quang Tri Combat Base, holding up the movement of foot and vehicular traffic with elaborate greeting rituals. We were convinced that the Third Force Marines had enough to worry about without being hassled by representatives of some counterculture.

Third, visits—other than official ones—to other units were also banned for reasons of operational security and drug-traffic potential.

Establishment of these policies was accomplished in an open and informative manner, including many face-to-face discussions with individual Marines who learned quickly that Hisler, Coffman, Morris, and I were approachable and willing to explain anything, anytime. While discussions were free, violations were quickly dealt with.

All of these complex actions occurred without reference to time, space, or sleep requirements. Operational teams went to the field and returned to find their unit moving. New faces appeared everywhere, yet a sense of belonging to something special was being created in the minds of the troops. To spice things up, a typhoon arrived during the last week in August 1969, and the company lived through 135-knot winds that ripped up living quarters, destroyed the mess hall, and stranded four teams in the DMZ for three days without any rations. Despite being interrupted by a typhoon, enemy action in the form of rocket barrages, and the steadily increasing operational tempo, change within the company continued. We went far out of our way to make sure that everyone involved could see that Third Force was changing into a far different organization than it had ever been before.

4

LOOSE ENDS

Important things that are left to chance, or to the good intentions of others, result in loose ends that must be tied off in a satisfactory manner if a unit is to function effectively. Unattended, such loose ends can result in death or can create an ambience that results in slipshod performances by tired and irritated men.

Some misguided souls actually believe what they see in war movies. For celluloid heroes, everything happens with subtle ease, confusion never reigns, and the good guys do not get bombed by their own aircraft or shelled by their own artillery. In real wars, things never happen that way. Even when it is done professionally, the complexity of the detailed coordination required for successful long-range reconnaissance operations is amazing. An interesting dichotomy exists. We find that we are trying to accomplish a truly secret task—running patrols deep in enemy-dominated terrain—yet nearly *everyone* needs to know where and when this will take place. If this knowledge is not shared with those who need it, there exists the very real opportunity for our side to drop explosive devices onto us as we slip through the underbrush.

While the professional doctrine, the military texts, and the leaders on high always emphasized in the Vietnam War that we were *all* working toward a common goal, that did not mean too much. In reality, it was a simple matter for a force reconnaissance unit to get hammered by some dolt who didn't get the word. In reconnaissance operations, proper coordination and education are absolutely essential—otherwise, Marines die. In August and September of 1969, as I prepared to take Third Force independent, it was clear that many loose ends needed to be tied off, many supporting elements needed to be educated, and plenty of room for terminal error existed. Many fine techniques were already in place for coordinating reconnaissance work, but it was essential that the entire process be reevaluated in light of the new missions that would be assigned to the Third Force teams.

At this time, Colonel Polakoff was in the throes of putting together the SRC at III MAF in Da Nang for General Nickerson. The Commissar had an enormous task to accomplish, against massive institutional resistance. From the individual photo interpreters who would be forced to provide analysis reports to the SRC to the Marines who monitored the NVA radio nets to the electronic warfare types who dealt in radar analysis, everyone had a reason why his unit should not report directly to the new center.

It was General Nickerson's view that they should—period— and his view eventually prevailed. Sometimes it was the Commissar's charisma that made things happen; on other occasions it may have been the memo signed by General Nickerson with his distinctive big green capital *N*. Whatever was required to motivate the necessary people, it happened, and the SRC began to take shape.

One of the prime values of the SRC was to be its coordination capabilities. In the beginning, however, that did not exist, and so some methods to accomplish immediate coordination of our newly initiated and far longer-ranging independent operations were essential to our survival.

Because we expected to operate reconnaissance patrols throughout the area bordered on the south by the Hai Vanh Pass, on the west by Laos, and on the north by the DMZ, my first order of business was to assemble a detailed listing of just who on our side could hurt us and how. That included everyone who could deliver fire or combat troops into Northern I Corps. That was one hell of a lot of people!

Starting with an examination of the coastal areas, we considered the U.S. Navy, which could shell certain sections with its 5-inch and 8-inch guns, and there was always the off chance that a battleship might turn up to provide 16-inch gunfire support. Regardless of the projectile sizes being used, we did not want them to shoot any of us by accident. Large numbers of carrier-based naval aircraft flew overhead, and they could be dangerous too. More frequently they were assigned to attack targets that were north of the DMZ and the seventeenth parallel, but those aircraft could easily be diverted by someone who needed an air strike. Without coordination, Navy bombs could kill reconnaissance Marines by mistake.

The U.S. Air Force, operating from bases within the Republic of Vietnam, Thailand, Okinawa, Guam, and God knows where else, could bomb us from high or low altitude. Fundamentally, we were opposed to that.

Marine and Army aviation might attack the teams if not kept current on their locations and the rules of engagement in force in our particular area. The Vietnamese Air Force flew sorties into our area of operations, and they too could kill us.

Artillery was used by the Army, the Marines, the Vietnamese Army, the Korean Marines, the Rural and Provincial Forces, and anyone else who could get his hands on a howitzer. Obviously, any reconnaissance work within the artillery fan could be dangerous.

Last, ground operations were in progress all the time. The units who might be found operating in the field against the enemy were diverse. They ranged from the Vietnamese Rural Force platoons patrolling outside their home villages to combat operations by large Marine and Army elements operating in concert against regular NVA forces. Without proper coordination—namely, a full, two-way exchange of information—these operations could accidentally happen upon a force reconnaissance team and kill it by simple tactical blundering. If they were not warned that the team was in their area, they would shoot first and ask questions later.

From my initial operational analysis as commanding officer it was obvious that we had our work cut out for us in Third Force Reconnaissance Company if we really expected to stay alive. The North Vietnamese would certainly make a diligent and professional attempt to kill us—that was acceptable. We knew that the few Vietcong elements we might encounter (only small, token VC units remained operational in Northern I Corps by 1969) would kill us if we let them, and that too was acceptable. We lived with the knowledge that everything we did on a daily basis was dangerous, and we could die from some stupid operational mishap—that was also acceptable.

What was not acceptable was the possibility that one of the

teams might die as a result of friendly fire. While the term is used to define the source of the fire that inflicts the casualties (our side versus the enemy), there is nothing friendly about being beaten up by your own ally! Speaking from experience, the bitterness, anger, and recriminations that follow an attack from your own side are terribly painful and terribly frustrating. The lesson here is that if you intelligently coordinate your combat operations, leaving as little as possible to chance, the needless loss of men and matériel can be reduced.

After compiling my huge list of all the people on our side who could kill us, I had to refine the methods already in use—and devise new ones—by which all concerned could be kept aware of where we were operating. This was done by defining, for dissemination far and wide, areas where other units fighting in the war could not fire or maneuver freely. This is never easy because everyone who delivers fire or plans combat operations reflexively resists the creation of "no-fire" areas.

Adding to the complexity of mission planning and coordination, every area that was to be made off-limits to the application of firepower had a start time, a duration, and an end time, after which firepower or maneuver could again be employed without any reconnaissance-related restrictions. This creation of reconnaissance-driven restrictions on firepower was most difficult when operations were planned close in, near the coastal enclaves. It was far easier when the range from friendly forces grew larger. Design of the restricted areas required that there be enough room in which a team could operate without the area under restriction adversely affecting anyone who had a legitimate reason to fire or maneuver in that part of the country.

The resulting Areas of Operation (AO) for each team's mission in the field had to be designed to fit that mission. For work along the Laotian border, for example, the AO might be long and narrow, as it covered team movement in search of trails and other signs of NVA infiltration along the unmarked boundary line. In some of the more open terrain we had to ensure that at least part of the assigned AO contained broken terrain or heavy undergrowth in which the team could go to ground at night with some expectation that no NVA unit would stumble over them while moving in the dark. Any AO that was close to friendly forces would also of necessity be much smaller and more restricted because we wanted to avoid interference with the legitimate concerns of the friendly unit for its own security and freedom of action.

Sadly, we had to face the reality that there was no such thing as a secret in the Republic of Vietnam. The AO provided to a reconnaissance team was deemed to be compromised the moment it was made known to anyone outside the company. Spies and sympathizers for the North Vietnamese were known to be working at every command/political level within the country, and we were forced to live with the knowledge that the NVA might be waiting for the Marines when they landed to begin their operations. To counter this potentially deadly situation, we held our messages of notification of assigned AO coordinates until the last possible minute. This was done in the hope that the NVA would not be able to react in time to foil the insertion. Despite that hope, every team landed in their assigned landing zone with an expectation of coming under fire in the first moments after touchdown.

Occasionally in selecting an AO, some nonoperational matters had to be considered, matters that one seldom finds in the field manuals. For instance, some wiseacre decided that for a Marine who was new in-country—an NIC—to lose his status as the new guy on the block, he had to dip his toe in the Ben Hai River, which ran directly down the center of the DMZ between the two warring Vietnams, or to walk on ground that was clearly on the Laotian side of the border between Laos and the Republic of Vietnam. Obviously, any NIC who was worth his salt would slip across the artificial boundaries of an assigned AO if he was close enough to either the river in the DMZ or the border of Laos in the western mountains.

Of course, I could have loudly issued draconian orders to prohibit this operational violation of safety and good sense, but sensing that this new tradition was important to the Marines, I never permitted the slightest official notice of the practice, choosing instead to use one AO boundary for the team and one slightly larger—opened in the direction of either the river or the border—for submission to the coordination agencies. Thus, if the team slipped out of its assigned AO to baptize an NIC, the men would have the delicious feeling that they had pulled one over on me, and I would be sure that no outside agency would fire on them while this took place. On top of everything else, the areas where an NIC might wander to cast off that hated designation were important, and good reconnaissance work could always be done in this terrain that needed checking.

While we were developing our coordination, we had to educate every entity that could deliver fire. They needed to understand our operational concepts so as to ensure that they would be responsive to the requirements of the recon teams should those teams be forced to ask for fire within one of the restricted areas. When firepower is wanted, it is wanted quickly, and the team leaders had to know that their requests would be honored, even when the firing might be needed right on top of their position. When minutes are critical, the man on the ground *must* have the final say. We made every effort to get that point across to all concerned.

Education between supporting elements and those who depend on their support is always a two-way street. From all of the various supporting forces we gleaned important data that we passed on to the troops. We held classes on aircraft capabilities and limitations, munitions effectiveness, and all of the rules on usage that were handed down from above. Everyone in Third Force was schooled on the careful, precise radio procedures that the artillery lived by, as well as the less structured ways that one talks to aviation folks, who are a bit more informal when they communicate among themselves. (We did not, however, ever say, "Real fine, gents, real fine!" or "Roger that": phrases we heard at least a thousand times from aviators of all services who found them voguish in 1969/70.)

One interesting facet of our education was the identification of dead spaces wherein artillery fires were rendered ineffective by their inherent trajectory parameters and the shadow effect of the taller ridges. The operations and intelligence sections prepared map data for all hands to illustrate these dead areas—both as a warning that support could not reach those locations and as information on where the NVA might be found. Their maps showed all of the identical dead spaces, carefully marked. None of us ever took the NVA for fools. Their leadership knew us well, and they intelligently used their knowledge of the strengths and weaknesses of the U.S. military forces to their advantage.

One way to establish detailed coordination with supporting elements is to provide them with liaison officers. We needed to be represented in the SRC, in the Army's XXIV Corps headquarters, at the 101st Airborne Division, and at one or two major commands of the Army of the Republic of Vietnam. Having liaison personnel works because you have a representative on site to advise and explain, to keep maps up to date, and to educate headquarters decision makers on the comings and goings of the reconnaissance teams. If the liaison officer is doing his job, the operational headquarters personnel will learn to appreciate his presence, and the recon teams will be happy to find that they are not bombed, strafed, or shelled by anyone who is purportedly on the same side.

For a unit the size of Third Force, with just twelve officers when manned to the maximum, to provide enough liaison officers to do the job was impossible. I selected key spots for those officers and/or staff noncommissioned officers that I felt we had to have detailed to liaison representation and made it my business to establish other ways to coordinate many other relationships. The need for liaison representation hurt the company, taking leaders away from their units and forcing less experienced Marines to shoulder the burden of field leadership.

Additionally, we found that a lieutenant with a total of eighteen months of active-duty experience was welcomed and accepted as a liaison officer, whereas a staff sergeant with twelve years in the Corps was violently resisted as a substitute for that officer. To preserve my sanity, I often sent Captain Hisler to reason with the staff officers who acted in this fashion. I do not know if he used reason or threats. I do know that he was able to keep our officer losses to liaison duty at a level that was almost acceptable.

When sending a liaison representative was not possible, we disseminated the necessary information through use of maps that would reveal to pilots at U.S. Air Force bases in Thailand and to Vietnamese artillerymen in the DMZ all of my reconnaissance AOs and no-fire areas, where fire could not be delivered without the permission of the recon team on the ground.

Shabby living conditions was another loose end that was adversely affecting morale, and Marines with lousy morale have shortened attention spans and will be more likely to make terminal errors of judgment. Third Force Marines were living just above the level of barnyard animals when I arrived in the company, and changing that became an instant priority. Because some units were already being shifted out of the war, we were fortunate in finding better living conditions for the troops each time we moved. From the miserably tight quarters they shared with 3d Recon Battalion we were able, after several moves (first within the Quang Tri Combat Base and later south to Phu Bai), to get control of enough space for the troops. They deserved to live in some comfort between deployments to the field.

Promotion inequities and the lack of defined promotion policies can result—with good reason—in disgruntled men. We had no time for that sort of nonsense, so the promotional loose ends had to be dealt with. Third Force seemed to lack any form of command-directed promotion policy. Some of the men appeared qualified on paper, and when interviewed they seemed to be fully ready for advancement. Yet, they had not been promoted when their peers had been advanced.

To deal with this situation I directed Captain Hisler to examine every record book in the company to identify anyone who might have been slighted by omission or by discrimination. He completed his examination in short order, and those who had been left behind improperly by the 3d Recon Battalion system had new stripes to wear. In addition to removing inequities, we established as a firm, well-advertised policy that meritorious promotion was possible for a job well done. Below the rank of sergeant this was easy: all we did was promote the man, enter it into his record book, and make a unit-diary entry so he would get pay appropriate to his new rank.

Routine elevation of anyone to the rank of meritorious sergeant, however, was not possible because of the control of the cutting scores. These scores were calculated through use of a headquarters-developed formula that assigned numerical values to time in service, time in grade, conduct marks, and proficiency marks in the individual's service record book. Cutting scores needed for promotion were made known to us by orders published from headquarters in Washington. Nevertheless, we did have the odd exception, when quotas came down from III MAF headquarters, of promoting one or two sergeants to that rank.

Lance Corporal Sexton, for example, had a most unusual experience within our promotion system. He had a fine record, and when he did an especially superb job in a firefight during which he was hit by an AK-47 rifle bullet that lodged in the sheath to his K-Bar knife, I spot-promoted him to corporal on his return to the company area. Not long after that, General Nickerson asked that Sexton come to Da Nang to describe the firefight to him personally. While Corporal Sexton was there, the general spot-promoted him to sergeant. Nobody could see any reason to argue with the general's logic, so we left well enough alone.

Another loose end related to the qualifications earned in the various special schools that the force recon Marines attended. When I arrived in Third Force there were *no* quotas for professional schools. This situation created a real bone of contention for those men who had come to us from other units: they were doing the work and wanted to be able to learn the special skills as well. Obviously, the company also had a vested interest in adding qualified personnel who could replace men lost to death, wounds, and rotation.

In addition, the men earned qualification badges, and extra pay went with those badges. For men who took great pride in what they were doing, neither the badges nor the extra money were inconsequential items when it came to morale. Besides the badge-producing schools for SCUBA and airborne qualification, there was an Army school in Vietnam—known as Recondo—that had a well-deserved professional reputation, and we wanted to obtain some quotas to that rigorous and valuable course of instruction as well.

To keep professional schooling and special qualification from being a barrier to promotion or team assignment, the Igor went to great lengths to educate everyone on the new policies, pointing out that quotas would be obtained and men would be sent for schooling on a fair and equal basis. We would allow competition for any training slots that we could get, but combat operations capability would always take precedence over detachment for training. We made it exceptionally clear that we would *not* tolerate anyone denigrating those who were unable, for whatever reason, to attend special schooling.

Despite our best efforts, however, many of the finest members of the company never were able to qualify for the distinctive badges, but that was a situation beyond our control. Combat took priority and the troops seemed to understand.

When Third Force was under the control of 3d Recon Battalion, the rest and recreation (R&R) quotas had not filtered down in an evenhanded fashion. Another loose end. Many of the team members' requests to take R&R in a specific location had been turned aside—a situation that did not seem to apply, however, to those who served in administrative billets, closer to the flagpole. Once we were operating independently, we established our own quotas. I then detailed Captain Hisler and Lieutenant Morris to organize our R&R program so that it benefited everyone equally—with priority of choice being retained for the more junior members of the company. I told them to run it like the chow line, privates first class and lance corporals first, corporals and sergeants second, staff noncommissioned officers third, and officers last.

As a loose end, R&R quota assignments may not sound like much, but we considered anything that damaged morale to have a direct and immediate effect on operational competence. We believed the axiom that any reduction in competence would foreshadow an increase in body bags heading east in the belly of C-141 aircraft.

In addition to time off for R&R, Marines often need emergency leave to deal with crises in their families at home. While every unit tries to expedite every emergency leave, Third Force added a small factor to ease the situation for the affected individual. We established a box—kept by the first sergeant—and salted it with about three hundred dollars. The cash was there for the taking by anyone who needed some extra money for his emergency leave in the United States. Contributions were voluntary, and repayment in full was expected. It was the responsibility of the man who used the money to replace it whenever he could do so from his pay. There was to be no formal accounting by the first sergeant—none! Yet, the faith engendered by this small act of trust resulted in a box that always contained more money than had been tossed in originally. When the company stood down from active operations, the box was still there, and it contained something over eight hundred dollars.

Another loose end that was bad for morale, in the long run, was a lethargic and unresponsive awards-and-decorations policy. Nothing any of us ever tried seemed to improve this worrisome matter. Not to my satisfaction, anyway. When one of the men of Third Force was written up for an award, we always had a sinking feeling when the recommendation left for higher headquarters—even when hand carried to Da Nang by an officer. We knew that many of the comfort-loving staff folks held us in contempt, and such petty-minded men would take that contempt out by denying a force reconnaissance Marine an award that had been justly earned. Except for those times when we could get the general's personal initial on the form, we never felt comfortable about the fairness of the awards system. Worse, nothing we did seemed to keep a number of these recommendations from disappearing into thin air.

Even today, across the intervening twenty-five years, I am angered by the fact that many Third Force Marines received no award—despite recommendations written and submitted—and others received lower awards than they merited, awards that had been downgraded by someone far from the desperate firefights in the Vietnamese mountains. Downgrading is not unusual, as every infantryman knows full well. If you write a Silver Star recommendation for a lieutnant and a lance corporal, citing the same level of bravery in action, the officer will surely get the award and the lance corporal's award will be downgraded one or two levels. Sadder still, when Third Force was broken up in May 1970, many of the men went on to other units, where they received nothing at all in the way of recognition at the end of their tour. The awards system did work splendidly for the rear-echelon pogues, however; I saw their decorated chests everywhere I went at headquarters in Washington.

For whatever reason, the awards system just did not work in a way that would appropriately dignify the efforts of those who dared greatly. The young Marines who actually did the work in the field against the NVA were shortchanged by a loose end that no amount of honest effort at our low level could bring under control. That was shameful, and certainly not in keeping with the professional quality of the combat service rendered.

5

SHIFTING THE OUTLOOK

In peacetime or war, every time a Marine unit gets a new commander a certain amount of upheaval, some strife, and a clear sense of change occur. In the case of Third Force Reconnaissance Company, a far greater and more complete change was needed than might have occurred under other circumstances. I intended to alter in every fundamental aspect the lives of those who were going to take part in the coming independent operations.

The attitudes and corporate culture that were in place in Third Force when I took command were unacceptable. The organization seemed to be functioning without obvious purpose and direction; slovenly performance by uncommitted men was the norm. From the top to the bottom there seemed to be no interest in living up to the standards—of dress, deportment, preparation for combat operations, operational reporting—expected of such a unit. I was convinced that the attitude was that of a group attempting to get by with just the minimum effort.

The rumors of faked patrols were one clear indicator that things needed to be changed. Allegedly, teams were reporting that they were moving through operational areas that they never even approached. Another indicator was the response to a fragging incident in the 3d Marine Division wherein a lieutenant was assassinated by someone who rolled a grenade under his cot. This story drew a thigh-slapping laugh from a few thugs in Third Force. Reacting violently to what we saw on arrival, Hisler, Coffman, and I made sure that *everyone* was quickly aware that this was going to be a time when the Marines of Third Force Reconnaissance Company would begin living new and vastly more challenging lives. Change was what I had come to accomplish, and revolutionary change is what came to pass. Not overnight, but more quickly than many ever thought possible!

While making virtual war on the personnel and logistics aspects of the establishment that was supposed to support Third Force, I was also dealing in a very firm, very specific manner with matters of importance to the internal functioning of the unit. It was necessary to drastically alter the way things were done, starting at the bedrock-level and working upward. A sudden purge of the thugs and those few who were considered to be non-performers among the Marines in the company created the first stir. I began that effort the day I took command, using high-visibility firings to make the point to all hands.

After that initial trauma, it was time to weed out a few unsatisfactory individuals who might have been able to do the work but who did not possess the moral fiber that was now to be the acceptable standard.

I had learned from a friend, a Marine gunnery sergeant assigned to the provincial-level CIA element in Quang Tri Province, that one of the force recon sergeants was deeply involved in currency manipulation schemes. He was offered the opportunity in a one-on-one discussion to come clean, but he denied ever trading in currency or Military Payment Certificates (MPC). A quick, obviously illegal—but we were not going to waste time fighting the search and seizure laws—look in his personal effects produced more than ten thousand dollars in U.S. and Vietnamese currency, a hoard of MPC, dope, and illegal weaponry, plus several cases of scotch, bourbon, and vodka. I had him put in irons and had him and all his holdings in the hands of the naval investigative types (who were standing by at my request) in minutes. It did not take long for the word to filter from one end of the unit to the other that things were, indeed, changing.

The extent of change began with the most basic aspect of daily life in the unit—language. To be considered proficient professionals, the Marines had to quit using jargon and slang. They were directed to habitually use standardized terms that had an understandable meaning to everyone we might contact. Because we were preparing to operate deep into NVA-dominated portions of the country, I demanded that words and terminology become as close to a repeatable standard as possible. Operating independently, we would be under constant hostile scrutiny from people on our side, and the use of unprofessional terms would leave us open to critical hassles from those who had little else to do profitably with their time.

The first chance to begin this education took place the day I took command. I was with Lieutenant Coffman in the rudimentary COC when the radio speakers carried one of the teams in the DMZ reporting the presence of "beaucoup gooks." Since this had no meaning to me, I asked the operations chief to tell me the precise definition of beaucoup. His embarrassment was total, and I let him off the hook quickly enough to spare his pride. Effective from that moment, however, the term was assigned a meaning, and *everyone* was made aware that beaucoup meant exactly 212—not many or a lot. If a force recon Marine had the good fortune to see a 215-man NVA unit in the DMZ, the spot report had better contain either the precise number or the acceptable alternative, "beaucoup plus three." To take the edge off the very specific criticism I was making, I had purposely resorted to humor—but no joke was intended.

As proof that this effort had a telling effect on those who were present, I cite a remark by retired M.Sgt. Danny Williams, who departed the company as a medical evacuation case. Our next meeting—at Marine Corps Recruit Depot, San Diego—occurred in 1992. That day he grinned and said to me, "Colonel Lee, I just want you to know that every unit I ever served with after Third Force learned to use language right and that beaucoup means 212, exactly, no matter what!"

After my edict on beaucoup, we quickly went on to other areas of language usage. Hundreds, perhaps thousands, of aviators have heard someone on the ground asking that firepower support be delivered against the enemy who "is right in front of us in the rice paddy." Now, aviators can often see thirty thousand rice paddies at any one moment, while recon and infantry Marines see those paddies one at a time. Training was needed immediately to wipe from the company vernacular any form of that variety of confusing and stupid radio transmission. Soon there were Marines at work looking at their wrist or pocket compasses, chanting things like, "From last impact, target bears 234 degrees, 50 meters" or "Free fire, bearing 080 to 140 magnetic from my mirror."

Part of this change in procedures was educational, part was

motivational, part was humorous—with a point—but most important, *all* of this effort was aimed at saving lives when it counted. Men die when time is lost. Survival might be measured in seconds, and confusion from misuse of terms or reliance on slang was not going to happen if I could prevent it.

Next on my agenda for corporate culture change was the area of *active* participation in the war. A force reconnaissance company has clerks, cooks, drivers, supply people, radio technicians, armorers, and an entire section of parachute riggers. These Marines, though working hard at their assigned duties, were not taking an active part in the company operations in the field against the NVA. The day I arrived to take command, I issued orders that *every* man in the company could expect to see duty in the field with the teams. This operational change included myself, my executive officer, and every Marine and corpsman in the company down to the most junior cook in the mess section. Most took it calmly; some few—including two supply chiefs—whined and cried bitterly. These men were summarily fired and replaced with volunteers from other units.

It was a most satisfying experience when the third replacement supply chief, James Tate (a staff sergeant), arrived and registered no great concern about earning his money as a Marine in combat. Tate turned out to be a magnificent Marine, performing all of his supply and combat duties flawlessly. But he did confide, many years later, that although he had no feeling that he should be excused from going "out there," it was not until his first helicopter ride to the Ashau Valley radio relay site that he really understood how far it really was to the there we had discussed.

None of this alteration of individual roles to a more active state was conducted as a pogrom against anyone. The idea was to bring everyone up to speed so that they could contribute—no feather-bedding allowed. A reconnaissance indoctrination program, known as RIP, was drawn up by Lieutenant Coffman for all hands, both new arrivals and those who remained in the company after the initial purging of the ranks. The Igor's program covered all the skills we deemed essential. It began with the most basic infantry skills (crucial among these was map reading) that needed to be reviewed, and it concluded with more specialized activities such as helicopter rappeling, prisoner snatch techniques, communications and ambush drills, sniping, sensor implantation, jungle movement, etc., etc.

We tried to make everyone aware of techniques we had acquired in schools or had picked up the hard way in previous combat tours. Coffman was a demanding taskmaster, and he cut no slack to anyone. Passing RIP meant that clerks and mechanics quickly became basic recon Marines. In addition, getting a check mark from Coffman was a great morale boost for every man who struggled to make the grade.

Training all men from the support elements of the company improved both capability and team availability. The operational platoons could expect to be reinforced, when it was necessary, with men who knew what they were doing in the bush. This meant that whenever a particular Marine might have a cold, his coughing and snorting did not make his team nondeployable. We could now fill the slot with a trained and ready man from one of the available pools and send the team to the field. We also created more teams, including one made up exclusively from the parachute riggers, who called themselves Team Lofty.

Additionally, the staff and support Marines were an excellent source for use on such specialized missions as downed aircrew recovery, clearance of explosive devices from bridges, bomb damage assessment, and sensor implantation. Using an operational team for these specialized missions reduced the amount of time that that team had for long-range patrolling.

A binding force grows within a unit when all hands are subjected to the same dangers, and I took full advantage of this psychological fact in building a cohesive, competent, and totally focused unit. The idea behind this upheaval was not original with me. As it was initiated, I had in mind some ideas gleaned from the Israeli view of leadership, with its emphasis on the leader's place being at the point of gravest danger. We just modified that thinking to include everyone in Third Force Reconnaissance Company. All of us could earn an equal share in the satisfaction of a job well done only if every last one of us was exposed to an absolutely equal share of the danger.

At the same time that Third Force was being forcefully shifted to an all-hands warfighting stance, the training effort was expanded enormously. It was Lieutenant Coffman's goal to virtually retrain and remotivate every Marine in the unit. In addition to the military skills training in the RIP classes, we wanted to bring everyone to a higher standard of personal dedication. That meant destroying old attitudes and replacing them with a steady diet of professional ideas about living like a Marine, winning like a Marine, and, if need be, dying like a Marine. We wanted to restore in the men pride in themselves, in their unit, in their corps, and in their country. We were not ashamed to teach pride as a positive emotion for fighting men to hold close to their hearts. We taught the Marines and corpsmen that openly caring about their comrades and their mission was neither out of style nor unmanly.

To ensure that all of this training was as valuable as possible we leaned on our personal experiences and openly pirated the best ideas from every school we felt could contribute to successful prosecution of the mission of Third Force. Between us, Lieutenant Coffman and I had a wealth of professional sources to tap. We both had trained with Army Rangers: the Igor had his Royal Marine training experience, and I had attended selected portions of the U.S. Army's Special Forces School. As a team, Lieutenant Coffman and I had endured the rigors of the British Jungle Warfare School at Johore Baru in Malaysia and the Australian Army's Jungle Warfare Training Center in Kanundra. These schools all taught military skills and the ethical truths of soldiering that we attempted to pass on formally and informally to every man in Third Force. There never were enough hours in the day!

Coffman and I were absolutely convinced that standardization within the unit and *constant* attention to detail would save lives. Individualism was fine in its place, but we would not accept it in matters of importance. We began with checklists at the individual level and made similar checklists at every level of unit complexity. The list, carefully detailed by the Igor, specified what a recon Marine would carry, where he would carry it, and how he would carry it. We felt that if every man's load was completely standardized it would be possible to find, merely by feel, any needed item on any Marine who was down, even on the darkest night you ever encountered.

Thus, attention to detail included the location of items on the load-carrying web gear (pressure bandage always on left shoulder of harness) and precise specification of the pocket where the radio codes would be carried (left chest pocket). With almost no exception, everything had its prescribed place, and we expected that item to be there at inspection before deployment and during operations in the field. Corpsmen were hardly exempt from this obsessive organizational thought process: the contents of their individual medical field packs was standardized in the same manner by the senior "Doc," who produced checklists too.

Using such lists may sound childish to the uninitiated, but they work in managing the takeoffs and landings of huge complex aircraft, and they work when you are dressing for war. We required that every individual and his gear be inspected by his team leader, who signed off that everything specified was present and in the correct location. We required that every man in the team be inspected by the platoon sergeant and by the platoon leader—when that officer was not required to be away from the company on some liaison duty or other. Last, before morning briefing and lift-off to the jungle, the operations officer or the executive officer would personally recheck everything, ensure that *neither* cigarettes nor gum were going along to the field, and sign off on the checklist.

Actually, the experienced force recon Marines did not find this particularly onerous, as many had been Ranger trained and had been to the airborne school—both of which live by, and teach survival by, the checklist. None of us who were parachute qualified had ever found anything degrading or childish in the checking and rechecking that riggers do before they let you jump out of aircraft in aerial flight. In fact, it gives one a sense of confidence to have someone else ensure that you are ready, and I too submitted to inspection before going out to visit with the NVA in the dark mountains of Vietnam.

Another aspect of life in Third Force Recon that we immediately altered was the required level of training between missions in the field. After a good night of sleep and a quality debriefing, the team members would begin work on one of the most important projects in the training syllabus, Immediate Action (IA) drills. Over and over again the teams practiced and played out various scenarios for the training section. Sudden cries indicating contact from one side or the other would be followed by physically doing the things that would be necessary in a real contact situation. For example, if the point man was declared to have been hit and downed, the team had to set up protective firing positions, his backup had to pick the man up and carry him to safety, and the team had to roll back out of immediate contact to break away, or at least to get sufficiently loose from the enemy force so that the team could be given fire support and an extraction from the fight.

IA drills were credited by many with saving their lives. They are not a panacea, but, like plays in a football game, if executed well after long hours of practice, more good things happen than bad things. When the level of risk is pegged at survival to live another day, the play contacts practiced over and over in the compound at Quang Tri and later at Phu Bai in Vietnam's sweaty heat or chilling rain made a difference. I am convinced that Marines made it home because of the IA drills.

Sitting around waiting for a mission was no longer tolerated. Training, as directed by the operations officer, was hard, it was constant, and the subjects were complex. That training had to take place while we continued to operate on missions assigned to us from above. Every aspect of reconnaissance operations was covered, and it was not unusual for Coffman, Hisler, or me to be holding school in the COC at 0100. Six or seven team leaders and an equal number of others would be picking our brains, posing detailed questions for discussion, and generally working together to soak in as much professional knowledge as possible before their next mission.

Reorganization of the company into more teams than it had ever fielded before, and preparation of those teams for longer-range operations into the far reaches of Northern I Corps, sharpened the level of competence of the troops and caused us to make training an around-the-clock effort. We always tried to accomplish more than the time would allow. We taught tactics as well as techniques, dwelling for hours on why certain tactics made more sense than others.

We forced the issue of terminology while teaching techniques, hammering home the need for every man to be qualified to talk on the radio with any element of air, artillery, or naval gunfire that might be able to provide covering fire support. It was not unusual for a Marine to be stopped suddenly by an officer or staff noncommissioned officer as he was passing by and asked to call an artillery mission on a nearby hill mass. We would just hand him the map, tell him that NVA troops were on the hill, and order him to call the mission. We would act as the radio set and would interject the appropriate mission responses. Not fun for all who stammered through the early trials, it nevertheless resulted in a company of men who could all call fires from artillery sources or from aircraft without babbling foolishly in confusion.

The Marine Corps normally uses officers to call and control air strikes. Third Force recon teams did not have that luxury, and we found that well-trained privates first class could do the job when it had to be done in the bush.

Fundamentally, once on our own we would be responsible both to react to tasking from above and to generate our own missions. To make this all fit into a sensible and understandable set of policies, the organization needed to be brought up to a planned operational tempo. Team deployment schedules and field-to-base camp ratios were developed and disseminated to everyone. Nobody laughed as the plan of operations was explained: they knew it was going to be more demanding than anything they had ever encountered before. I established an eight-day cycle of operations as company policy. It was an ambitious plan, with six of every eight days scheduled for operational deployment to the field. The remaining two days would be spent getting ready to go again!

In practice, the cycle proceeded through eight specifically named days, each with its anticipated activities. Thus, in compliance with the policy, on the morning of Day One the team would be given a written warning order describing the forthcoming mission, the team leader would get an overflight of his assigned AO, and intelligence photos of the AO would be ordered. The SRC would be alerted and would gather from various sources all available information on the AO and its surroundings.

The night of Day One would include issuance of the formal written order directing the team to conduct the assigned mission, the initial two rounds of inspection, and the detailed briefing for the team in the COC. All available photos would be studied at this time.

Day Two would be insertion day, and before dawn the Marines would assemble their gear on a line of squares painted on the ramp where the helicopters would park, and more inspections would follow. Of course, test firing was always conducted in the test-fire pit. Also before dawn, the heavy ordnance—Claymores, bulk explosives, CN gas grenades, M-72 shoulder-fired rockets,

M-60 machine guns, etc.—was issued from the company explosives bunker.

When the helicopters arrived, the team and all of the aircrews were briefed together for final coordination. Lift-off and flight to the AO usually took place in the morning hours, both for the improved lift effects of the cooler air, and because in the daylight it would be easier for a team to fight its way out of trouble than it would be if insertion was in the evening and the fight took place after dark. We did insert in the dark too, but it was a great deal more dangerous and hardly more productive in intelligence gathering.

Days Two through Seven were patrol days, with extraction usually scheduled for the morning hours of Day Seven. This too was driven in part by the better lift during morning hours and by the fact that NVA soldiers might try to leap on the team during extraction. To pound away at NVA troops more effectively when we encountered them, we definitely preferred to work in the daylight. Day Seven, after extraction, was devoted to a hasty debriefing, collecting, and forwarding to the SRC any data or physical items that were time sensitive, cleaning up, and relaxation.

On the morning of Day Eight the team took part in a highly detailed debriefing, and the team leader and his assistant jointly wrote up a report for the intelligence officer, Lieutenant Robertson. The S-2 also required that they update the master map as to trails located and any other features that would affect later operations in that area. Midday, Day Eight, would find the teams working on IA drills, cleaning and packing gear, writing letters, and getting ready to start the cycle again. The evening of Day Eight was designated as free time for rest and recovery.

Establishment of this ambitious plan of operational cycles all took place during active combat, and it is important to note that planning is just that, planning. Due to a wide variety of events, a number of the teams sent on patrol were unable to complete their missions in accord with the planned cycle. Teams got shot out of the zone on touchdown and returned to base without a day of patrolling. Teams were kept on patrol when weather precluded any aerial extraction, and, on occasion, a team would run into so much trouble that it would have to be extracted for survival. Some teams were inserted for a specific mission and came home in two or three days, having completed the mission.

Regardless of such exigencies, the eight-day cycle was instituted to provide a strong sense of predictability to the lives of the men of the company and to permit my staff to do more planning and less short-notice reacting to the needs and desires of those for whom we worked. Each member of a team knew that whenever he came back to the Third Force Recon base area from a patrol, that day was immediately designated as Day Seven. He could expect to rest the next day, after which he would, once again, be back into the cycle. This plan provided some structure for those who would live it, with enough flexibility to absorb events that could neither be controlled nor predicted.

Third Force Recon changed. A direct appeal to pride in personal and professional performance worked wonders. Clear enunciation of goals piqued the interest of everyone, causing them to pay closer attention to those goals. Major overhauls were made in the areas of personal appearance and adherence to simple decency.

The most petty matter that required attention was the equitable distribution of such beer and soda as happened to come into our possession. One or two individuals just did not understand the concept of fair distribution to all hands. To alter this I was forced to formally order that the number of cans received be divided by the total number of men, officers, staff noncommissioned officers, noncommissioned officers, and remaining enlisted men. The separate officer/staff noncommissioned officer beer and soda cache was closed forevermore. Certain members of the company who felt that junior Marines did not rate this type of treatment bitched, but the point was made. Equal access by the major and the privates to whatever good deals, if any, came around for the company had considerable appeal to the rank and file.

Third Force Recon needed to be altered in order to meet the challenge of independent operations. We did it quickly and thoroughly because no time could be wasted on niceties. I knew that major U.S. ground forces were scheduled to leave the Republic of Vietnam in late 1969. One unit on the departure list was the 3d Marine Division. The void left by its departure would be covered only by reconnaissance patrols, ones that we would be required to deploy. Once the twenty thousand Marines of 3d Division went back to Okinawa, NVA units would be free to maneuver almost anywhere they chose in Northern I Corps. Only along the coast would they find any U.S. forces—an Army mechanized unit (1st of the 5th Mech), and that unit was not scheduled to operate anywhere inland along National Route 9. Third Force would be their only resistance west of the foothills.

Another reason for wanting to alter the company was my desire to create a more fully professional unit, one that could be expected to perform with honor and attention to duty when asked to dare greatly. I knew full well the level of risk that these men would be facing, and I remained convinced that the road to maximum survival was through constant pressure on everyone: pressure that caused each man to focus on performing at his professional peak. Nobody was going to live to be much older if they sought to sleepwalk through combat operations in Northern I Corps in late 1969 and early 1970.

6

YOU ARE TOO EXPENSIVE

Long-range reconnaissance operations—if supported properly—are frighteningly expensive. An incredibly small number of Marines can use up the things and stuff expended in a war far faster than many deem appropriate. Proper and effective support of these small units also requires an enormous expenditure of time by supporting elements, all of whom are normally already stretched thin by the missions levied on them. But worst of all, support for operations such as ours required men, matériel, and money from elements of the III MAF, the U.S. Army, the U.S. Air Force, and the Vietnamese military, all of whom were decidedly unwilling to work with us and/or were totally uninterested in what Third Force Recon was going to be doing in Northern I Corps.

For a small unit like Third Force, with only a major in command, the submission of detailed requests for support of special operations was an exceptionally difficult and complicated situation. Almost no one responds favorably when you make the rounds, hat in hand, looking for support for secret, special operations. Creating an independently operating force reconnaissance company forced me to touch all the bases in assembling the necessary support, and it was no surprise to find a wall of dollar-related, manpower-related, and resource-related resistance to virtually everything we considered necessary.

First, we did not have the right individual equipment, period, and what we did have was in poor repair. This reflected both the hard use of three years of combat as part of the 3d Reconnaissance Battalion and insufficient matériel in the first place. While Lieutenant Coffman toiled in the operational world, Captain

Hisler and I began to assemble the equipment we needed. Some could be obtained by legal and normal means, other items took an application of initiative or the talents of an old-fashioned horse trader.

We felt impoverished, and we sought every imaginable item used by troops in the field. We needed additional sleeping shirts (an Army-developed item that made life more tolerable for those sleeping in the rain and cold of the mountains), two-quart canteens, compasses (in pitifully short supply), strobe lights, flashlights, signal mirrors, bush hats, pen-size flares, K-Bar knives, grenade pouches, gloves, and more and more and more. Until we had collected these things, the company really would not be ready to fight effectively.

What Third Force Reconnaissance Company really needed in 1969 we did our best to beg, borrow, or steal—rather successfully, I am proud to say. While we seldom found all the things that we wanted in the supply system, we eventually got an issue of new equipment that was part L. L. Bean, Eddie Bauer (via the CIA), and military issue.

Second, the company needed to replace many of the major items issued to it as part of the approved Table of Equipment. The rifles, the radios, the binoculars, the machine guns, the vehicles, for instance, were plainly worn out. A great deal of the company gear was long overdue for the scrap heap. A return to the official, authorized equipment levels, however, would still not meet our needs. We wanted, and demanded, more of the standard-issue items plus the addition of many more pieces of equipment not normally found in a force recon company. Each of the things that we wanted to add met needs that we had identified, needs that had not been considered by anyone who had assembled the company's equipment list. When the shooting starts, such a list—drawn up in peacetime—often is at variance with the needs of the troops doing the fighting.

For Third Force to become a fully independent element, as envisioned by General Nickerson, we had to have new equipment that fit the mission and for the additional teams carrying out that mission. We needed greatly increased allowances of specialized items such as night-vision devices, seismic detectors, encryption devices, and a host of minor items such as the thirty-round magazines that we wanted for everyone who walked point on patrol.

Our battles with the supply folks were long, hard, and intense. When we asked for items that we "did not rate," we often got a lot of yap, yap, yap.

I was reminded, then, of an experience I had when I was preparing to go to Vietnam in 1965 with Regimental Landing Team Seven. Serving at the time as the 2d Battalion, 7th Marines logistics officer, I asked for two extra recoil springs for each of the machine guns in the battalion. Supply announced that I could not have the recoil springs because I did not have an AMRD. Not speaking the arcane language of supply, I asked just what in blazes an AMRD was and learned that it meant Average Monthly Recurring Demand. No amount of calm, or not-so-calm, explanation of the difference between firing blanks at Camp Pendleton and being ready to change recoil springs in a firefight in some jungle in the rain registered with the bureaucrats in supply. What was required was the signature of the colonel, which we obtained in a matter of minutes. Following that, the recoil springs came almost magically into our hands.

Something similar took place in Da Nang when Captain Hisler and I were replacing worn-out items and getting extra ones that we needed. When we happened to appear at a supply source with a requisition signed by the commanding general, the floodgates would open. But even with that high level of command interest, we did not win all our battles over matériel. All in all, though, we did well, but after each encounter, we heard one form or another of the litany "You cost too much!"

Worry over costs was hardly restricted to the supply world. The force personnel officer himself voiced the opinion that it would cost too many men to fulfill our requested manpower increase. To be fully effective, I felt strongly that we would need about 115 percent of the Table of Organization strength of a force reconnaissance company on paper. It seemed logical to me that we would need some additional manpower because of the vast expansion in our operational area and the attendant responsibility for surveillance by additional teams over that area.

I was prepared, however, for the reality that it was normal for the big headquarters to be staffed at 200 percent of paper strength while the fighting units lived with chronic shortages in personnel. In 1965 and 1966 the rifle companies that I had commanded (E-2/7 and F-2/7) averaged 135 effective Marines in the field. That was roughly 70 percent of the 206-man Table of Operation strength, while the 1st Division headquarters had 2,300-plus Marines assigned for 1,250 billets.

I was also quite familiar with the attrition that a unit lives with on a daily basis in combat. Besides the obvious losses to death, wounds, and operational accidents, manpower shortages are caused by R&R, emergency leave, leave granted to volunteers who extend their tour of duty in the combat theater, sicknesses of all types, and the school-related absences that are a necessary part of keeping the unit capabilities up to par.

We were, of course, turned down by the personnel folks. Our strength levels were not raised when our mission was made larger and more complex. We were not surprised, but we looked at the effort that we had expended as a necessary attempt. We owed it to the troops to make the case for more men. Our lives in Third Force would have been eased, and some of my Marines might be alive today, if we had not been denied the increase we requested.

Even in the intelligence community we found that our requests for more maps, more photos, more this and more that were greeted with incredulity. It was as if we were asking them to reinvent the wheel. When I told them that we wanted low-oblique aerial photos taken every day of prospective operational areas for the following day's missions, they were utterly astonished. Before this all began, Third Force had been far, far away from these folks, and the company had not directly presented demands for anything. If 3d Recon Battalion had made such requests before, it was not reflected in the records of Third Force.

Things were going to be done far differently under my direction, however, and the intelligence elements found us to be pushy and demanding as we began laying out new requirements for support of our operations. As was the case with the simple compass, some personnel believed it was proper for a reconnaissance team to deploy to the field with merely one map. Nonsense. We finally got what we wanted, albeit not without creating some enemies.

Effective communication is the lifeblood of reconnaissance operations. We needed more radios, more frequencies, and more cryptographic equipment. This need was not hard to explain when one looked at the number of teams to be fielded, the requirement for two radios per team, the number of liaison elements that were required, and the increased tempo of our operational deployments. Here too, however, we found our requests quickly pared down to levels with which the force communications officer could be comfortable. This result was not to our liking, and we went forward to solve the problems through our own efforts. We begged, borrowed, traded for, and stole equipment to keep the company going. By the middle of September 1969 we had obtained about 200 percent of our rated number of radio sets and the associated equipment for those radios. Our needs were being met, but not from any normal channels of supply.

Frequencies were requested for the purpose of permitting us to operate our various communications nets. Submissions of our frequency requests opened another unwanted Pandora's box, one filled with pointless opposition to our identified requirements. Needing and being denied a considerable number of frequencies beyond the number allotted, including a couple in the ultra high frequency (UHF) range, I resorted to subterfuge. Books were available that listed the frequencies assigned to a vast array of units: those in the Republic of Vietnam as well as those in Japan, Hawaii, and the United States. Being resourceful, we carefully selected our own frequencies. Using our handy lists, we could happily tell an aviator to preset his UHF radio to three zero five, decimal six, and call it Button Green. We knew that 305.6 was not in use in our area of operations and was assigned as "squadron common" to an aviation unit that was many miles from the fray.

This whole silly need to be deeply involved in frequency napping vanished when the 3d Marine Division left the war in October 1969. After that we had access to whole books of division frequencies that might be in use in Okinawa but which nobody was using in Northern I Corps—with the possible exception of the NVA, who did not clear its frequency usage with any of our bureaucrats.

Possession of radios always carries with it the need for call signs. In the Republic of Vietnam the U.S. forces switched call signs every so often to fool the NVA. Of course, no NVA soldier worth knowing was ever fooled by the changes because the units lived in base camps with huge signs on the gates proclaiming their identity. In the early part of the war, units came to fight using their call signs from peacetime training. I remember that when the 2d Battalion, 4th Marines—commanded by then-Lt. Col. P. X. Kelly, who would one day be commandant—arrived in our area in 1966, they were known as "Bendix." Hearing them on the radio was like finding an old friend in a huge crowd, for nine years before that time I had spent more than two years of my life answering radio calls in the 4th Marines that began with the Bendix call sign.

Although we did not believe that all this call-sign shifting fooled the NVA for one minute, we had no choice in the matter, and call signs were passed out to us by the communications bureaucrats who acted as if they were dispensing gold coins.

Looking over the list, I was stunned to find out that Third Force Reconnaissance Company was now to be known as "Coconut Candy." That made me Coconut Candy Six, Captain Hisler Coconut Candy Five, and the huge frame of the Igor Coconut Candy Three. Despite the obvious humor, this was unacceptable. Coconut Candy was an appellation that I was unwilling to bear for myself or for the company. The communications officer, Lieutenant Murphy, was sent to rectify this unsatisfactory situation. He returned from his mission without success and was harshly chastened by officers on the force communications staff.

I then went myself to deal with these folks and hit a stone wall of hostility. They had found time to yell at Lieutenant Murphy, a shy and earnest young man who possessed limited confidence in his abilities. That was offensive and unprofessional, and it was my intention to do something about it when I went there. When I arrived in the land of the communications big shots, they did not yell at me, but they were not interested in my anger at the treatment of my lieutenant, nor did they give me any new call signs. What they did was pull rank (colonel vs. major) and announce that the discussion was closed.

My response included some remarks concerning the effect of appropriate call signs on fighting spirit, citing units of the Army's 101st Airborne Division known as Stiletto and Striker as examples. My comments were ignored, so I shifted to point out the deleterious effects on morale and discipline that could happen if some Third Force Marine killed a couple of communications types who teased him about being a piece of coconut candy. I also pointed out that I had seen fights break out over call signs in the past when one unit with some black Marines took violent umbrage over being teased about being members of a unit with the call sign "Senior Digger"—which had been trashed to "See Ya Nigger" by a number of red-neck illiterates. Nothing I could say seemed to be of any interest to the communications folks. They had power and they chose to exercise it. Since the colonel retained his rank position over me, and always would, I chose to leave without shooting any of them. Not a mean feat, considering my level of frustration.

Having wasted energy trying to work cooperatively within the system, we decided to make our own call signs to suit ourselves. Harking back to the Mangudai who served the great Genghis Khan some seven hundred years ago, I decided that Ancient Scout would do nicely as my personal call sign and for the company as a whole.

Once that was decided, Captain Hisler and Lieutenant Coffman created a long list of team calls that would be easy to use on the radio and that would not embarrass or irritate anyone. Team names like "Boxhill, "Snaky," "Arctic," "Atlas," "Lofty," and the like were acceptable to all hands. More importantly, Third Force Recon now had an identity that could not be easily derided—one that we could use with pride. I became Ancient Scout Six with pleasure.

Antennas were another part of our supply woes. Using radios, as we did, at ranges that were frequently double the intended transmission distance required the best antennas available. Since the Third Force Recon equipment table did not contain enough long-range antennas, and we could not seem to shake them loose from Marine sources, it was necessary to scrounge them from the Army. As all Marines know, the U.S. Army always has lots of gear—normally ten times as much as the Marine Corps. The situation in the Republic of Vietnam was no different, and we were quickly able to equip the company with the desired long-range antennas. In fact, we found that we merely had to ask for some help in this area, and the Army supply officers were glad to assist us in meeting our needs.

Weapons were the easiest items to acquire. If we wanted some that we did not rate, it was a simple job to find all we wanted. Extra weapons were everywhere in the Republic of Vietnam: they were in U.S. warehouses, in the hands of the Vietnamese Army and paramilitary units guarding villages, and among the covert operations elements operating in the war. Many of the weapons that were available were in mint condition, and we were glad to add them to our armory. Requirements ranged from more M-16 rifles to items like a 60-mm mortar and some .50-caliber machine guns for the relay site. My armorer was a quiet, effective sergeant who did not need to be oversupervised. I told him what I wanted, and got quickly out of his way. Within hours, the requested weapon would be available for inspection, usually in its original container, with spare parts.

Our armorer exceeded the company's requirements in night-vision devices as well, returning with six more AN/PVS-2 Starlight scopes than I had asked him to get. In addition, he returned with an agreement from an Army repair unit to directly exchange any night-vision equipment that required repair.

A force reconnaissance company always owns some motor transport, but with liaison teams all over hell and gone, serving with higher headquarters and the nearby major Army commands, we needed a couple of additional Jeeps. Our approach to the force motor transport officer was met with a chilly response. He saw no reason why we needed more wheels for the officers and/or staff noncommissioned officers who were posted to other units. Within the company lay the solution to this minor shortage, and his name was Sergeant Reifinger, a tall, tough-as-nails southern Marine who had extended and reextended to stay in the combat theater. Reifinger could lay claim to having held, at one time or another, almost every billet in the company, having been there nearly three years. When I posed the problem to him, he gave me the famous "No sweat" response and left the compound a few minutes later with two other Marines in a Jeep.

After an hour or so, Sergeant Reifinger returned with a small column of three vehicles: his original Jeep and two new M-151s, with the characteristic paint job and tactical markings of the U.S. Army. The two new arrivals were quickly repainted in the approved flat Marine Corps green. A rumor reached me that the Jeeps were the result of a trade that included two Russian SKS rifles, a double-barreled shotgun, and a Swedish K submachine gun that was coveted by an Army major. True or not, we no longer had to fight with any motor transport staff officers who were not really interested in our problem.

Many, many other pointless arguments within our own service proved to us that we were almost universally seen as a fringe unit that was more trouble than it was worth. Our sudden elevation to independent status, with all the attendant needs for costly support, seemed to cause otherwise rational officers and staff noncommissioned officers to react with a great deal of anger and hostility. The postal folks were angry about setting up a separate delivery system for our mail. The engineers said it would cost too much and we did not rate a boiler for hot-water showers. (We got one from the Seabee unit the next day.) The food service folks thought it would cost too much for us to open our own mess and suggested that they did not want to deliver fresh food to another facility. The classified material control folks got rather testy about setting up a separate system for Third Force Recon. The staff judge advocate had legal worries about our going independent, the administrators had trouble with the concept, and a host of other staff sections and support elements all held firm to the view that we were costing too much.

Third Force Reconnaissance Company was also going to be an expensive item for the Marine air wing, and we visited them to set forth our needs. Our long-range operations were going to need a great deal of air support, both fixed wing and helicopter. To get what we needed we began initially to develop cordial relations, but that was not always easy. One lieutenant colonel on the wing operations staff seemed to speak for his boss and the entire air wing when he suggested that supporting Third Force in the far corners of Northern I Corps would be too costly and was not worth the effort. Needless to say, disregarding comments of that nature was not simple.

We never felt hostility from the Marine aviators we flew with, though. The pilots on the actual missions were almost always young lieutenants and captains. We primarily had a problem with the officers who held more senior positions. Regardless, we made our wants known and accepted the reduced level of support that was offered. We did have an alternative. If the Marine air wing could not, or would not, support us fully, we could seek help from the ready-and-willing Army aviation assets of the 101st Airborne Division. Having had considerable previous combat time also eased my concern because I knew that in an emergency, with Marines under fire, the Marine air wing would pour in every resource they had—even if the aviation staff officers did not approve of what Third Force was doing in the reconnaissance world.

Outside the Marine Corps we occasionally met a number of other service members—like a few of the officers in Saigon on General Abrams's staff—who believed emphatically that we were costing too much. The difference, however, was that they met us, not as poor relations, but as presenters of the desires of General Nickerson. That made it all easier. We came forward with a plan of action that had the approval of the commanding general of all the Marines, and even those who disliked the whole idea had to see their way clear to provide what we wanted.

From the U.S. Air Force we sought three kinds of support, one of them being very expensive and the other two being fairly cheap. We wanted a huge quantity of aerial photographs, and we wanted them in a timely manner. I asked them to provide my team leaders with split-vertical photographs of assigned operational areas, with an eighteen-hour interval from our initial request to the delivery of the prints. If the Air Force could do that, we could hand the team leader both vertical and low-oblique photos of his AO at the time he received his formal order for the mission. We had no real precedent for such a large request from a minor unit like Third Force, but we were given every assurance that the Air Force would accept our requests and attempt to meet our deadlines.

I pondered this for some time after our visit with Air Force personnel, wondering how things would have been altered if I had been as well supported while I was in an infantry unit earlier in the war. In 1966 my rifle company was in a brutal firefight with a considerably larger force. The situation that day was chaotic, and the outcome remained in doubt for some hours. If I had been given aerial photos before that battle, I might well have been far more successful in maneuvering my unit against the NVA, who tried to surround and destroy us all.

We muddled through, well enough, to eventually create a win from a fight that could have easily turned the other way. Perhaps good aerial photo coverage might have helped me save some of the men who died that day. The maps we had in 1966 were rotten; it was virtually impossible to gain the essential infantryman's understanding of the terrain from them. Photos would have shown the routes used by the enemy and would have made it easier to prepare to fight him and/or chase him down and kill him. Partially because of that painful experience, it became a priority of mine to provide the team leaders in Third Force with the opportunity to work from fresh photography when they faced the NVA.

The second thing we needed from the Air Force was a communications backup capability. One part of the airborne command and control network used to handle aircraft heading toward North Vietnam was a C-130 flying a racetrack pattern over northern Thailand. This aircraft, known as Moonbeam, was packed with communications equipment and operators. What I asked for, and received, was a frequency and recognition code that could be used by a team in trouble and out of communications with Zulu Relay in the Ashau Valley or with the COC to call the aircraft. Operators on board Moonbeam could then reach out to us in Phu Bai, or to other stations within their range, to report the team's situation.

Although during any given hour Moonbeam would probably be out of range to Third Force teams for twenty-plus minutes because of its assigned flight path, it was always comforting to know that out in the night sky there was one more way that the teams could call for help if they needed it desperately.

The third thing I needed from the Air Force was almost a duplicate of the second. We wanted communications access to the EC-121 (Constellation) aircraft that were in constant orbit over Northern I Corps. One of these aircraft, operated by the Air Force for the Defense Communications Planning Group, was always on station to read out the electronic sensors emplaced in the DMZ, along National Route 9, and in Laos. Since Third Force was going to be involved in the sensor business, it made sense for us to be able to talk to these aircraft, particularly since their orbit near our operational areas made the EC-121 a perfect communications backup for teams that might not be able to reach Zulu Relay.

My request was granted, and we were also offered the frequency and code words with which we could communicate with Nakon Phanom (NKP) in Thailand, where all the sensor data analysis computers were located. To communicate with NKP would require that the team be equipped with high frequency (HF) radios, but that was always a possibility when teams operated in areas that were chancy in terms of normal radio reception and transmission.

From the U.S. Navy we needed similar support. If General Nickerson required Third Force to send teams into North Vietnam or into portions of Laos, we would not be able to communicate with them from any of the coastal enclaves in the Republic of Vietnam or from Zulu Relay. If faced with deep missions of that type, I needed an alternate means of communications, and the Naval Communications Station in the Philippines seemed to be the logical answer. I asked that that communications station provide us, on request, with high-frequency listening support on our frequencies.

We also needed to set into place a plan for retransmission of any team messages that had to be routed via the Philippines to Da Nang for further routing to the SRC, where Colonel Polakoff would sort them out and keep me abreast of the situation. Eventually, this too came to pass.

From civilian resources in the Republic of Vietnam—that is, the various organizations operated by nonmilitary elements of the U.S. government—we asked primarily for cooperation and the free exchange of information that might be of assistance. So many kinds of civilian elements operated in that country that I doubt anyone even knew the names of all of them. Nor do I believe that anyone had any idea whatsoever what they were doing to aid the prosecution of the war.

I found friends among some of the small, covert organizations operating in I Corps and shamelessly exploited my previous service with them for the benefit of Third Force Reconnaissance Company. We saw these agency types and their associates in the pacification business as magnificently wealthy in material things and, therefore, overburdened. Whenever we could, Third Force tried to lighten their load by adding some of their vast resources to our storehouses. Again, we cadged, scrounged, borrowed (forever), pleaded, and stole. It was worth it because we got many useful items like special radios, special weapons, special cameras, and a lot of not-so-special items that we could not get any other way.

The Australians gave us food. For reasons known only to some mild-mannered logistics planner twelve thousand miles from the battlefield, there was a dire shortfall in the number of Long Range

Patrol rations (LRPs) that we could get by normal requisition. This forced everyone who deployed into the bush to take some of the standard (canned) rations along as part of his survival load. The added weight was a penalty that was unfair to the man who carried it, and consequently, we prescribed a reduced ammunition and hand grenade load. The LRPs were favored by nearly everyone, so a hunt was initiated for those who might have more than they needed.

It so happened that a small Australian advisory team of five or six sergeants was located near the 3d Marine Division (rear) headquarters in Quang Tri. The Igor and I dropped by to chat a bit and see what they were doing so far away from the rest of the Australians assigned to Vietnam. We found that these fine fighting men were well situated indeed. They had splendid living conditions, superior communications equipment, a challenging job, and, best of all, pallets of LRPs. From the look of it they had rations enough to stay in place for several years. Since the Australians were few in number and not particularly interested in the LRPs—and because the Vietnamese troops that the Aussies were advising would not eat LRPs—we saw our way clear to accept them as if they were addressed to Third Force. While we never had enough LRPs, ever, we did reduce the shortfall drastically.

I wanted my Marines to stay away from other units and out of their recreational clubs. This meant that Third Force should have its own club where beer could be consumed by those not on watch or preparing for deployment. Of course, everyone in the club business was convinced that adding us to the system was proof that special units cost too much. Our idea was nixed without so much as a comment. To me this was not acceptable, because clubs of other units had drug problems and race problems—two things with which I was not willing to permit my Marines to become involved. We had a war to fight; nothing else could be allowed to detract from that.

The club problem was solved in a wonderfully simple manner. Certain Air Force officers who flew C-130 aircraft wanted a rubber boat to play with at their base in the Philippines. We wanted beer. Bingo, trading time. I wrote the rubber boat off as a combat loss; the pilots flew in two pallets of San Miguel beer. Sergeant Henderson took charge of the beer, and we had an instant club.

Part of what happened to Third Force at this time was rooted in the simple fact that there will always be those who are hostile toward units that engage in special operations of any type. Another part of the lack of positive response related more to simple inertia than to hostility. The unit on whom the request landed had often been doing things one way for some years, and change was not easily accommodated. Third, part of the reaction was my fault. I had no time, insufficient manpower and matériel, and an overpowering sense of fatigue from these stupid little, unnecessary conflicts. Working twenty-plus hours per day did not make me a charming person—quite the contrary. I was described by one senior officer as loud, pugnacious, unpleasant, and greedy. Perhaps I was most of those things, but I *would* quarrel with the word greedy. Regardless of the view of outsiders, Third Force needed every damn item I ever requested.

7

COMMAND AND CONTROL

Reconnaissance teams from Third Force Recon were asked to take great risks, to go far into harm's way, with nothing more to assuage their fears than an internal belief in their ability as Marines and their trust in our side's abilities to respond should the combative, well-motivated enemy close with them. Because I did not trust anyone else to place the interests of the men of my company in proper perspective, it was my policy that Third Force teams must always have one of their own in control of their insertions and extractions. That person would be in the proper place to make operational decisions and to manage all forms of support. If the reconnaissance teams were to be effective and were to survive, they needed to know that they could depend on the command structure to be responsive.

All of the misconceptions as to the roles and missions of a long-range reconnaissance unit come to the fore in movies with a Rambo-type hero dashing off to do battle with countless bad guys: all alone, with no plan for insertion cover, no plan for fire-support coordination, and without the foggiest notion about how he will come back alive from the mission. Civilian management types today would call members of a reconnaissance unit nonexpendable assets. I called them family.

Every man in Third Force Recon Company was someone to cherish and protect in as many ways as possible. To do that, I established control and coordination procedures that precluded decision making by outsiders—to as great a degree as possible. It was my job to protect my Marines from well-intentioned but ill-informed individuals who might kill them through errors of omission or commission. This included strike flight leaders, direct support air center controllers, fire support control center officers, and commanders of other maneuver elements. We considered all such outsiders to be potentially dangerous.

The time of gravest danger in a reconnaissance operation comes during the gut-wrenchingly tense moments when the team is being inserted into or extracted from an assigned area. Vulnerability is greatest when going into the AO because no amount of knowledge of the terrain and climate, no careful analysis of the enemy's capabilities and limitations and the tactical situation, and no compilation of electronic intercepts can assure you that the team will not meet a hornet's nest of fire upon landing. At least during extraction the team is on the ground and can brief the pilots flying cover and conducting the extraction lift as to the presence or absence of enemy contact at their particular location.

When briefly outlined in this manner, the subject sounds simple, but there is nothing simple about it. Reconnaissance operations are filled with unknowns, and the unexpected will frequently rise up to destroy the complacent.

My policy in Third Force Recon was that every airlifted insertion and every extraction would be controlled from above, not from the company COC some forty, fifty, or more miles away. Obviously, other techniques applied to drop-off-and-stay-behind insertions wherein the teams would be inserted into their assigned AOs as part of an infantry maneuver. The majority of our missions, however, began and ended with the helicopter. Only by placing a force recon decision maker overhead could we be sure that all of the various elements for coordinating their efforts to complete this specific mission stayed coordinated.

Additionally, we were always concerned that some self-centered nitwit might happen on the scene and unilaterally decide that my ground Marines were not worth the potential cost to him in precious matériel that might be expended to ensure that the team came out alive. This had actually happened to 3d Reconnaissance Battalion on one mission when aerial extraction was unilaterally scrubbed by an aviator without even minimal coordination with the battalion commander. Their team was left to walk out of the DMZ because of the possible danger to the helicopters. We never wanted the aviators to throw their lives away, but we did not want our lives thrown away either.

The mind-set of those who openly compared the value of machines to the lives of Third Force Marines, coming down on the side of the machines every time, concerned us all. This was not only professionally insulting, it was totally unacceptable.

In plain language, we were not going to let one of the Third Force teams pay the price for any misunderstanding or any lack of aggressive effort on the part of the insertion/extraction elements. In many cases this merely took careful briefing to educate all hands as to what was expected. On other occasions we met with individuals who violently disagreed with and confronted us. Typical of the latter was a helicopter unit commander who demanded that the reconnaissance Marines jump from the rear ramp of the CH-46 helicopters as they hovered over the landing zones—instead of riding the helicopter down to an actual touch-the-earth landing. Jumping from a hovering helicopter is not smart in the first place, but to do so while carrying an eighty-pound pack, into grass of an unknown depth, in a landing zone in enemy territory was one of the dumbest ideas we ever encountered. Many bitter, threat-filled harangues later, we won the day.

The only policy that I would accept was fifteen seconds on the ground to permit the team to debark and the enemy to open fire if he chose. Using this commonsense technique, the team could leap back on the aircraft if fire was initiated—avoiding a later and possibly more costly return to haul them out under fire. Eventually, the logic behind the fifteen-second policy earned us reasonable respect from the officer who took over that particular squadron, and from then on relationships were most cordial.

Mission command was the designation selected for the on-scene presence of me, Captain Hisler, or Lieutenant Coffman over the insertion/extraction. That term, however, did not always mean the same thing to everyone taking part. Marine Corps aviators profess to love their fellow Marines, but they abhor taking orders from ground people at any time. We used to laugh and make light of the attitude problem, but it was often a difficult matter when some lieutenant colonel would arrive and explain to me that he had five reasons—including his rank—why his helicopters would not go where we wanted, nor would they land in the zones we had requested in the first place. That attitude played hell with our assignment of specific teams to specific landing zones and AOs.

The Army aviation elements were far more flexible in attitude, although occasionally a soldier-aviator might feel that ground people had no business telling flying folks what to do, or when to do it. Working with these Army aviators was eased because the questions of rank were less important. The majority of them were young warrant officers who were quite attuned to being directed and controlled by ground commanders. The few senior Army fliers we came in contact with were all branch qualified in some other specialty besides flying and had, for the most part, a fairly reasonable approach to the question of control over the battlefield.

Once the shooting started on any mission, the time for tactful education was long past. So, to avoid pissing contests during the expected firefights, we always tried to provide as much detailed explanation in the pre-mission briefings as possible, outlining why various actions were expected and others were not acceptable. Misunderstandings or refusals to cooperate did occur from time to time, but with our taking an inflexible, hard-nosed stand from the outset, these hassles became non-events.

Mission command was both exhilarating and frustrating for those of us who flew it. We knew very well that the NVA was watching us wherever we flew over the wide expanse of territory they dominated. We often learned of the enemy's presence by spotting smoke from a charcoal fire or by sighting newly installed underwater bridges where trails crossed the many jungle streams. Working with the rotary-wing attack helicopters and the jet attack aircraft was impressive, as one could see proof of the American military power arrayed against the NVA.

When teams operated within range of friendly artillery, fires could be massed in a matter of minutes and support for the teams was assured. From our vantage point in the air, we could shift those fires to best support a team that was in fight or shield the extraction of a team from a hot zone.

Obviously, every one of the three of us who flew mission command flights was frustrated by the separation between ourselves and the action taking place on the ground. After all, we were three experienced infantrymen, and being in an aircraft far above the actual fighting was foreign to our basic urges. As the commanding officer, I felt it was my job to be in the mission command slot whenever I would get away from other duties such as patrolling in the jungle to observe a newly designated team leader at work. I would also put Lieutenant Coffman or Captain Hisler in the mission command seat when I was deployed on a bomb damage assessment, aircrew body recovery, sensor implantation, or any one of the other unusual missions that came to us from above. Occasionally, I was forced by various circumstances to be away from Third Force to attend to administrative and command matters at III MAF headquarters.

We could establish our mission command position over the teams in four basic ways. The first of these was for one of the three of us to ride along on the CH-46 helicopter making the insertion. This would happen when no UH-1E helicopter was available. Although this was the least desirable method open to us, it did afford the mission command officer the chance to see, firsthand, the situation in the landing zone as the team was inserted. Being there allowed you to take a self-interested part in peering through the jungle for possible NVA firing positions, and you were in a position to quickly affirm the pilot's desire to make a hasty exit if the team came under fire and had to reload aboard the aircraft.

The primary disadvantage of riding the insertion/extraction aircraft is self-evident. If you are that personally engaged in a mission, you cannot get an overview, nor can you work to provide support as events unfold. Even worse, the CH-46 was not a particularly good observation platform. It contained only a jury-rigged communications setup, and there was no direct access from the mission commander's helmet to air or artillery communications nets. That meant that we had to use a ground radio—the AN/PRC-25—with the antenna sticking out the porthole on the side of the helicopter. We did occasionally use the insertion CH-46 for mission command, but only with a strong feeling of concern regarding the shortcomings of this method.

A second method employed a UH-1E helicopter from the Marine Observation Squadron Six (VMO-6), operating in the DMZ. This aircraft came to us with a crew of four—two pilots and two door gunners. The internal seats had been removed, along with the large sliding doors that normally close up a Huey in flight. The mission commander had the entire area behind the pilots to roam around in and could hang out either side of the aircraft, held in by a gunner's belt. The Huey had radio capability for use in calling air or artillery fires; an AN/PRC-25 radio, whose antenna jutted horizontally out the door, permitted conversations with the teams on the ground.

More important, this method allowed the mission commander to stand clear of any fighting, to call fires as necessary, and to observe the action with the proper detachment from which correct decisions might follow. Unfortunately, in the hot, humid weather, the UH-1E would be operating outside its safe performance envelope if asked to lift off the ground successfully with a six-man team, the mission commander, and the crew. It just did not have enough power. In short, this mission command aircraft could not be depended upon to snatch an entire team out of trouble, and a second empty lift bird was usually needed. That limitation made for some extended waits for teams under fire, but the laws of physics do not bend easily to military necessities, and we had to live with the difficulty. Despite lift limitations, use of the UH-1E was highly acceptable, and we flew many missions in that aircraft in the summer and early fall of 1969.

A third method of exercising mission command entailed the use of a U.S. Army UH-1H, and when the Marine units left Northern I Corps, this was our primary command technique. The H model had all the advantages of the VMO-6 helicopter, but it was far more powerful and had a bigger rotor system. It could be taken into a zone, when necessary, to extract a six-man team in one lift, and as we came to depend more and more on the Army for aviation support, we often did just that.

With the UH-1H provided from the 2d Battalion, 17th Air Cavalry (2/17), came our command pilot, Maj. Chuck James. Assigned to fly me every day that we used Army aircraft, Major James was a magnificent addition to Third Force Recon's assets. We came to know him as a professional fighting man and as a friend over many hours in the air. He and the many other Comancheros of 2/17 flew for us hour upon hour, refueled, and returned to the battle with the true warrior spirit. Major James became an integral part of Third Force Recon, taking part in planning sessions, discussing ground and air tactics, and assisting us in every way possible. Unquestionably, use of the UH-1H with Major James at the controls was a most satisfactory arrangement for mission command.

The officer to whom Major James reported was Col. Vern Bindrup, and I never encountered a more supportive and professional officer. He never wasted time on the colonel-major power struggle garbage. Instead, he made it a point to treat me as a fellow combat commander to be respected and supported. Throughout our association, Colonel Bindrup made me feel that no other mission was as important to his aviators as flying supporting missions for my Marines. When asked, he committed assets to my needs without question and then sought out additional ways to help. We loved him like a brother Marine and gladly accepted his invitation one night to don cavalry hats, lift a toast to absent friends, and become honorary Commancheros.

The fourth method involved using the observer's seat in the OV-10 (Bronco) aircraft of VMO-6. This was a superlative way to get the job done. The OV-10 was well known to me, as I had seen drawings of the concept aircraft years before. Two Marine officers, Lieutenant Colonels Rice and Beckett, had spawned the idea of a small, light reconnaissance aircraft, known as LARA, which would be based far forward, close to the battlefield, and would be used primarily in close support of the infantry commander. The two men preached that idea to anyone who would listen, finding great favor among infantrymen.

In early 1963, as a member of the Weapons Planning Group, I had been asked for my opinion regarding this aircraft, and that gave me the opportunity to urge some of the leaders in the Defense Department's Advanced Research Projects Agency to fund it. The OV-10 was eventually developed from the LARA concept. Interestingly, the aircraft grew and grew over the years. More missions were postulated for the OV-10, and that meant that the entire aircraft became bigger, heavier, and in need of much more power. It was thus considerably less likely to be based on some dirt road awaiting some ground commander's requirements for observation and light attack. The LARA became a much bigger and more complex bird than the one dreamed of by the original proponents of the idea.

In 1968 the OV-10, now a flying reality, was brought to Quantico for certification as a parachute delivery platform. The aircraft was still growing when it came to the development center. Lieutenant Coffman and I used the last engine hours available on one of the intermediate-size engine configurations (715 horsepower)—

they were to be replaced within fifteen hours of operation with engines that were 15 percent more powerful—for the requisite parachute jump certification testing. Therefore, when Third Force had the chance to use the OV-10 for mission command, I accepted the opportunity with great pleasure.

The OV-10 aircraft was a superb observation platform for our mission: the backseat was arrayed with numerous radios for talking to the teams and calling fires when needed. While the cockpit was hotter than hell when you climbed in for takeoff, once in the air it became bearable. Over the years the little LARA had grown up to be a most capable aircraft for use by force reconnaissance. Because of our successes with it the troops often vocally approved, with loud cheers, the presence of the OV-10 in the insertion/extraction package of aircraft that arrived at the company parking ramp for the pre-mission briefings.

I should note here that all of the missions flown by all of these various aircraft would have been impossible in a less permissive air environment. The shoulder-fired antiaircraft rockets available on the modern battlefield preclude today's commander doing the things that I did every day, month after month. Had the NVA been able to introduce the SA-7 Strela in 1970 instead of 1973, when it was first encountered over Vietnam, they would have shut down 90 to 95 percent of our aerial insertions. That would have coerced Third Force to spend countless hours in cross-country trekking in order to survey the Ashau Valley and other areas that lay far from friendly forces.

While we loved the aircraft, we never forgot that Third Force Recon owed a debt of gratitude to the pilots who flew for us. The VMO-6 officers who risked their lives to put the mission commanders overhead in the right place at the right time would also come down to treetop height to deliver rockets and machine-gun fire in support of the teams. They never failed us.

8

DEATH ON A BEAUTIFUL
MORNING

By the nature of their mission, force reconnaissance Marines often find themselves amassing considerable flight time. Flying mission command over the Ashau Valley or the DMZ nearly every day added two to six hours (one day the flight time totaled nearly fourteen hours) per day to my personal accumulation of flight time—depending on whether I had made one OV-10 flight or three or four helicopter flights. Spending so much time in the air made me acutely aware of the dangers faced by the aviation community and the stresses faced by young pilots, all of whom were living wretchedly and flying far too many hours per month. Regardless of this understanding, my level of knowledge was rudimentary at best. It took a tragic event to teach me even more about the cost of doing business in aviation, the hard way.

Interestingly enough, the first time you ride in the backseat of an OV-10 you get a flying lesson. Mine came one afternoon in August 1969. The first OV-10 pilot assigned to fly for us, Captain S., carefully pointed out during his preflight briefing that I had a lot to learn in a short time. He also pointed out that although I might have ridden up to jump altitude many times in the back end of the OV-10, I had never flown in the cockpit, and there were things for me to do if I wanted to ride with him.

Captain S. got me suited up, attached to the aircraft correctly, and took me out flying. He lifted the agile OV-10 off the runway and climbed out over the Vietnamese coast to an altitude of about four thousand feet. He worked hard at making me sick, was partially successful (but I would not admit it), and began to show me things I needed to know. During rocket passes to mark targets, or low-level flight while we took a closer look at something that interested us, Captain S. was clear about what was required for survival.

"Major," he said, "just rest your feet lightly on the rudder pedals and your hand lightly on the stick. If you hear things hitting the aircraft, pull back and kick rudder as hard as you can! Once we get to altitude, you and I can fight over who is flying this sled." His advice made sense because he was looking out the front through Plexiglas that NVA bullets could easily obliterate, along with his head. I, on the other hand, had the distinct advantage of being behind both Captain S. and his armored seat.

To educate me, Captain S. practiced jerking the poor OV-10 all over the sky as he simulated being hit during near-vertical rocket runs and during low passes across the coastal ridge lines far from any NVA rifleman who might want to bag himself a practicing airplane. He then had me try to duplicate the maneuvers he had just completed. I made a lousy pilot, but with Captain S.'s calm guidance, things began to improve without the wings coming off during the high-G maneuvers required as part of the lesson.

Next, Captain S. hit me with a truly confounding and disturbing news flash: I would have to land the OV-10 if the pilot was incapacitated for any reason. This was an unsettling idea for an infantryman. The OV-10 ejection seats work in a planned sequence, with the pilot normally leaving last. If necessary, the pilot can elect to toss himself and the observer out, with the observer leaving half a second or so ahead of the pilot. The rub comes when the observer reviews his options: he can eject himself, but he cannot punch the pilot out. It is plain that this leaves room for catastrophe. If the pilot can no longer fly the aircraft, the observer is "it." He cannot abandon the pilot to die in the aircraft, nor can he get the pilot out in his ejection seat. The GIB (guy in the back) has only one true choice—to land the aircraft.

Once he had explained all that, Captain S. then completed my fragmentary education in things aeronautical by having me shoot landings until I was plain sick of it. I never lost sight of the fact that this was neither a fun time nor was it designed to make a ground Marine into an instant fighter pilot—it was serious survival business for the pilot to entrust me with his life.

Shortly after my flight lesson the press of events in August

1969 forced the daily tempo of reconnaissance operations to increase, and teams were going in and out every day of the week. I quickly began collecting a considerable number of flight hours. Whenever the OV-10 was available to me, I was pleased to make use of it, enjoying both the flying and the effective operational control that the aircraft gave me. I flew with whatever pilot was assigned but most frequently with Captain S. He and I were comfortable together, and we became rather close friends.

One morning a rainsquall passed through at 0500 and washed the dust and haze from the air, making visibility over the mountains of Vietnam nearly unlimited. Mission command was scheduled that morning for the OV-10, and I was looking forward to the flight.

After the last-minute morning briefing in the COC, Captain S. and I flew the mission as it had been planned, without a single problem. We covered the insertion of three teams and the extraction of two more from the DMZ. On the way back we did some low-level visual reconnaissance over areas that teams would be assigned to patrol in the near future, and we expended the on-board ordnance against some occupied trench lines along the edge of the Ben Hai River, at the point where the river enters the coastal plains.

When the time came for our return to the airstrip, we both relaxed to a degree and took a good look at the countryside around us. We were both struck by the beauty in the freshly washed day, and we shared an appreciation of the endless variety of colors in the rugged hills and valleys between the coast and Laos. We chatted quietly on the intercom about how odd it was to find the whole area so beautiful, right in the middle of a war.

The morning was completed with an uneventful landing in the growing heat and some good-natured teasing by Captain S., who swore that I must be taking copious amounts of Dramamine since I would not get fully sick, no matter how many G's he pulled in tight turns and rolling climbs. Of course I was sick, I was just too pigheaded to let him see me throw up. Keeping my insides from rebelling violently was not easy, and it had become a matter of pride for me to avoid disgracing myself while in the air.

After we landed, Captain S. taxied the OV-10 up to the edge of the parking revetments and shut down one engine to let me climb out of the rear cockpit. I rapped him on the helmet, offered my thanks, and climbed down onto the ramp. A 3d Marine Division aerial observer from the artillery regiment climbed up into my seat. Captain S. grinned from beneath his raised face shield and gave me a goodbye wave. He restarted the engine on my side of the aircraft and taxied away. I went into the VMO-6 operations area, turned in my survival vest, spoke to one or two pilots, and took time to bum a drink of cold water in the hut used as a ready room.

As I left the area in my Jeep, I drove along a dirt road that was separated from the end of the runway by only a few yards. I stopped to watch as the rearmed and refueled OV-10 taxied into position for takeoff. While waiting for clearance, Captain S. glanced my way and gave me a quick salute, which I returned in the manner of the ground crewmen, who always sent the pilots out with a sharp salute that was cut away with the hand pointed in the direction the aircraft was to travel.

The tower must have issued clearance for takeoff at that moment, and Captain S. quickly turned the snarling green aircraft onto the active runway and accelerated away from me. As the aircraft began to lift off, something in the starboard engine disintegrated. The OV-10 jerked and emitted a terrible noise as it suddenly rolled to its right and crashed into the wall of a sheet metal hangar that was roughly halfway down the runway. I saw it roll, heard the impact, and watched the fireball roaring upward into the sky. It was not possible that either of the two Marines in that cloud of flame had survived. I learned later that Captain S. and the observer had both ejected, but the aircraft was already so far into the roll that they were well inside the hangar when their seats separated from the wreckage. Both were killed instantly.

I returned to Third Force Reconnaissance Company with the feeling that I would never again, ever, see beauty in that land—no matter how many squalls came through to wash the skies clean and settle the dust. At 0600 the next day I was in another OV-10, with another pilot, and mission command went on as usual. Mission command went on because the war went on, with teams to insert and teams to extract. But there was not the tiniest shred of beauty to recommend that day or any of the others that followed. The part of me that could see anything beautiful had been lost in that heartbreaking, pointless fireball.

Captain S. was buried in Arlington National Cemetery by other Marines, and out in the Republic of Vietnam we went on with the war. In 1970, when I was ordered to headquarters for duty, I often stopped at his grave to pay my respects.

9

THE IGOR TEACHES SCHOOL

Third Force Reconnaissance Company was often assigned missions on very short notice. The immediate response that was required totally precluded any and all forms of preparation that we felt should be the norm for successful reconnaissance operations. We were convinced that about 80 percent of these quick-response missions were being dumped on us just because it was easier than planning ahead. To sugarcoat the process, some valid reason would always be forwarded from above as to why we had to jump through hoops. All of that posturing was more for the staff weenies, however; we just ignored the frosting and fuzz, trying to respond with our best possible performance to every mission we were assigned. We often felt that we were being treated without the respect due us, but bitching was not going to solve anything among senior staffs who did not feel like providing advance warning of potential missions.

One such mission, a bomb damage assessment mission, was levied on Third Force on a hot, dusty September morning in 1969, just after completion of a routine insertion/extraction operation. We had not had an unusually eventful morning, despite the considerable amount of fire exchanged on one extraction. Fortunately, the fight had been resolved successfully without loss of life, without wounds, and without any damage to the supporting aircraft. Churchill was right—getting shot at without result is exhilarating.

At about 1100 we received a flash operational-immediate message ordering Third Force to stand by to run an assessment of a B-52 strike in the DMZ area just south of the Ben Hai River.

Since most of these strikes were planned days, or even weeks, in advance, I was angry to get news of our involvement less than three hours before mission time. I got sympathy from Colonel Polakoff at the III MAF SRC, but he had just gotten the requirement from Saigon minutes before tossing it on down to us for execution.

Meanwhile, Third Force Recon was gearing up as quickly as we could for the mission. Bomb damage assessment missions were despised by the entire command. We willingly accepted that it was our mission if higher headquarters wanted to order us to do this type of work, but we questioned the basic mission rationale. When an enemy force is bombed, it is seldom—if ever—destroyed down to the last man. Frequently, numerous survivors remain who have the ability to butcher a reconnaissance team when it arrives in their area to take a quick look around. Even when survivors are few, neighboring units will quickly filter into the bombed area to hunt down and kill any small units examining the damage inflicted by the air bombardment.

In Vietnam we found that if the bombs did not happen to fall on anyone, the NVA would often move quickly into the bombed-out area, living, in part, by the concept that lightning and bombs seldom hit the same site twice. No matter how well or how poorly the targets were covered, the end result was almost never favorable for reconnaissance Marines who were ordered to assess the damage. The chances of getting killed were astonishingly high. Most of the troops looked on all of these assessments as basically useless forays into harm's way that were required by unthinking senior officers who did not understand that it was a no-win situation for those who were nose-to-nose with the NVA.

Now that the company had an assessment mission in hand, any opposition to the concept was obviously without merit. A quick evaluation of available teams resulted in the selection of one led by Corporal Heffington. His team was not fresh, but that was not unusual. As the 3d Marine Division was pulling out of the back country and preparing to leave Vietnam in October, we had to increase our operating tempo. Every member of the company was starting to show the strain. Ready or not, Heffington was the logical choice. A stolid and competent Marine, he was an Indian from central Oklahoma. Like most Marines of Indian descent, Heffington was automatically designated by the other troops as

Chief, a title he bore without any obvious signs of resentment. In fact, he was somewhat aloof and carried himself like the strong, silent image one equates with an Indian war chief. When called into the COC, Corporal Heffington was quick to agree that his team was the correct choice for the mission, and he and his five Marines were quickly briefed and sent to get their gear, test-fire their weapons, and get ready for a fragmentary order before lift-off.

Because of a temporary shortage of available aircraft in I Corps the Army could not support us with any lift helicopters. For this mission Marine CH-46 aircraft from Marble Mountain, near Da Nang, were scheduled to arrive at 1315, with mission takeoff slated for 1345. Since no packs would be required, the team could take an extra man. Coffman slated himself to join Heffington. He would not command the mission but would, instead, add a pair of well-qualified eyes for observation and the firepower of a real killer for team security. Captain Hisler would rotate into the COC, and I would be overhead in the OV-10 as mission command.

From both the warning order and the follow-up execute order, we learned that the B-52 strike would be directed at an area south of the Ben Hai and to the northeast of the old Marine combat base at Con Thien. We had on hand good photo coverage of that area, and Lieutenant Robertson banged together a mosaic of the grid squares that the bombs would fall into, along with several copies of what was essentially a strip map similar to one that you might get from an automobile club if you were planning a summer's jaunt.

Our mission was clearly no such picnic. We were going north to an area where the NVA was often found in great numbers. The 1st of the 5th (Mech), an Army unit running screening operations in the northern regions of I Corps, was already reporting heavy enemy buildup along the Ben Hai, with some movements southward suspected to be in battalion strength or larger. Screening by the Army's mechanized unit consisted of swiftly moving infantry sweeps designed to locate any major NVA forces moving south from the DMZ. While this was not a classic textbook example of screening operations, that was the way it was always described in the message traffic that we saw in Third Force.

Part of the area that the B-52 strike was targeted against was rolling ground with scrub growth on it, and part was open flatlands. These flatlands had little in the way of concealment, and I was skeptical about the concept that any North Vietnamese unit would venture out there in the daylight. In the night, yes, but not in the daylight.

As always happens in combat, time was one of our major enemies. The team had to be readied, the order issued so that all seven men were sure of the mission requirements, and both the team and the lift and attack helicopter pilots briefed together. Meanwhile, I had to leave for the airstrip in order to get my seat for the show. Captain Hisler ramrodded the Third Force preparations, and I headed out of the compound in time to draw my flight survival gear and get airborne in the OV-10.

Mission command was to be overhead the target area well before the arrival of the team in its transport helicopter. The valid military reasons for this included operational aspects like insertion zone selection, actual versus planned strike coordinates, effect of windblown smoke and dust on the mission, and a host of other matters, all of which were considered in this case. Additionally, a B-52 Arc Light strike was a display of awesome power that had to be seen to be appreciated, and the best seat in the house would be in an aircraft like the OV-10, with its expansive canopy. Particularly when the aircraft would be flown by a pilot pressing his luck by flying close to the planned impact point of the first bomb.

I had observed, at close range, several Arc Light strikes from ground level during the time I was dispatched to Khe Sanh in February 1968. In fact, I was in the eastern trenches with a fire team from 1st Battalion, 26th Marines, the night the decision makers in Saigon permitted one strike to be dropped 750 meters from the protective wire. Concussion from the huge load of bombs caused layers of sandbags to dance in the air, and secondary explosions from the NVA munitions went on and on. That strike, the brainstorm of Capt. Mizrah "Harry" Baig, proved that the enemy was using hugging tactics against the combat base, digging themselves and their munitions deep into the ground, well inside the previously sacrosanct three-thousand-meter safety line. Having been bounced and rendered partially deaf by that Arc Light while on the ground, I was more than ready to climb into my aerial ringside seat for this particular strike.

When I arrived at VMO-6, the OV-10 was ready and the

assigned pilot had already checked (preflighted, in aviation parlance) the aircraft in readiness for takeoff. He had not flown me in mission command before, so we had a short educational discussion about how the OV-10 had come to be used for this mission and how important it was that he understand its role in the reconnaissance mission taking place on the ground. He was unusually receptive to my views, and it wasn't until later that I learned that he was an experienced infantryman who had seen combat in 1965 in Vietnam. We lifted off without incident, although I admit to a moment of controlled apprehension when the aircraft began to accelerate to rotation speed, remembering Captain S. and his death on the same runway.

We arrived over National Route 9 about ten minutes before the CH-46 and the two accompanying AH-1 Cobras. The pilot and I checked in on all the appropriate radio nets to establish both the aerial UHF communications and ground communications on the VHF frequencies used by the Third Force teams while out on missions. All aircraft had received Direct Air Support Center (DASC) warnings—repeated every few minutes—of heavy artillery north of Con Thien. They were further directed to stay clear until the warning was lifted. All of our communications worked as advertised, and we circled Dong Ha while we waited for the rest of the flight.

Shortly thereafter the blocky transport helicopter and its shark-like attack helicopter escorts arrived and established an orbit below us that would have as its northern edge a line about five kilometers south of the intended target. Since we anticipated an east to west heading by the three B-52 bombers at the time of bomb release, the plan was for the OV-10 to fly parallel to the Arc Light drop line, about fifteen hundred meters to the south of that line, timing the flight to permit us to turn immediately north to overfly the first point of impact. At the same time, the CH-46 and the Cobras would begin their low-level run in concert with the bombing, planning to arrive to insert the team at the edge of the first bomb crater soon after the dirt and big chunks of debris had fallen back to earth.

Being at a higher altitude in the OV-10, we would see the big picture. The helicopters would be down in the dust, getting the team in as quickly after impact of the first bomb as possible. As soon as the Marines were in place, the transport helicopter would return to orbit over Dong Ha to wait. The Cobras would orbit directly over the team in order to provide immediate fire support if that became necessary.

Just as advertised, at 1410 everyone made schedule. The B-52 flight of three aircraft was somewhere up there in the glare above thirty thousand feet. We were just south of the planned drop line, ready to turn north over the first impact, and the team was on its way in the CH-46. Unseen by those of us at four thousand feet or less, the B-52 bomb racks quickly emptied their 500- and 750-pound bombs, and the big aircraft began the long, long flight back to Guam. A drop warning on the Guard Channel—the emergency UHF radio frequency monitored by all aircraft at all times—told us that the bombs were in the air, and we tensely scanned the earth for the first explosion.

Suddenly it blossomed, exactly where it had been planned. Each explosion was huge, producing a dark brown upthrust of earth and debris that had a harsh red center. Despite preparing your mind for the event, when you actually see such power, it induces fear. The pilot cranked the OV-10 over into a hard left bank, and we raced over the shimmering dust cloud as the shock waves began to buffet us in great lurches in the sky. Below, we could see the CH-46 flying a low and fast route to its landing on the edge of the first bomb craters. Corporal Heffington's team was quickly out of the CH-46.

As soon as they had piled into the first crater, Heffington established communications with me and with the COC as well. He reported that the team had been safely delivered into the AO and that no fire had been received on landing. The Arc Light impacts to his west were still driving shock waves through us all when I passed back to the COC my assessment that the mission was under way without incident. And it remained so for some time. Obviously, the luxury of air mobility gave our side the advantage in that we could easily send a team to examine the damage wrought by the B-52 strike. The NVA would have to walk in if they wanted to look the area over. In theory, our examination of the strike was to be quickly begun and quickly completed.

As soon as his team moved out on its crater-by-crater search, Heffington began reporting grisly findings which proved that the intelligence had been good and that an NVA unit had been in the area. The team noted that entrails, several heads, a scattering of legs, and other chunks of NVA soldiers were splashed along the undergrowth surrounding the first bomb craters they searched. The simple assessment was that human beings had been there, but they were now dead.

While Corporal Heffington was working in the first eight or ten craters the Cobras reported from their orbit overhead that they were taking fire from entrenched troops on a small ridge roughly one thousand meters north of the team. We went down low with the OV-10 and were also taken under fire from the same area. As we were pulling out of an evasive turn, another group of about fifteen to twenty NVA soldiers were seen moving toward the team from the east. Using the radio in the backseat, I warned Heffington of their approach while the pilot directed the Cobras against the moving troops and then got on the air support net to DASC to call out the hotpad F-4's from Da Nang. While they would come as quickly as they could, it would take start-up and flight time to get jets on station for close air support. This meant that it was essential that I echo the pilot's request for air support with one of my own for ground-based firepower.

Shifting the radio in the rear seat to the artillery frequency for that day, I alerted the available artillery assets that we had targets, and over the conduct-of-fire net I used the first of what turned out to be a considerable number of fire missions. From my vantage point over the battlefield it was easy to adjust the artillery impacts to those areas where NVA troops had been sighted, but the results were hard to gauge because of the heavy brush. I reported loss of visual contact with the troops moving toward him to Corporal Heffington and told him to ignore the artillery impacts to his northeast, as these were my contribution to the fracas. He returned a short "Roger" for the information and continued the mission.

By the end of the first thirty minutes on the ground, Heffington decided that he was finished with any form of bomb damage assessment. He was taking an increasing amount of small arms fire, and his supporting Cobra gunships were taking machine-gun fire, while I was reporting from above that more NVA ground troops were on the way. He called and told me that he had decided to terminate the mission because his team was about to become engaged in a fight for its life. The NVA forces moving toward him outnumbered his team ten-to-one, or more, and it was time for them to come out before being cornered for good.

I quickly agreed with Corporal Heffington that the time had come to get out of Dodge City. The seven Marines on the ground maneuvered to a bomb crater that they liked—one that would be defensible and on terrain where the CH-46 could land for the extraction. Overhead, we intensified the work of the AH-1 Cobras, called more artillery, contributed some fire from the OV-10, and made DASC aware that we would need more Cobras and more attack aircraft, *soon*! The stage was set for another hairy tale for the company archives.

Within five minutes the team in its crater was under heavy fire. Heffington had long since transmitted the radio code word switchblade, meaning that contact had been made with the enemy and reports would follow as the situation permitted. As soon as that word was declared on the company radio it was policy for the COC and mission command to back off and stop any requests for reports from the team leader. We felt that he needed time to do his job without interference.

Using this code word also got the COC moving. They alerted everyone who needed to know, from nearby artillery units to staffs as far away as Saigon, that a team was in a fight and might need help. For example, our hospital care for wounded Marines came from a small Army medical unit based in the Phu Bai complex. A switchblade call would place them on alert.

Internally, our company reaction team would be prepared for insertion in case we had to fight our way in to recover Heffington and his Marines. Whenever we had a team in contact with the enemy, everyone in the company who was not on patrol prepared himself for possible involvement with the fight on a moment's notice. All of this was in keeping with our philosophy that Third Force was a family, and if someone jumped on any one member of it, all the other family members would stand by to leap in themselves to kick the bully in the tail.

As the enemy fire thickened, the Igor stepped out of his role as an observer and began to function as only he could under fire. Corporal Heffington related that Lieutenant Coffman seemed to reach a peak of happiness when the number of bullets passing over the crater began increasing each and every minute. He became more animated, more cheerful, and generally seemed gleeful about this enjoyable turn of events. Everyone who was in the hole agrees that they were buoyed beyond belief by Coffman's calm and absolutely unruffled demeanor. He had been in so many firefights in his life that every Marine in the crater saw him as the supreme example of how to act when the enemy is trying his damnedest to kill you. Lieutenant Coffman moved back and forth, spending a moment with each man to steady him and to point out targets. He then paused to teach school.

Chief Heffington later recalled that Coffman had literally lifted him with one hand and dragged him some five feet to the edge of the crater facing roughly northwest. The lieutenant then stood up, fully exposed to the passing bullets, and said, "Now, Chief. I want you to stand up here with me so I can teach you something important." When Corporal Heffington complied with the request—by his own admission, shaking in his boots—he was told, "Look over there by that dark bush. There is an NVA soldier in there, and he is going to move. When he does, I am going to shoot him." Just at that moment the enemy soldier did try to move to another location. Lieutenant Coffman calmly shot the man in the head as he ran for new cover.

Then the Igor turned and announced to everyone in the crater, using his best parade-ground voice, that, "You never use only one round. Got that? Never! Never ever shoot anyone once. Always make sure that once he is down, he stays down. Once you have the bastard stopped, put another round into him to make sure he doesn't come back to stick a knife in your gut when it gets dark!" With that admonition, Coffman calmly stood amid the passing bullets and fired from the target shooter's formal standing position, placing another well-aimed shot into the head of the unfortunate NVA soldier who was still lying where the first round had dropped him. Once that was done, Lieutenant Coffman grinned a huge grin and said, "Okay, Chief. School's out. You can get down now."

Heffington was still shaking from the experience some five or six hours later when he related his day's schooling at the capable hands of the Igor. From such acts are legends made!

When the F-4 aircraft arrived on station, the pilot of the OV-10 got them working quickly. Soon the perfectly placed Snake-Eye retarded bombs clustered across the area where we had last seen NVA movement. That was followed by the delivery of napalm.

With the arrival of the blazing hell of burning jellied gasoline, the NVA fire directed against the Marines with Heffington in the crater dropped to about 10 percent of the previous level. The pilot of the OV-10 directed that the Cobras get down low and wheel in tight to take the remaining NVA troops under fire while the CH-46, which had been called from orbit, prepared to extract the team. When the F-4 aircraft were out of the area, I restarted the artillery support as the CH-46 dropped down to collect the team without any further delay.

The extraction of Corporal Heffington's team went flawlessly because the Marine helicopter pilot was a brave and clever man. He literally backed his twin-rotor helicopter in against the rising hillside so that the fuselage was partially protected from NVA fire by the crater's upthrust earthen lip. In the infantry a similar use of available terrain for cover is known as moving into defilade. A highly unusual flight maneuver, it placed the helicopter almost on top of the Marines in the crater. In fact, the rear end of the helicopter was sharing part of the crater with them! To board, each Marine would dash around the rear of the aircraft, avoiding the path of the rear rotor, and enter the helicopter. Once all seven were safely aboard, the CH-46 made its departure down the hill at grass-top level to avoid further exposure to the enemy's firepower.

Despite an hour-long flight, Third Force suffered no casualties from this mission. We chalked it up to another piece of good fortune that resulted from paying strict attention to lessons being taught under fire. Lieutenant Coffman came home a happy Marine who took great pride in his day's work. He kept the cheery grin on his face for days. The six young Marines of the team that had accompanied him had lived through an unusual combat experience while learning from the best teacher that they would ever see in Vietnam.

10

A HARD DAY FOR THE INFANTRY

No matter how inflated their egos, no matter how fancy their equipment, and no matter what missions they are assigned, force reconnaissance Marines belong to a combat support unit, with the emphasis on support. In Third Force Recon we hammered home that we, like the aviation, artillery, and supply units, had no reason to exist except to support the Marine infantry. It was both a policy and a practice that was designed to keep each man in the company aware of why we were taking on the demanding and dangerous missions that we did.

During August and part of September 1969, Third Force Recon provided combat support by taking part in extensive patrol work along the edge of the DMZ, north of the various fire bases manned by the men of the 3d Marine Division. Some of these fire bases were famous, like the Rockpile and Vandegrift Combat Base, around which a number of major battles had been fought. Others in the chain had little to recommend them. Both large and small fire bases were scattered east to west along the Vietnamese National Route 9, and it was from these bases that the infantry operations were mounted against the NVA.

The company was operating full blast. We had not shifted to an independent status, in the formal sense, but we had begun the essential shift in operations. We accepted all the long-range missions, and 3d Reconnaissance Battalion concentrated on the close-in work that would be conducted under the protection of the artillery. Third Force was permitted to accept responsibility for the deeper patrols in the DMZ and on the Laotian border. At the same time, the 3d Marine Division was conducting infantry sweep maneuvers along the southern edge of the DMZ.

Of course, every single Marine in the division was hoping that he could avoid being the last 3d Division Marine killed in I Corps. In order to keep casualties to a minimum, therefore, some of these forays were of short duration and quite restricted in scope. Occasionally, our mission assignment required us to become directly involved by working north of the infantry units, warning of approaching forces and calling fires when appropriate.

To perform these missions effectively required that we insert several teams in a basic fan shape across the northern approaches to one of these sweeps. These insertions could be conducted in three ways, all of them with serious disadvantages. The first technique called for the teams to walk to their assigned area of operations. Walking in from one of the fire bases was time consuming, and the rugged terrain, coupled with the horrible heat and humidity of the last month of the dry season, sapped the energy of the Marines and made them far less effective. Bone-tired Marines make mistakes, and mistakes often result in sudden death.

Second, teams could be inserted by helicopter. In the central and western portions of the DMZ this was not an easy solution. Few suitable landing zones were available there, and the NVA often had units in well-prepared bunkers and trench lines assigned to react violently against helicopter landings. Of course, some wags pointed out that if a team was "shot out" of a landing zone, we had provided intelligence data already; namely, we had proven that the NVA units were there, answering the first question always asked, "Where is the enemy?"

Third, we could drop teams off from moving infantry units and sneak them into observation sites where they could spot possible enemy reaction to the movements of the ground forces. For several operations in August 1969 we chose the third course of action. The teams would fly in to the forward elements of the sweep force aboard a logistics helicopter, go to ground in some hiding place, and then stay behind when the infantry moved away. This gave us a clear shot at anyone following the unit and placed the team in a position to begin providing northern reconnaissance cover.

August 15 dawned, yet another hot and humid day in the hottest month in Northern I Corps. That morning, Third Force was conducting operations in seven locations, with four insertions related to the third day of an operational maneuver by the 3d Battalion, 3d Marine Regiment. This unit of about 850 Marines—designation 3/3—had been ordered to press north to the Red Line (which delimited the southern edge of the DMZ), swing east, and sweep several large ridges that lay to the north of National Route 9. To support this operation we employed two insertion techniques: two teams were airlifted to their patrol areas, and the other two were dropped off from the battalion's first-night position.

One of the helicopter-lifted teams was taken under fire immediately upon landing and was extracted from the insertion zone without loss of either reconnaissance Marines or helicopter crewmen. The second airlifted team lasted for two days before coming in contact with a vastly superior force. They shifted to an evasion mode and crept southward for later extraction by helicopter. I had two more teams dropped off from the battalion's second-night bivouac position, and the sweep continued with four Third Force teams sliding north to continue covering 3/3 against surprise.

Midway through the morning of the third day, all teams reported movement in their operational areas. This movement of enemy forces continued throughout the day and was relayed repeatedly to the SRC and directly to the 3d Marine Regiment and the maneuvering battalion. During the night, two of the teams had to be extracted under fire, with the helicopters landing by the light of aerial flares. It was obvious that the NVA had considerable strength in the area. A third team had a contact with the NVA and withdrew to the southwest for survival. By midnight August 15, these small unit actions had reduced our participation to one team in place to the north of the infantry battalion.

During the course of that same night, one of the infantry companies taking part in the sweep came under heavy attack, suffering a large number of casualties from small arms fire and mortars. Additionally, it was being shelled by artillery fired from across the DMZ. The company established a defensive perimeter and dug in to fight for their lives. Reconnaissance was no longer playing a role. We had spotted the enemy movement and reported it; there was no further need of informational support as to whether or not the enemy was present and ready to fight.

In the predawn planning brief, I ordered the team that was moving southwestward away from the NVA and the team that remained on patrol in the area north of 3/3 to be extracted as part of the day's operations. At first light we prepared to do just that and to insert three teams into areas to the west to learn whether or not major formations of the NVA were coming into the Republic of Vietnam from Laos. In the early dawn haze, mission command lifted off in the OV-10 for another day over the DMZ.

Insertion of the three teams in the higher mountains to the west—not far from the stark remains of the Khe Sanh Combat Base—went quickly and without response from the NVA. No fire was taken in any of the zones, and the teams slipped away into the jungle after the appropriate wait for possible NVA reaction. We also recovered, without incident, the team that was southwest of the battle area. Thus, we had an indication, which was dutifully reported, that the NVA had not yet surrounded the battalion.

Our flight east to recover the last team operating north of the hard-pressed Marines of 3/3 was made with every expectation of a heavy fight during the extraction. We were amazed, however, to find that not a single NVA soldier was around to contest the activity. The day's *planned* operations for Third Force were now complete.

In the OV-10 the pilot, a major I did not know and who had not flown a Third Force mission before, indicated that we would not go back to the airstrip, as we had fuel and a full load of unfired ordnance remaining on board. This was not unusual. In fact, the more feisty OV-10 pilots would often take me north of the DMZ to look for artillery positions and to shoot Zuni rockets at the huge NVA flag that was always flying from a building north of the DMZ on the coastal road, National Route 1. I settled in to bear up during some make-the-guy-in-back-sick acrobatics and some low-level flight where it gets bumpy as hell as the morning coolness is driven away by the heat.

All this freedom of action was quickly rendered moot. We immediately got a call for help from DASC, which was relaying a request from 3/3 on the ground. The battalion wanted an aerial observer to assist in calling fires to cover a medical evacuation flight that was going in to the most heavily committed rifle company. The OV-10 that had been scheduled for this mission, along with the assigned aerial observer, remained on the ground at

Dong Ha awaiting aircraft repair. Technically, I was not an aerial observer, but that had no bearing on the matter—we were airborne and in the area already. Fires needed to be called, and I was going to have to call them. If, in the process, some of the more sophisticated fire mission techniques were left out of the transmissions, the firing batteries and their fire detection centers were just going to have to cope.

The pilot stood the aircraft on one wing, and we roared across the dark, cratered landscape to lend a hand. The rifle company that needed our support was in danger of being destroyed by the NVA. It was cut off from the necessary mutual support of the other 3/3 companies, and from the jumbled traffic on the various radio nets that I listened to, it was obvious that several of the key decision makers were down. The pilot called the DASC for air strikes as we came on station, and I began to make contact with artillery batteries that were within range.

Soon after our arrival F-4 and A-6 aircraft began flying all around us, and the pilot ran twelve flights of fixed-wing against the NVA surrounding the company. In the slots between air strikes, I employed the services of five different batteries of artillery to dump concentrations of fire on the NVA. This was an extremely messy proposition, as I wrote firing coordinates in grease pencil all over the map in my lap, on my hands, and on the inside of the aircraft canopy. Keeping track of just which batteries were still adjusting fires, who was firing for effect, who should shift fires, and who was standing by, ready to fire, kept me busy, and I never had time to worry about being airsick from the tight turns the pilot was making and the jinking about in the sky he was forced to do as he tried to avoid being shot down. We were taking a lot of small arms fire and some 12.7mm machine-gun fire as well.

When the CH-46 helicopters of the medical evacuation lift arrived, the flight leader took a look at the situation and then contacted the rifle company's forward air controller with an immediate request that the company commander move the wounded to another landing zone, one that was not under fire. The voice that responded was that of a very young, very tired, and very scared Marine. He was polite, but firm. He said, "Sir, our six (the commanding officer) was killed last night, our new six is an oscar one, with two months in country (second lieutenant, and new to the war), my actual (the officer forward air controller) is wounded, and we can't fight and move anybody at the same time. Request you either come help us or *go away*, over!"

His transmission wasn't even acknowledged on the net. Without replying, the CH-46s and their accompanying Cobra attack helicopters began a steep descent toward the zone, the lift birds landing in sequence and the Cobras shooting hell out of the NVA firing positions. The aviation Marines didn't even chatter among themselves on the radio; they just proceeded to risk their lives for those who lay wounded under the merciless sun. The acting forward air controller gave each aircraft specific landing instructions and wished each a good morning as it lifted off the landing zone. In a short time all the wounded were en route south, and the young enlisted Marine was on the net again, saying, "Thanks for the help! Have a good flight home."

Listening in to that transmission from my eavesdropper's seat in the sky, I was forever touched by the raw courage of that young Marine who was demonstrating exactly what professional performance under the ultimate pressure of combat is all about. That night I wrote my impressions for the regimental commander of the 3d Marines. I never learned the 3/3 Marine's name, but twenty-five years later I can still remember his calm, steady, professional work as he found himself the acting forward air controller.

After the medical evacuation flight was out of the zone, a flight of CH-46 aircraft arrived with reinforcements: a reinforced platoon from another regiment. They fared poorly in the landing zone, taking heavy casualties. Despite suppressive fires from the accompanying Cobras and from the artillery firing under my direction, the NVA fire was insufficiently suppressed. The already suffering Marines of the rifle company were not assisted by the additional troops; rather, they were merely laden with additional wounded to care for and to process for later evacuation. Looking down on the scene and hearing the details pouring through my earphones nearly broke my heart.

Meanwhile, the OV-10 that I was sitting in was no longer a functional flying machine. We had heard several whacking sounds as we took small arms hits, and a number of red lights on the instrument panel told the pilot that if we did not depart soon, he and I would be ejecting into an area that was clearly in the hands of the NVA. Luckily, a pair of fresh, rearmed OV-10s arrived, and we were ordered south to get our butts on the ground before something vital gave way.

Reconnaissance patrols from Third Force had provided the requested combat support: we had announced that the NVA was there. We had answered the basic question. Beyond that, the decisions that had been made were ones that took place far outside our sphere of influence. By pure coincidence I happened to be in a prime seat to observe the final result at the rifle company level, and I felt that it was important that every Marine in Third Force learn what had happened, and why.

This entire sequence of events need not have come to pass; it had been avoidable. Movement in rugged terrain by widely separated units of rifle-company size was a particularly poor choice when every intelligence-producing element reported the enemy operating in large formations. The Marines of the badly mauled 3/3 company and those in the reinforcing platoon had been part of an action that violated one of the basic principles of warfare—concentration of force. The understrength Marine rifle companies did not possess sufficient combat power for the mission, and they had been spread over such a wide area of difficult terrain that they could not provide mutual support. Additionally, the reinforcement selected had been far from the powerful combat force needed to save the day.

This battle was easy to explain, however, and it illustrated points that were important to teach my reconnaissance Marines. I used it consistently thereafter as an operational example that would make everyone in the company acutely aware of the difference between combat support troops and those who fight the real wars, the infantrymen.

Oddly enough, about a year after the events described above I learned that the major who had flown the OV-10 had been recommended for the Navy Cross for his heroic delivery of support to the surrounded rifle company. I had not been asked for any form of corroboration of the major's heroism, even though I had been three feet behind him in the backseat the whole time. I found the idea of a unilateral Navy Cross quixotic at best and fraudulent at worst. It both saddened and infuriated me when I compared it with awards given to Marines on the ground. Nevertheless, that major did receive his award, and Ancient Scout Six got one hell of a flight!

From a historical perspective, I will always wonder if the brave young Marine of that rifle company who acted so professionally lived another day, another week, another month, or was he among the last Marines to die in the 3d Division?

11

COFFEE WITH THE NVA

Prisoners of war (POWs)—especially if they willingly choose to talk to their military interrogators—frequently provide valuable intelligence information. In fact, that information is often both timely and time sensitive. Everyone at every command level above us wanted quality information, so we placed a high emphasis on the capture of live prisoners. While everyone knew that such a capture was particularly challenging, they were not deterred from pursuing this means of intelligence collection.

In fact, during a trip from Quantico to Saigon in 1968, I once visited with an acquaintance who worked on an exploitation team at the headquarters of the commanding general of all of the forces in the Republic of Vietnam. That particular team had been organized specifically to take charge of, and debrief, captured enemy officers of field grade (majors and above). They were known by some magnificently arcane title having to do with "asset evaluation in the short term." I doubt that they ever had the opportunity to do much of this exploitation work, as field-grade prisoners were few and far between, but the team was ready, willing, and able to fly anywhere at a moment's notice.

Command emphasis on collecting prisoners is frequently translated, at the operational level, to incentives and awards for an individual or a unit who can successfully bring home a real live POW. This can, of course, create within a reconnaissance unit a mind-set that becomes overly focused on rewards and ignores survival. This can lead to operational errors of judgment that have the potential to produce some hazardous and trying times.

Incentives and awards do have a motivational effect on the

troops. In Third Force we used the concept, as did everyone else I knew, to increase the possibility of POWs being brought in for interrogation. In theory, we were employing the incentives to clarify for the troops that we wanted them to use judgment during firefights and that taking an NVA prisoner was preferable to killing him. That was, of course, pure nonsense, as the teams who were in firefights seldom had the opportunity to apply judgment during such a fight for their lives.

We felt that any incentive that was offered must be sufficiently valuable to the men in the reconnaissance teams to cause them to make an honest effort to snatch a POW when the odds were in their favor. On the other hand, we did not want the prize to be so valuable as to cause a loss of judgment with the potential loss of life that would surely follow.

From the perspective of hindsight, I am not sure that the incentives really added anything. Third Force Recon team leaders took their orders seriously, and if directed to try to bring in a POW, it was their habit to make as professional a response as possible. They were not in the habit of shooting people just to be shooting them.

By 1969/70 it was no longer fashionable for a commander to reward his troops with lands and titles, and it would also have been a bad press-relations decision to pay the men off with war hatchets or other unseemly items in the way that Lieutenant Colonel Emerson of the Army's 101st Airborne had rewarded his men in 1966. So we used what we could lay our hands on in the world in which we lived. In Third Force Recon I gave fundamental rewards: promotions and time away from the war for rest and recreation. One or two men in the company might have preferred a barony or a duchy, but we refrained from conferring any such titles on those who were successful. Nevertheless, we did find humor in the concept of dubbing a couple of the more inventive team leaders as "Sir Snaky of Tiger Mountain" or "Sir 'Come-With-Me-Asshole' of the Valley." Fanciful investiture ceremonies were created by Lieutenant Coffman for amusement purposes. Laughing never seemed to hurt.

Because we took the capture of POWs seriously, everyone was carefully trained in a number of special POW-collection techniques. Some of these techniques were right out of the field manuals; others were acquired by the Igor and me among the Gurkhas at Johore Bahru in Malaysia. Some were taught to us by the British Special Air Service practitioners of the art, and still others were either our own creations or inventive concepts developed from ideas brought to us by the troops. Although we practiced and practiced, the opportunities for actual application of the training were rare.

A memorable exception to that rule came one bright, clear morning in the Ashau Valley when normal insertion/extraction operations were followed by a full-fledged attempt to take some prisoners. Team Coffee was presented with what seemed to be a magnificent opportunity, and we all busied ourselves in collaborating on what we hoped would be a super snatch of some unsuspecting NVA. But the course of events seldom unfolds as expected.

Team Coffee was prepared in the normal manner for an intelligence-gathering mission to the central Ashau Valley. They were to examine a portion of the valley where four small watercourses emptied into the main stream line that drained the Ashau. Primary interest was in some well-traveled trail networks that seemed likely routes for infiltrators moving from the north.

Preparation began with a written warning order that was issued to the team leader on the morning of their Day One. That evening he and his assistant overflew the valley in an Army helicopter and conducted a visual reconnaissance of the assigned area. His written operations order had with it all of the requested aerial photographs that had come up from the SRC in Da Nang. Before dawn on their Day Two, Team Coffee, along with two other teams, had been inspected and reinspected prior to the standard morning flight briefing.

On this particular day we were flying with the Army, and the surprisingly young and energetic—most of them were roughly the same age as the Third Force troops—warrant officers of 2d Squadron of the 17th Cavalry brought a feeling of energy to the COC as they trooped in for the briefing. The flight included two of the sinister and powerful AH-1 Cobras and four UH-1H slicks. Three of the lift helicopters were for Coffee and the other two teams going into place and for extraction of two teams that were due to come home. The fourth UH-1H was my mission command helicopter, and it was to be flown, as usual, by the boss Commanchero, Maj. Chuck James.

Should we need immediate help during insertion/extraction, two pink teams would be operating nearby in the Ashau Valley. A pink team consisted of one OH-6A and one AH-1 Cobra, and their tactics were simple. They went out hunting trouble. The OH-6A, a light observation helicopter, would work at treetop level, and the Cobra would lurk at a higher altitude from which it was always fully prepared to pounce on targets of opportunity or any enemy dumb enough to fire on the small observation helicopter. Pink teams, and a similar aerial hunting unit called a red team (which employed two Cobras instead of the Cobra and an OH-6A), were frequently used by the Army to engage the NVA in the Ashau. Additionally, the 101st Airborne was always ready to send their all-volunteer recovery platoon of sky-soldiers, known as the blues, should we need to call for ground assistance.

Our day began with test-firing weapons, a detailed final briefing for both the aircrews and the force recon Marines, and the normal precombat butterflies. As usual, everyone did a bit of swaggering as they tried their best to cover their natural fears with competent preparation and light banter aimed at easing the tension. No one was fooled, but we all felt better for the effort.

Team Coffee, like most of my teams, had a resident character around whom most of the teasing and laughter would revolve. In this case it was a long-faced Marine of Greek extraction, whose last name was Supious. Corporal Supious took heat from all concerned about his nose, his skin, his face, and just about everything else from his big feet to his unique bearlike rolling gait. Supious would grin his lugubrious grin and play the dozens with the best of them, but when the shooting started, he was a proven performer. As we all filed to our aircraft, we had no idea of the rough day that "the Greek" had in front of him.

When the three Third Force teams to be inserted had manned their aircraft and the Cobras had taken off, Major James fired up the mission command helicopter and we were off to the wars. We flew some forty-five miles to the northwest, across the steadily rising ground, until we crested over the last ridge line that formed the eastern edge of the Ashau Valley. To the north and across the valley rose Tiger Mountain, where we knew the NVA maintained a radio direction-finding unit, an engineer unit, and a transportation unit. The radio direction-finding people were there to hunt us electronically and to direct enemy ground forces trying to find and destroy the teams that were calling air strikes on any NVA they could find in the valley.

The NVA kept engineers there to repair the Tiger Mountain Road, a well-traveled route of entry from Laos into the Republic of Vietnam that was attacked frequently by the Air Force with heavy bombs. Successful bombing would often blow sections of the roadway off the side of the mountain, but the enemy's engineers, working only with hand tools, would repair the road and fill the craters. This repair effort would allow the enemy's transportation people to resume moving supplies to NVA units operating in the Republic of Vietnam. We knew all this from a combination of direct observation, photo-interpretation reports, and the Marines of Radio Battalion who listened in on the NVA communications networks.

Entry into the Ashau always evoked a feeling of mystery—mystery and a palpable sense of trespass. This was NVA country, and we knew that for fifty miles to the north or to the south there were no occupied civilian habitations, no agriculture, and absolutely no friendly faces—only the dark, heavy jungle and the dirt roads and airstrips that remained from another time in the country's history. Everyone who worked in the Ashau Valley seemed to share this sense of personal awe with regard to the valley's desolation, silent loneliness, and danger. We all took things quite seriously when on a mission in that foreboding place. Other than the small contingent of relay-site Marines from Third Force, perched on their mountaintop, anyone you met there would do their best to kill you dead as a hammer.

Thousands of men had fought there over the previous twenty-five years, and only bits of scrap iron from shrapnel, pieces of equipment, and bomb and shell craters remained to tell of their passing. The Ashau was tough country; we were there to map the enemy's routes and to kill him if we could. It was our hope that we might also be presented with an opportunity to collect a POW or two.

Our flight of six aircraft scattered across the sky as we approached the selected operational areas. Major James and I were at an altitude of three thousand to thirty-five hundred feet above ground level (AGL), both for a better picture of events and to ensure clear communications with all parties. The last thing we needed during the critical insertion/extraction evolutions was to be so low that some hillside could blind our communications. Team Coffee was first on the list. The team was inserted on a hillside on the eastern side of the Ashau, exiting the helicopter on the third of four landings, made to confuse any watchers as to the precise location of insertion. Coffee, in the form of the calm, quiet voice of the Greek, reported that the team was all secure on the ground and that they had solid communications with the relay site.

From the command aircraft, I entered the net to check out communications with the team and to wish them good hunting. Two clicks in my headset affirmed that the Greek heard and understood.

We swung off to the north to continue the day's work. Team Coffee was to move into one of the side valleys entering the Ashau from the east, where their reconnaissance work would begin. The other two teams scheduled to be inserted were successfully dropped off—no fire was exchanged—and we began extraction efforts. Because of a reported mechanical problem, Major James released one of the UH-1H aircraft, directing immediate return to Camp Eagle. The other two UH-1H helicopters collected one team apiece from remarkably quiet zones and departed, each in turn, for Phu Bai to drop off the Marines and then to fly on to their base at Camp Eagle.

Basically, our morning's work was on schedule, with no untoward events to mar the sunny morning. We took the mission command aircraft and the two Cobras down to fifteen hundred feet AGL and flew northwest to conduct some visual reconnaissance in the northern Ashau. When we had been gone from the area a mere fifteen minutes, Zulu Relay called and changed the course of our day dramatically.

On Tactical Net 1 came the softly spoken message, "Ancient Scout Six, request you return south to Coffee AO. Possible prisoner snatch." I replied quickly to the call, and our three aircraft headed south to give Team Coffee any assistance they might want. Major James entered the helicopter net and notified the two pink teams that our flight would be coming south and that we might need them to join with us on short notice. They both answered his call, giving him information on their fuel status and their ability to respond, should they be asked to come to the party.

"Coffee! Coffee! Ancient Scout Six. How can we help you?

Over." Once within radio range, I called to alert the team that we were nearby and that we were ready, willing, and able to provide assistance if needed. By this time we were heading back toward the team but were still eight to ten miles north of its area of operations. Any NVA in Coffee's area might hear the helicopter blades making their characteristic whacking sound, but they would be unlikely to understand that we were on our way back to that specific location. Major James turned the flight eastward as we moved to the south, doing so to give us an easier low-level flight route into the east-west-oriented side valley in which the team was operating.

Back came the response in that sibilant whisper used to keep the voice as low as possible while communicating from a hiding place and trying to stay alive. From Supious's voice it was obvious that they were working in close proximity to the enemy forces. "Six. Coffee. Affirmative, Boss. Got four confirmed NVA taking bath in stream. All are transport troops with gray uniforms, all with heavy rucksacks stacked on the bank, all armed with AK-47s. Copy?"

Corporal Supious was telling me that he had a small detachment of logistics troops, the men that the NVA used to man-pack equipment and supplies south to the war, perfectly positioned for a prisoner snatch.

"Coffee. Six. Roger. Copy. Stand by one." After this reply I conferred with Major James and obtained a feel for the time left to us in the Ashau, which was dictated by the amount of fuel remaining in the tanks of the participating helicopters. Comfortable that we had enough time to pull off a dream POW snatch, I called Team Coffee.

"Coffee! Six. We are six miles north of your position, with two Cobras and the slick. We will approach from east at low level, two Cobras at treetop at edges of your valley, this bird down the center at 'zip point shit' AGL. Use our noise to cover move. Jump the bathing beauties in the water. Kill two and take two for lift in this bird. Get all four packs. Copy?"

"Six! Coffee. Solid copy. Wilco. Say ETA [estimated time of arrival] overhead." Again, the whispery singsong of his voice betrayed both his tension and his solid professional abilities as a reconnaissance Marine. He was wound tightly, but he continued to perform as steadily as if he were doing a tactical problem at Camp Pendleton in far, far away California.

"Coffee! Six. Three minutes from now. Get ready for the show! Out." With that transmission our flight of three helicopters swooped downward until the skids were nearly in the leaves of the tallest trees. The Cobras spread wide to snake back and forth along the edges of the valley, and Major James took us right down the middle. As we sped toward Coffee, I ordered Zulu Relay to get the COC busy requesting both rotary-wing and fixed-wing support on an emergency team-in-contact basis. I felt it was better to get things going at that time than to wait for the fight to develop. Major James did the same, calling on the two pink teams to rendezvous with us over Coffee. Working together in this fashion, we both knew that there would be all manner of powerful help on the way should it be needed. Both of us also had the option to cancel these requests later if things went 100 percent our way.

Everything was happening at blazing speed! The trees and finger ridges seemed to blur past as we came down the stream line, yet there was a strange quality of slow-motion choreography about the maneuver. Major James jinked us smoothly through the trees in what seemed to be a dance pattern. The companion Cobras executed a far more extroverted set of direction changes as if they too were dancing, responding to a different rhythm. The two young soldiers behind the machine guns in our helicopter were crouched forward as they joined us in searching the jungle flashing below us for any sign of the enemy. Although this was a seriously dangerous enterprise, there was enough adrenaline flowing in all of us to keep fear from unbalancing our focus on the task at hand.

Suddenly the bend in the stream where Team Coffee was prepared to snatch the unwary North Vietnamese soldiers from their bath came into view. Major James pressed our luck further as he flew the helicopter even lower into the topmost branches of the trees in order to give the team as much noise as possible. As we slashed out of the trees and across the stream, happily scattering noise everywhere, Major James began a climbing turn to the right. We had barely started to climb when the door gunner on the left side opened up with a long burst of fire. Without missing a beat in his steady firing, he shouted into the intercom, "Taking fire! Tracers at eight o'clock! Break right! Break right!"

Chuck James was not an average pilot; he was a great one! In the next five to ten seconds he demonstrated that unique level of skill under great duress that sets the great ones apart from the common men who are mere mortals. The helicopter was taken to its limits of maneuver, jinking through all three degrees of freedom as he snaked us through the sky while the NVA tried to blast the UH-1H into scrap. For the moment we were the primary target for every NVA rifleman and machine gunner who could get his sights aligned in our direction and pull his trigger. The hillside was alive with winking muzzles, and tracers leapt up toward the UH-1H from several machine guns.

Basically disregarding the danger during our break to daylight, Major James never forgot that Team Coffee would shortly replace us as the primary focus of the NVA's violence, no matter if we were shot down or if we escaped to fight again another day. Right in the midst of the most wrenching maneuvers, he was calling to the Cobras, directing them to move to support the team, calling to the two pink teams for added support, and taking time to suggest that I call Zulu Relay and double the request for aerial fire support. He was, of course, also carefully directing his gunners to fire at a maximum rate at any targets that appealed to them—as long as they did not fire on the south bank of the stream where Coffee was hiding. It was a magnificent display of airmanship, courage, and professional aplomb under great stress. I was proud to entrust my life to the skills of such a man.

In a few seconds the danger passed. We flew clear of the tracers and quickly were outside the effective range of anything that the NVA seemed to be packing that morning. Our helicopter was not untouched by the NVA fire, however: we had been hit several times. Luckily, none of the hits seemed to affect the flight characteristics of the aircraft. Regardless of how good things seemed, Major James and his copilot were immediately busy checking for engine and airframe damage as I got on with my part of the war by summarizing the situation for the Marines sweating this one out on Zulu Relay.

During the most dangerous moment of our flight among the bullets came the first report from Team Coffee on the ground. The unflappable Supious reported, "Six! Coffee. Switchblade!" This code word signified that the team was in contact with the NVA and that fire was being exchanged. Now it was Coffee's turn. Those of us in Major James's helicopter were not the only ones getting shot at by the NVA.

The virtual torrent of fire made it quite evident that a significant NVA force was present for duty. They were tucked away in the thick growth on the north bank of the stream, holding positions on some gently rising ground where they had lain undetected by Team Coffee as the Third Force team had approached from the southeast. The sudden appearance of the helicopters and the attack by the Greek had probably surprised them into firing on us. Normally, they would have remained hidden, if possible: that was their most effective method of avoiding U.S. airpower. Instead of a four-man courier element from a transportation unit that had halted to rest and take a quick bath, it appeared from the volume of fire that Team Coffee had jumped headfirst into a firefight with at least two companies of regular NVA infantrymen. I called Zulu Relay and asked for all the firepower that could be made available.

In my ear—at full volume, when all pretense of secrecy was gone—Supious gave me both good and bad news. "Six! Coffee. Confirm two NVA kilo. Two NVA Papa Oscar Whiskey. Got the packs. Receiving heavy RPG and AK fire. Two whiskey! Request air support and extraction." Team Coffee had done it! We had two live NVA captives. We also had two Marines wounded. Now all that was necessary was for the team to survive long enough for us to snatch them out from under the NVA guns.

As he gave me this report, I noted that the tone of Supious's voice on the radio was altered to a flat and reedy sound that was unlike his normal delivery. From this it was an easy leap of intuition to conclude that Supious was one of the two wounded Marines. The nature of his wounds, and those of the other Marine who had been hit, could have a life-and-death impact on the chances of survival for the rest of the team. Despite the confusion of the firefight, I had to press the Greek to clarify the situation for me.

"Coffee. Six. Say status of two whiskey!"

"Six. Coffee. Boss, we got one shoulder wound, bullet, unconscious. One minor foot wound, frag. Me. Can't walk. We are taking heavy fire from across stream. Request you get it hosed down so they don't get south of us."

As we orbited above the fight, Major James quickly did what Supious asked. In a very short time the Cobra gunships were hard at work pounding the north bank of the stream. The NVA reacted with violence, filling the air with tracers that reached out for the Cobras as the helicopters maneuvered to fire their rockets and machine guns. It was a short and impressive show, the Cobras withdrawing eastward with superficial damage after expending all of their ammunition.

Good fortune smiled on us at this moment. Just when it appeared that Team Coffee was going to be fighting against twenty-to-one odds, the two pink teams arrived overhead. Major James quickly got them into the fight. The Cobras from the pink teams arrived with a full ammunition load, which they immediately began to expend against the enemy while the small OH-6A helicopters joined the fracas with their miniguns blazing.

All of this firepower display concentrated the NVA's attention on the attacking aircraft and kept the bulk of the fire off the necks of Team Coffee. That was all well and good in the short term, but in the wider scheme of things, the immobility of the team, with Supious unable to walk and another Marine unconscious, forced me to make an immediate decision. We had to use the command UH-1H to extract the wounded. This was necessary in order to give back to the team its ability to maneuver away from the superior enemy force. That force was ready to slaughter them at the first slackening in the effective aerial attack that the helicopters were pressing home so strongly.

Adding to the complexity of the situation was a significant time pressure. Major James warned that we were soon going to be leaving the Ashau because of our fuel state. We could not wait for any helicopters that were reportedly coming from the Army's Camp Eagle, some thirty minutes' flight time away. I gave my decision to Major James, who calmly nodded and began setting up the supporting aircraft of the two pink teams to cover our landing on the south bank of the stream.

"Coffee. Ancient Scout Six. Extraction in four minutes. I want the two whiskeys, the four packs, and the two POWs in this aircraft on touchdown in this zone. Assistant team leader to take command. Do you understand?" I was being very directive in what I ordered done to avoid the possibility that Supious might opt to stick with his team out of loyalty—despite the fact that he could not walk.

"Six. Coffee. Wilco." At least there was no argument from the Greek on our side of the stream line. Major James ordered the Cobras to cover our landing, and we began to make the approach. I scrambled out to the limit of my gunner's belt and hung out the right side to begin firing my M-16 as an adjunct to the firing by the door gunner on that side. Tree limbs and brush whacked against the skids as we made the dash to what was clearly a lousy landing zone, one that had the added foul disadvantage of being in plain view of the NVA—who packed many guns.

Major James again displayed his superior airmanship as we smoothly transitioned from twisting, dodging flight to sudden landing, with one skid planted firmly on the hard ground at the edge of the stream. We were down, about six feet from the smoke grenade thrown to mark the pickup site and to provide wind-direction information. Overhead, the Cobras were wheeling in to pound the enemy, but some fire was still being directed toward us as we settled to earth.

The sound of automatic weapons fire directed at you, personally, is one that none of those who have ever heard it in combat will ever forget.

In seconds, two apparitions—force recon Marines with dirty camouflaged faces and bodies covered with mud from the POW snatch in the stream—appeared before me and handed up a wounded Marine to be stowed aboard the helicopter. Right behind came the Greek. He was ashen faced and hopping with great difficulty toward the helicopter. In one hand he held his rifle and in the other he had two fat rucksacks of the kind normally carried by the NVA. His comrades unceremoniously shoved him into the helicopter as he made the effort to climb aboard. They then tossed two more, blood-soaked, packs onto the helicopter. As they did so, both pointed skyward and dropped from view into the thick undergrowth. No NVA prisoners were handed up, but there was no question that it was time for us to leave. I said into the intercom, "All on board. Go!"

Major James had kept the power near peak on the helicopter, and at my command he announced, "Coming up!" Each door gunner responded with the word "Clear" (right or left, as appropriate) to denote that none of the team Marines was going to be killed by the helicopter as it took off. The UH-1H always appeared to me to have an odd look, somewhat like a scorpion lifting its tail, as it tilted forward on takeoff, but this time we nearly overdid it. The deck seemed to approach the vertical as the tail came up and the helicopter dragged us forward and upward toward the safety that lay above. We dodged, twisted, and corkscrewed as we climbed to avoid providing a zero deflection shot for any gunner nearby. The NVA had their chance, but they muffed it. Many tracers passed the helicopter. All of them missed: some by fifty feet, others by mere inches.

Once out and away from the fight, we took stock. None of us had heard any hits on the helicopter, but that meant very little. Major James repeated the basic checks to be sure that some stray round had not made the machine unflyable. While he did that, I checked on the two wounded men. The Marine who had been shot through the shoulder was now coming back to consciousness. He was not in shock, but his eyes betrayed his pain, and he did not respond when I shouted in his ear to learn if he had any other wounds that we could not see.

Corporal Supious was leaning against the armor plate that made up the back of the copilot's seat, tears streaming down his face. His trouser leg was damp with blood oozing from fragmentation wounds, and his boot was torn where shrapnel from a rocket-propelled grenade had entered his foot. My clumsy efforts to give him solace as we bounced around the sky had little effect, and I was worried for an instant that the Greek had been broken by the pain. I should not have worried, as I learned when I leaned over to hug him. He sobbed deeply and told me that he was ashamed to leave his team behind, and worse, he was ashamed to have failed me by not being able to bring out the two POWs. Nothing I could offer would serve to reassure him that things were all right.

The Greek was hurt far more psychologically than physically by his wounds. He had great pride in his performance of duty, and he felt that the mission had gone sour because of some error on his part. That was not the case, and clearer heads prevailed when it came time to analyze the patrol and its actions. In the long term Corporal Supious came to understand that he had been wrong to feel ashamed, and that what he should have felt was more pride in the accomplishment of his team in holding off a large formation of NVA who wanted to blow them away. Both the Greek and the other wounded Marine recovered fully from their wounds.

The fates smiled once again on Third Force Recon. As the mission command helicopter was still climbing away from the hornet's nest of fire, we got help. A flight of four attack helicopters from the 101st Airborne Division arrived to take a whack at the NVA. These were aircraft from a unit that the Army called the Aerial Rocket Artillery. Each helicopter had nearly twice the ordnance load of a normal gunship, with the bulk of its armament stations being loaded with 2.75-inch folding fin rockets containing flechettes. The flechette rounds, filled with what looks to a layman like so many small arrows, were famous for their effect on personnel targets. Called in the slang of the time "nails," these were wonderfully effective weapons for the kind of fight we had on our hands, and the flight leader went to work quickly.

Major James briefed the attack helicopter leader on the team's location and the enemy situation as we saw it. Then, being fuel short, we headed east to deliver the wounded to the hospital. During the transit toward the coast we passed a flight of two more UH-1H from the Commancheros, and they were ordered to coordinate with the attack helicopters and extract the remaining four Marines of the team from their position on the stream line. There was little value to be gained in asking them to continue the mission at reduced strength and a great deal to be lost if survivors of the NVA unit tracked them down and attacked again. After all, we had wanted to know if the NVA was using those particular stream lines and valleys as routes of travel from the Ashau Valley to the coastal plains. The question had quickly and clearly been answered in the affirmative.

When we arrived in Phu Bai the first priority was delivery of the wounded to the U.S. Army field hospital. We had alerted the company first sergeant, and he was on the pad to oversee the handling of the Marines as the Army medics rushed them to treatment. Once that was accomplished, Major James flew me back to the Third Force pad where he shut down and came to the COC for coffee and a rehash of the events we had just survived. While he did that, his copilot and the two door gunners taped over the various holes in the helicopter so the eerie whistling would stop as it was flown back to Camp Eagle.

Shortly after we had settled down again in the COC, the rest of the team was delivered home by the smiling warrant officers of the Commancheros. All four of the Marines were unscathed, despite the heavy volume of fire that had been directed on them by the NVA. They reported that once the nails were delivered by the Aerial Rocket Artillery, the NVA broke and ran—leaving their wounded behind. During extraction the team did not receive one round of fire from any survivors of the NVA unit on the north bank of the stream.

Once again we were skunked in the POW game. The team and Corporal Supious reported that both of the prisoners had gone down when the Greek got hit in the opening moments of the fire-fight. No one had seen them rise at any time, and the supposition was that both had been killed by the AK-47 fire of the NVA. Of course, once the team was in a fight, they cared for their own (for which no one could fault them) as opposed to daring to move among the flying bullets to learn the fate of an NVA courier.

While we had no POW for the exploitation folks to interrogate, we did have four large packs filled with papers and maps for the intelligence types to examine. Our job was not to analyze, only to catalog and forward the materials on to more sophisticated intelligence units. As we prepared to do just that, we were surprised to find that one of the couriers must have been a paymaster of some kind. He was carrying voluminous records, all with monetary amounts noted therein, and a large number of sheets of gold leaf as well. Gold was often seen in the marketplaces at the village level in Vietnam—jewelry being crafted while you watched—and carefully weighed gold was used often in the vegetable market transactions. Obviously, the courier who had died carrying this gold was taking it south to the Republic of Vietnam to pay someone off. To bribe someone was, and I suppose still is, rather a normal part of life in Southeast Asia.

I sent the intelligence officer, Lieutenant Robertson, to personally turn the materials over to the analysts in the III MAF headquarters. He flew to Da Nang where he turned the pack, papers, and gold over to the intelligence staff. He returned with a receipt for all of the items and prepared a detailed report that we would send along to amplify the finding for the higher headquarters. Once that was finished, we basically relegated the entire incident to our historical file. About three months later we learned, by accident, that the gold had vanished while transiting through the intelligence system between Da Nang and Saigon. I received a call from a highly positioned officer on General Abrams's staff. This colonel had read the report of the translator's analysis of the materials, maps, documents, and such, but only in our report was the gold mentioned. It seems that someone made a profit on his time in the Republic of Vietnam.

Needless to say, it was hard to convince the troops that turning the gold over to higher headquarters had been the best course of action for the company. Their reasoning was impeccable. Third Force Recon could have financed a rather fine bash with those few pounds of gold!

12

IT'S CHRISTMAS.
WHERE THE HELL IS SANTA?

On special occasions during the Vietnam War—Christian and Buddhist holidays and the like—formal cease-fire periods were proclaimed by those who were far, far from the sound of the guns. The fact that they had issued the proclamation, however, had zero influence on whether or not one could die a violent death in the fighting units on those occasions. In fact, for reconnaissance and other special elements involved in intelligence data collection, the cease-fire times were some of the most active periods we faced. The command chronology for December 1969, for example, contained sixty-seven separate entries denoting specific operations that were conducted by the company during those hard days.

So from the tower of babel in Washington the word went out to suspend offensive operations, halt the bombing campaigns, and restrict ground operations over the Christmas holidays. Santa was due and 1969 was tottering into the history books. As always happened when the U.S. forces eased up, the enemy began moving troops and supplies as fast as they could to take advantage of our failure to interfere.

For Third Force the tempo redoubled, and we spread far and wide across the mountains and valleys of Northern I Corps in an attempt to answer General Nickerson's questions about where the NVA was moving, in what strength, and whether its concentrations of forces were a danger to his Marines deployed around the population centers on the coast. To find out, we fielded teams to examine the network of roads and trails leading south through the

Ashau Valley; we peered again into the DMZ; and we tried to cover as much area as possible near National Route 9 in the vicinity of Khe Sanh. A few patrols were run to the south, along the mountains near the Hai Vanh Pass, but our reconnaissance missions emphasized those routes that led from Laos into the valley and those that provided routes of access eastward within the Republic of Vietnam toward Dong Ha, Hue, and Phu Bai, where the company was based.

The availability of air support for Third Force was also greatly restricted, being, in the main, limited to whatever was needed during emergency extraction of teams that were under fire. For us, the major difference during the cease-fire period was that aerial firepower was not being applied to the north, nor was it pounding the Laotian routes used by the NVA. We could not freely hammer NVA forces in any meaningful way unless they ran one of our teams to ground or they massed and moved threateningly toward the coastal enclaves. Despite the lessons of Tet 1968, the enemy was allowed a freedom of movement that had absolutely *no* relationship to either tactical or strategic common sense. Concepts of that sort are not hatched by those who are in contact with the enemy.

In Third Force we made every effort to accept the possibility of a holiday death without dwelling on it. I felt that we could positively deal with the stress by looking reality straight in the eye. No lies, no evasions, just simple truth for the troops who were asked to accept the missions and the concomitant dangers without flinching. The Marines and corpsmen of Third Force may have been just eighteen to twenty years old, but they measured up fully.

The company neither obtained nor expected any respite from the pounding operational tempo, and certainly we anticipated no reduction in the level of danger to ourselves from any cease-fire or stand-down ordained by the National Command Authority, by the Pentagon, or by Saigon. In fact, we extended our reach during this time, patrolling farther than ever before away from friendly forces—and taking greater risks in the process. To meet its obligations, Third Force was operating at full throttle.

In the spirit of the time of year, I allowed some personnel who were due to rotate home in late December to stand relieved of field duty before the arrival of Christmas. Among these men was one of the more experienced team leaders in the company, and his replacement had to be checked out by direct observation. I accomplished this in the normal manner, accompanying him on his first patrol as a team leader, going along as an additional, seventh man, a technique known in the company as riding gun. The objective was to let the newly designated leader run his team with minimum interference, while concurrently observing his every move and providing for the team an experienced backup should the situation overwhelm his ability to cope successfully.

For Corporal B., his team's Day One was Christmas Day, and he was given a warning order for an area-surveillance mission in the mountain chain that made up the western side of the Ashau Valley. This area encompassed a portion of Tiger Mountain where a wide, well-used road entered the valley from Laos, and it extended south toward the slopes of a mountain known as Dong Ap Bia. This high ground had been made infamous in the spring of 1969 when it was christened Hamburger Hill during a large battle that took place while the U.S. Army was operating major ground forces in the Ashau. Photos of the area revealed many vehicle tracks on the roads and the presence of an extensive trail network. The NVA had forces in the area, and the questions were, Which way are they going, and in what strength?

Team preparation was exceptionally thorough, as Corporal B. was concerned about the chance of heavy contact with the NVA and by my presence in his team. His prior experience during twelve to fourteen patrols had given him some of the confidence that I sought in team leaders, and he paid appropriate attention to details, using all the required checklists during his inspection of our packs and equipment. Also, in deference to my being a silent specter in his midst, and based on the written order prepared in the operations shop by Lieutenant Coffman, he prepared and issued a comprehensive and well-structured team operational order.

Despite his thorough pre-mission efforts, I felt a certain unease. This corporal was too breezy and had a disquieting way of shifting suddenly from a calm, competent professional to something better characterized as a wise guy. As we moved through the preparation phases, I confided my concern to Captain Hisler. As much as possible, I stressed the good points Corporal B. exhibited. Nobody is ever absolutely ready for his first combat command, and I remained hopeful that he was going to settle down as he gained experience. After all, he was merely twenty years old and was facing, for the first time, *personal* responsibility for the lives of Marines entrusted to him. He had every right to be a little bit nervous and jittery.

For this patrol, Day Two arrived with broken cloud cover, gusty winds along the coast, and the possibility of heavy rain predicted inland for the mountainous regions where we would be operating. As always, the last-minute checks of equipment were conducted in silence as each man held his own thoughts close within himself. We placed our gear on the designated spots on the ramp where it was inspected once again, test-fired weapons, and gathered in the COC, along with the aviators flying the insertion, for the briefing by Lieutenant Coffman.

The insertion lift was made up of only two teams, and we were flying with Marines from Marine Medium Helicopter Squadron 262 in the CH-46 aircraft. Mission command would be in a UH-1E, and Coffman would occupy my normal slot while I departed for the field. Later, General Nickerson would strongly suggest (actually, it was more a direct order) that I stop taking part in patrol actions at the team level, an edict that I occasionally was forced to sidestep, but at Christmastime in 1969 he had not learned of, or was willing to overlook, my personal participation, on the ground, in reconnaissance patrols.

Lift-off for the Ashau was uneventful, and the two CH-46s bumped along at four thousand feet as they were shepherded west by two AH-1 Cobras and the mission command aircraft. Corporal B. was given a crewman's helmet, and he talked to the pilots on the intercom. The rest of the team sat on the bare metal floor or kneeled at the open portholes where the Plexiglas, like the seats and cushions, had been removed for weight reduction. The assistant team leader was busy checking face camouflage and adding a bit to those who needed it.

In what seemed to be only moments (it was actually forty-plus minutes of flight), we arrived over the central portion of the Ashau Valley and prepared for insertion. All weapons were loaded, but everyone rechecked to see that rounds were in the chambers, the safeties were on, and straps were pulled just that one iota more for last-minute comfort. Reacting normally, we all shared the wish that we had stopped another time at the urinal tube to lower bladder pressure.

Our team was scheduled for the second of the two insertions, so our fat green CH-46 settled into an orbit while the other lift aircraft and the remainder of the parade headed south to make the first insertion. The team primary radioman, Kaintuck, a country boy from the hills of Kentucky, stuck a tape antenna out the port on the starboard side of the aircraft and made a five-second communications check with the relay site. He gave a thumbs-up sign to the team leader and sat back down on the aluminum floor to wait it out with the rest of us. After a few lazy orbits, the crew chief and Corporal B. both waved for our attention and pointed down at the ground, following that sign with the thumb and forefinger pressed to form a circle, signaling okay. Our sister team was down and their insertion was deemed successful. It was our turn.

We all shifted our packs and made ready as the CH-46 left orbit and began to drop toward the treetops. Looking out of the port, I spotted the Cobras skimming along among the taller trees as they led us first to a false insertion on the east side of the valley. Our pilot chose an open ridge on the east side of the Ashau for his deception touchdown, and we landed lightly in the grass as he kept his power at takeoff levels for a quick departure. We drew no fire during the deception, and the aircraft lifted off after the normal fifteen seconds on the ground. The gunners at the windows and the crew chief all displayed relief to be back in the air and grinned at us as we made ready for the real landing.

Within five minutes we had begun the final approach to the assigned landing zone in the hills to the west of the Ashau. As we descended, the ramp was partially lowered to slightly below the level position, affording us quick and easy egress from the aircraft. Again, the pilot made a smooth and careful approach for his landing. When the struts began to take the weight of the helicopter, Corporal B. pointed out the back door, and we deplaned as quickly as our loads would allow. Dropping immediately to the ground, we executed our landing drill, each carefully scanning a portion of the landing zone while the team leader stood close to the rear ramp, where he could see the crew chief. After fifteen seconds with no fire received, Corporal B. gave the crew chief the thumbs-up, and the helicopter, now free of our fifteen to eighteen hundred pounds of weight, virtually leaped out of the zone. We were now on patrol in the Ashau. Merry Christmas!

My initial impression of team discipline was quite positive. Each man seemed to function without need for direction by the team leader. Even though this was precisely how I wanted it to work, I was still pleased to see that it did happen when the team was out in bad-guy land. In less than thirty seconds after the CH-46 cleared the zone, both the primary and secondary radiomen had solid communications with the relay site, and Corporal B. gave the signal to move out.

Standard practice was to clear the landing zone as quickly as possible and find a nearby defendable site where the team could wait to determine whether the enemy was prepared to react immediately to the reconnaissance insertion. We did just that. The point man—our team leader—led us away from the touchdown area to a rocky outcropping where our footprints would no longer be present for all to see. After crossing about fifty meters of rocky ground, we slid quickly into some tall grass above the rocks, where we would have fields of fire if anyone came at us from the landing zone.

All of us went to ground facing outboard: those nearest the rocks ready to take any following enemy troops under fire, the rest of us providing all-around security. Now all we had to do was wait until the team leader felt it was safe to start into the AO. We sat, silently strip-scanning our assigned portion of the perimeter. This was a methodical scanning of terrain in which enemy troops could lie hidden. One starts at the point of gravest danger—usually nearby bushes—in the assigned sector, then sweeps his eyes across that strip from right to left, shifting emphasis out to forty to fifty meters, then back again. Next, he sweeps out to seventy-five to one hundred meters and follows that by scrutinizing the near strip again.

Time was passing, but now it seemed to be doing so at a snail's pace. While we were prepared for an enemy approaching from any direction, we all had in our minds that the danger lay in the direction of the landing zone.

After about fifteen minutes of waiting in this temporary position—just long enough to get fully uncomfortable—we heard voices. Voices speaking Vietnamese. Aha! The wrong direction! The voices were nowhere near the rocky ground, and the speakers were not approaching from the direction of the landing zone at all. They were on the ridge with us, in the area above where the open ground gave way to heavy jungle cover. By now we could hear the clink of equipment and the sounds of men pushing through light brush and grass. Nobody moved a muscle, and I wished (and I am sure every other member of the team had a similar wish) that I was facing in another direction so that I might get off the first shot without moving.

Wishes never come true when you need them to, so I mentally made ready to roll to my right when contact was made, choosing a fighting spot better oriented to firing up the slope. The chattering NVA kept coming in our direction, and we made like statues in a sculpture garden. I could see Kaintuck, the primary radioman, lying to my left; he was breathing—as I was—slowly and shallowly through an open mouth to minimize any possible sound from the nasal passages. We had no enemy in sight, but they were now within ten meters of our position; the tension was palpable.

In our favor, this approaching NVA unit seemed to contain just ten or fewer members. If they stumbled upon us, we would suddenly reduce their numbers at the moment when we started the firefight. Before there was any need for us to open fire, however, they stopped, dropped their packs, and sat shooting the breeze and smoking while seven armed, very dangerous, and reasonably nervous U.S. Marines were lying—trigger fingers ready—less than twenty feet away in the shoulder-high grass.

Since they were above us, and we had not moved through that area yet, it was unlikely that they were talking about our footprints, so we stayed silently ready and waited still longer. After what seemed an eternity, we heard an officer or noncommissioned officer issue some orders in Vietnamese, and our pals got to their feet grunting and probably bitching, as troops in any armed force will bitch, and they moved away to the east, staying off the rocky ground that lay between us and the landing zone. Even silent recon Marines can heave a quiet sigh of relief, and we did so with an exchange of grins all around.

A few minutes later Corporal B. reported to Zulu Relay this passage of an NVA unit, and we moved out uphill to the west to examine the tree line from which the NVA troops had just come. When we gained the edge of the jungle, it was not long before the entire matter came into clearer focus. There was a major trail in the trees, one that was invisible to aerial observation or photography. By major I mean a trail that was large enough for troops to walk on four abreast or for six-by-six trucks to travel on with little obstruction. The NVA had cleverly rigged the jungle for camouflage purposes, with cables pulling treetops together in those places where the jungle did not afford full overhead coverage. Our recent visitors had evidently been on the main trail when we inserted and had left to take a look at the area where the helicopter had landed. Only good fortune and Corporal B.'s careful choice of terrain had prevented them from blundering into us as we waited to see if anyone had followed us into the brush from the landing zone.

The team leader made a spot report on the trail we had discovered, and we moved quickly away to avoid the chance of our bumping into another NVA force in an area that they knew well. We crossed the trail carefully, without leaving so much as a boot mark on it, and moved deeper into our operational area.

The remainder of the day was spent patrolling and observing possible NVA transit sites. We moved every two hours to selected new positions from which we could observe stream crossings or trail intersections on the Ashau floor below us. The objective of this work was to learn what we could about the NVA movement patterns. We needed to know about their direction of travel, types of units, number of men, equipment carried, etc., etc., etc. We were not particularly successful the first day, but this lack of success was to be expected, because the NVA knew that another recon team had been inserted either in the eastern hills or the western hills overlooking the valley floor. Using common sense, they would reduce logistical movement while their tactical units tried to ferret out the Marines and destroy them.

Darkness was coming soon, and with it, the rain. It was time to find a night harbor site and hunker down. Frequent movement by the team and an early selection of the night harbor site was all part of survival by avoidance, and we began a careful move toward higher, more difficult ground.

Corporal B. continued to impress me favorably, as we had now been in the field for eight hours, and other than his necessary radio transmissions of information and routine movement reports, his team had yet to speak a word. We already seemed to have the kind of cohesive efficiency within the team that bodes well. I was proud of these tough, capable young men, for they had taken to heart all that Captain Hisler, Lieutenant Coffman, and I had tried to teach them about the attention to details that make for a cohesive and effective fighting unit. Each man covered his assigned area, strip scanned steadily, covered every move of his fellow Marines, and seemed to have fully accepted the teamwork aspects of quality small unit operations.

As we headed into some broken, brushy ground for our night harbor site, I felt a calm sense of pride in seeing another team that was truly professional.

Our first night in the bush passed uneventfully. We had slipped into the selected harbor site after visibility had dropped to a few feet, at best, making a question-mark maneuver just before going to ground. This was simply a looping movement on the ground that would bring the team back around to a position a few feet away from the trail our passage had left in the brush. That way, any NVA force that was following that trail would walk right into our prepared defensive position—with no warning. Corporal B. had arranged the team so that our harbor site was not only close to the route we had taken on arrival, it overlooked it as well. The seven of us created a tight perimeter that was oriented to provide all-around security, with emphasis on coverage of the route that we felt was most logical for an attack by the NVA. We wanted to ambush the enemy if he chose to follow us into our harbor site.

Rain was pouring down, and each of us made a cold meal of rations and wrapped up in an attempt to keep as much water as possible on the outside. We had Claymore mines out, trip flares were set up, the night-vision device was working well, and four seismic detectors were implanted on likely routes of approach. The seismic detectors, known as Patrol Seismic Detectors (PSIDs), were something Lieutenant Coffman and I had great interest in, since we had tested them at Quantico for the Marine Corps.

Seismic detection works. It does have drawbacks, but so does most equipment. A rainstorm is a disaster when using the PSID because each drop gives the listener an input signal from the buried geophone—the same signal that a footfall would provide. Corporal B. was no fool, and he quickly directed the security watch to set aside the PSID earpiece for later use, should the rains stop. With two Marines on watch at all times, each of us took our turn staring into the dripping darkness and monitoring the radio net for traffic.

Around 0200 the relay passed to me, since they had obviously been told to do so by Lieutenant Coffman. The message: "Ancient Scout Six, you are totally unsat! Igor sends." I replied with three closures of the microphone key and accepted the teasing in silence, as I was expected to do. In the verbal horseplay between me and Coffman, to be unsat was good, and anything that was totally unsat was as good as it was likely to get in this or any other life. Lying there in the rain, I appreciated the humor of the message and the chuckles which the radioman at the relay must have mustered when he sent it along—all the while wondering just how much wetter and how much more uncomfortable the next few hours would be. Eventually, I was relieved of radio watch, and I rolled tighter into a ball and tried sleeping. I tucked a fold of poncho liner into my teeth to reduce the chance of a snoring bout, a trick taught by the British at the Jungle Warfare School in Johore Bahru. A trick, although not always successful, that was passed on to all members of Third Force.

At first light the team moved out, and Kaintuck reported to the COC that we were boot, the term for on the move, continuing the mission. After some rather nasty cross-compartment movement that took us down one steep slope into a narrow valley and up another steep slope to a ridge that ran parallel to the one we had just left, Corporal B. had the team in position to observe three major areas of interest on the Ashau floor. We were on a ridge that gave a view of a large streambed, an improved road network, and the opening of one of the east-west corridors leading from Laos into the Republic of Vietnam. We waited and watched. Nothing moved. The team was in the right place, but the NVA was not cooperating. After two hours of observation, Corporal B. moved the team to a new observation site from which the same areas could be seen.

Our movement across the difficult terrain paid off quickly with an enemy sighting. Just after noon the observation element—two Marines with binoculars—picked up the first NVA movement below us on the Ashau Valley floor. It was a sighting of six to ten men in gray uniforms moving south. They were too far away for even the most sharp-eyed to spot weapons on. They appeared to be uniformed like the transportation and support troops we had contacted before. Just as the report was sent in, there was another sighting, then another. All the NVA troops were going south, and all were on the same trail in the Ashau. Without any air strikes authorized for interdiction of this enemy movement, we merely reported the number of troops spotted and the direction of their march. We watched and allowed them to pass on to their destination.

As the day waned, it was again time to settle into a night harbor site. The team leader again chose an excellent site; again, we executed the question-mark maneuver and established ourselves as best we could to defend against possible following NVA troops. The rain continued, and we got as comfortable as possible. Around 0300 all of us were awakened by a new danger. Out of the darkness to the south came a sound that damn few people of any profession ever hear in the wild. A tiger had begun roaring into the night sky!

The sound was partly a roar and partly a chuff-chuff-chuff noise that convinced us all that he was just a few feet away. After a time the tiger grew quiet, and we all then wondered if he was silent because he saw NVA moving to attack us, or was he silent because he had every intention of eating one of us? None of this was academic speculation. In one documented case, a tiger took a staff sergeant from the center of a reconnaissance patrol, carried him away, and ate him. There were also two or three instances of tigers being shot by recon units who happened on them in the mountains. Our concerns were also based on the absolute worst-case reality that any tigers near the battle site on Dong Ap Bia would have had ample opportunity after that bloody fiasco to taste human flesh and would likely enjoy the chance to continue adding a bit of Marine "steak" to their diet.

Our good luck continued, however, and morning came without either NVA bullets or tiger teeth making a mark on any of us.

Over the next few days we continued to see evidence of NVA movement: footprints, wheel tracks made by bicycles or carts, and detritus left by the passage of troops on the trails we crossed. No more tigers roared at us at night, which we were pleased to note. We did see some NVA, and we heard many more as they shouted for some reason or other in the valley below us. In addition to shouting, the NVA trail watchers in the Ashau often communicated via shots fired into the air. An AK-47 would crack off two shots to the south and another would answer with three spaced shots from the north. This was standard practice, and we had all heard it before, but it was still unnerving to think that perhaps this was all a big plot to suck the team into some fatal mistake.

Meanwhile, I observed that the team was steadily functioning in a silent and competent manner right in the enemy's backyard. So far, Corporal B. had demonstrated to me that he had the qualities of leadership needed to be elevated to team leader. Despite my initial misgivings about his judgement, all of the decisions he had made while I watched in silence were dead-on professional. Now it was all downhill. Just a couple of days more on the slopes of Dong Ap Bia, and we would be extracted on New Year's Eve.

The evening before our planned extraction, we were working across the eastern side of Dong Ap Bia, watching the road network in that part of the Ashau and looking for an area for our last night in the bush. When the team leader selected his site, we carefully maneuvered through the question-mark movement, setting up to ambush any NVA foolish enough to follow us into the brush. Our site was perfectly chosen—miserable ground where moving troops would be unlikely to stumble upon us in the dark. We moved into position amid some head-tall grass whose heavy stems produced noise as we entered and would produce noise if the NVA came after us. The idea was for us to lie still and for the NVA to make the noise if they wanted to run into our Claymore mines and our firepower.

We settled in, each man assigned a sector of the defense and a watch period. The year was only a single day from completion, and I suppose that all of the men in the team were wondering what 1970 would bring—life, death, or any of the stations between that are characterized by the effects of disabling and disfiguring wounds. We all had destinies, and like the men on both sides in the Republic of Vietnam, we had no inkling of what those destinies might hold.

My defensive sector of the perimeter was at the northern end of the oval-shaped position, and I selected a firing position where a knuckle of two sharp-edged boulders pushed up through the nose of the ridge line. I felt that if we had visitors from that direction, I could roll right and fire from below the larger rock or roll left and fire from above. I placed the PSID device just a few feet beyond the larger rock and trailed the wire back to the center of the position. My Claymore mine was installed just past the edge of the smaller of the two rocks in a location where I felt I could fire it without having to worry about being killed by the back-blast effects.

Once again, the rain precluded the advantage of the seismic device, and we were left with only the early warning protection of the night-vision device and our own senses. Regardless, the position was well chosen, and the chances for successful defense if the NVA came to destroy us were good. The routine of rations and watch setting went on in the customary silence, and we prepared to sleep as much as the situation and conditions would allow.

Almost immediately after the seven of us had settled down to our assigned spots to sleep, while two Marines stood watch, the tiger called from just below us on the ridge. Sounding the same as when we last heard him, only a great deal louder, he was evidently a cheerful tiger, not a hungry one looking for loin-du-Marine as his entrée for the evening. He alternately roared and chuffed through his nose for an hour or more. It was good to note that he seemed to be moving away from us, but his direction would take him downwind of our position, and I considered just how strongly we all must smell to a tiger home in his own jungle.

Long after his noises had faded away to the south, every man on the team was sitting upright, listening with full attention for whatever sound a tiger makes as it leaps into a reconnaissance team to treat himself to a Marine for dinner.

By 0100 everyone not on watch seemed to have slipped off to sleep, and I handed the radio handset over to the Marine who had next watch and resumed my defensive position. While it was just a few feet away, it seemed a long distance because of the care I had to use to avoid making any noise as I moved. Once comfortable in my chosen spot, I was just in the process of preparing for sleep when loud voices—ten or twenty exceptionally loud NVA voices, less than twenty feet from my position—canceled any further thoughts of sleep.

My first mental reaction was to silently question how the NVA could have crawled or somehow snuck up on us so quickly. My second thought went to the survival equation. If the NVA soldiers were that close in large numbers, and if they knew exactly where we were, we should fire now! If they did not have us pinpointed, we could hold fire and await developments while they blundered around trying to lock us down into mismatched, close combat. It was a frustrating and frightening situation, with a number of scenarios to consider, although it was disheartening to note that most of them just happened to be *bad* for our side.

The voices continued, and Corporal B. wisely refrained from ordering us to open fire with the Claymore mines. With the Claymore firing clacker in my left hand and my rifle in my right, I slipped, an inch at a time, along the underside of the larger of my two rocks. When properly positioned, I would be shielded from back blast if I fired the Claymore, and I could quickly open fire with the rifle. Rain was pouring down, and it was noisy as hell, but that background noise permitted some movement, and the team reoriented more toward my side of the perimeter as we waited to see what was going to happen.

Suddenly, I was shocked to see someone using a flashlight about ten feet from my rock. The light came toward me, and I prepared to kill the man carrying it, along with any others in his vicinity. Just as I was deciding that when he took two more steps I would kill the flashlight carrier with my rifle and hose down his area with a Claymore, the light swerved away from me and started down the hill. Easing back my finger on the trigger, I watched in amazement as another flashlight came along; then an oil lantern swung around the turn and headed downhill. As all this went on, I began a count of the passing men, a count that went on for roughly two hours.

On and on they came, in twos and threes and larger groups as well. Since I was closest, it was my job to count them for the report that would be made as soon as it was safe to transmit. Some of the NVA passed silently, bearing their infantryman's loads and moving with the infantryman's steady, purposeful gait. Others were yammering away like magpies, probably bitching about the luck of the draw that placed them on that muddy, slippery hillside in the rainy dark. Those with lights used them freely, for the ceiling was down to zip-point-shit, and the danger of an overflying U.S. aircraft seeing the light was nil. With rain pouring down to cover their footfalls, many of those who passed us without lights likely went uncounted. Additionally, it was only possible to estimate the numbers when a group moved silently along.

By 0300 the movement had stopped, and the team leader reported to the relay that 169 confirmed NVA had been counted passing our grid coordinates, moving east into the Ashau. The team leader also added an estimate that 250 or more NVA had actually passed our harbor site. This information, along with that collected from all the other intelligence sources, might help Colonel Polakoff and his SRC people understand the big picture as to NVA movement patterns.

As tired as we were, sleep did not come again, and the team remained on full alert until dawn. At first light, two of us moved quickly forward to see the place where the NVA had been passing. The trail was about eight feet in width, and the mud was packed hard by the passage of many feet. This particular trail was not visible in our aerial photos, which were only days old, and it had obviously seen much use in the last few days. There were boot prints, sandal prints, and the marks of bare feet as well.

Many men had passed that way, and all visible prints were oriented eastward toward the coast and downhill toward the Ashau Valley floor. The NVA regulars and their supporting transportation people were obviously not headed home for the holidays. We looked, but we did not touch so much as a toe to the enemy trail, where the characteristic cleated boot print left by Marines would instantly give our presence in the area away to any inquisitive NVA who happened that way in the next few minutes. The traffic on that trail was impressive proof of the enemy strength that was being shifted into the Republic of Vietnam during the cease-fire period.

As we prepared to begin moving into the area of our anticipated extraction, we heard much noise and commotion from the valley floor. Needless to say, we could not let that pass without taking a look, or at least a closer listen. While we did not close within five hundred meters of the enemy, who were clearly there in strength, we moved close enough to hear loud talk, radio messages being sent by operators, vehicle engines, and all the other noises one would expect from a large unit in bivouac in the jungle. Charcoal smoke from cooking fires hugged the ground, where it filled our nostrils, and we could hear considerable chopping of wood as the NVA warmed themselves with fires under the double protection of the heavy jungle canopy and the low-hanging clouds.

We would have enjoyed a fire of our own making, to warm our chilled posteriors, but our request for an aerial attack by A-6 aircraft—using the electronic wizardry of the RABFAC Beacon for a napalm drop on the NVA unit—was denied at the DASC without comment. If the strike had been permitted, our beacon would have given the A-6 aircraft the ability to drop accurately through the clouds to the target area we designated. Since we knew that the air strike would be denied, we were already on the move when the DASC said, "No."

Actually, leaving was a rational and tactically sound thing for a reconnaissance element to do in this situation. We now knew as much as we could expect to learn, without taking them under fire, about the size and capability of the enemy force, and their direction of movement was obvious. We withdrew in a wide circle, giving them plenty of space to have their cookout while we maneuvered to reach the extraction landing zone at or near the correct hour.

Extraction was planned, but it was hardly a sure thing. First, the weather was just plain rotten. Second, the NVA was all around us and might have antiaircraft weapons with them to thwart any helicopters from landing at all. Third, we had no knowledge of the weather on the coast; it could easily be clear and sunny or as rotten as what we were standing in at the moment. Corporal B. brightened all our spirits when he put down the radio handset, made helicopter-blade motions with his fingers, and the okay sign with his thumb and forefinger. We moved to the landing zone immediately.

On arrival, we found the zone to be wide open, and there were several handy bomb craters in the tree line to give the seven of us shelter if a firefight ensued. We moved into what was probably the crater left by a two-thousand-pound bomb and waited. Corporal B. went to each of us and told us in whispers our sequence for boarding the aircraft, which would be a USMC CH-46.

Using the CH-46 made sense, because all the Marine pilots were instrument rated. Most of the U.S. Army warrant officer pilots came to the war without that particular skill, and operations in the evil weather in the Ashau were hazardous for those who were not instrument rated. In fact, the Army UH-1H helicopters did not have the same radar altimeter that the Marine aircraft had in their avionics suite. Lacking that instrument, even the bravest of the Army pilots could easily waste his life in heavy weather. Senior Army aviators like Major James, who flew me in his aircraft on almost a daily basis, did have full instrument capability, and he and I spent many a hairy moment while he shepherded flights of his young warrant officers back to the coast when the fog and clouds closed in unexpectedly in the Ashau.

While I was strip-scanning my assigned portion of the jungle, I felt a tugging at my sleeve. Kaintuck was looking at me with a wide-eyed, fearful expression. When he had my full attention, he leaned down at my feet and pointed to several tracks in the muddy crater walls, tracks that led down to the water that filled the crater's center. Our nighttime friend the tiger had stopped in this crater for a drink, and Kaintuck was plainly worried. I could not resist the moment and leaned close to his ear and broke silence by whispering, "What do you think it was?"

He stared at me speechless for about a minute, then the humor of the situation took hold. He grinned widely and whispered into my ear, "Short fat gook with four toes?" I almost choked holding in the laugh that I wanted to let loose, and our team leader glared at us across the crater as we returned to watching the jungle for unwelcome guests.

Exactly on schedule the relay reported the lift-off of our extraction flight, and we got ready to go home to Phu Bai. Quickly thereafter, the sound of Cobra gunships could be heard, and we spotted a pair as they set up the wagon wheel around our zone. We had no contact with the NVA regulars, but that did not mean that they might not be waiting in the trees for the helicopters to land. An appropriate warning was passed to the flight leader telling him that the NVA was not far away and might choose to take them under fire.

Extraction was always a tense moment for Marines who were tired, wet, hungry, sleep deprived, and piano-wire tight. This extraction was no exception to that rule. More can go wrong then than at any other time, and we knew the enemy was damn close by.

Suddenly, out of the gloom, came the fat nose of a CH-46, and it was only seconds before it had landed about thirty feet away, with its open rear hatch pointed directly at our crater. In our prescribed sequence we dashed for the open hatch, boarding in front of Corporal B., who was responsible for being sure that all seven of us were on board. In less than the planned fifteen seconds, we six had been counted, and the team leader leapt aboard and gave the crew chief the signal to lift. The CH-46 tipped its tail upward like a stinkbug, and we went immediately into the clouds. Unless the NVA happened to have a radar-controlled ZSU-23 in the jungle below, we were out of danger from the enemy forces on the Ashau Valley floor. We had cheated death one more time. The flight back was choppy and uncomfortable, but we did not care.

After this patrol was debriefed I signed off on Corporal B. as a team leader, and he continued to be successful for some time. Sadly, he did have a certain flair for judgmental error, and one day, some eight to ten patrols later, he got into trouble. He found another huge trail on a ridge in the Ashau area, and as he was looking at it, two NVA happened by, walking casually along at sling arms. Corporal B. leaped out onto the trail, shouting "Chieu Hoi" (a version of surrender, or "come to our side," in Vietnamese) while pointing his rifle at them. They were taken totally by surprise and likely would have surrendered had not the NVA in the unit following them decided to shoot the corporal twice in the leg.

That ended what might have appeared to Corporal B. a Medal of Honor action and turned the whole thing into a chaotic extraction fight that lasted for several hours. After the expenditure of many pieces of aerial ordnance and the commitment of a platoon from the 101st Airborne Division, we got all our Marines out alive (three wounded, including Corporal B.)—with no prisoners. The Army lost an OH-6A helicopter and nine men either hurt in the aircraft or wounded in the firefight—none killed.

Corporal B. was brave, resourceful, and tough. Perhaps if I had it to do over again I could have developed a creative way to teach him to modify his aggressive spirit with a bit more calculating judgment. Regardless, when I went into the jungle with him, Corporal B. performed as a team leader should, and I would still sign off on his promotion to that billet.

13

SILVER EAGLE RETURNS A CALL

As the year 1969 stubbed its toe on the way into the history books, Third Force Recon prepared to greet the arrival of 1970 with good humor. We exchanged many cheery holiday messages among ourselves, most of which would never have been used as prepared samples in any of the communications officer's training manuals. I was in the Ashau with Corporal B.'s team, and at 0001 on the next to last night of the blood-drenched 1960s, Zulu Relay sent the following message: "Ancient Scout Six, Ancient Scout Six, priority traffic for Grog from Igor. Acknowledge!"

Now, laughter and good humor do have their place, but it is essential to understand that we continued to take the war very seriously. In fact, the war was growing more pressing for us each day as the NVA arrayed more forces in the eastern mountains of the Republic of Vietnam. Many of those forces had only one mission—eradication of Third Force Reconnaissance Company. Therefore, for me to speak openly on the radio in response to Zulu's message might have been suicidal at worst and damned inconvenient at best. I did what all the radio operators were trained to do. I keyed the handset to break the squelch in the ear of the sender, released the transmit switch, and waited, listening.

Key clicking was not foolproof by any means, but it was superior to any type of speech whispered into the handset. For some reason, whispers carry for inordinate distances, and that could give away the presence of Marines lurking there in the jungle darkness. We used various short key-depression codes: nothing fancy, just enough to respond to simple questions and/or to signal that team silence was needed at the moment.

Of course, the teams used voice traffic when it was appropriate and safe to speak. Often the voice communications traffic was scrambled by cipher-coding devices when we were able to live with the transmission range reduction that the ciphering machines inflicted upon our equipment. Everyone knew that every radio transmission that was not encrypted was being monitored by the NVA.

After I had been passed the handset, I keyed twice, waited three beats, and then keyed six times in rapid succession. This would tell the relay communicator that he was really talking to Ancient Scout Six—me. Convinced that he had reached the intended party, the communicator sitting huddled in the dark on Zulu Relay passed on, "Grog, Grog, see the red fish. Happy New Year a day early. You are still totally unsatisfactory! The Igor sends!"

That particular message harked back to an underwater communications test that Buck Coffman and I had conducted off Catalina Island in California. We had been evaluating an engineering prototype of an underwater communications pack for reconnaissance swimmers. The eggheads in the Bendix design shop had fitted us with bone-conducting microphones and speakers that purportedly allowed the user to both transmit and hear through the bones behind his ears. In use, you spoke during exhalation into a modified rubber face mask, and the sounds picked up from the bones in your skull were processed by the waist-mounted instrument and transmitted to the other swimmer. Arriving on the bottom for our first test, I tried it out by telling the Igor to see the red Garabaldi fish that was trying to crawl into my face mask with me. The equipment was not ready for test, and it garbled up that simple message.

Hearing the Igor's message gave me a feeling of comfort in the knowledge that despite all the miles of jungle, the hard cold rain, and the presence of many NVA nearby, we were still part of the band of brothers that was Third Force.

While the rain continued to pelt down heavily, we were relieved to find that we had been blessed, on the last day of the old year, with a ceiling that was just barely high enough for the aircraft to operate in, and we were going home to Phu Bai. Extraction was without incident, although we did hear many signal shots in the valley as the helicopters swooped toward us over the ridge lines. By 1000 we were more than forty miles from the dark, forbidding Ashau; we were all reasonably dry, quite safe, and laughing as we told tales about our latest adventures in the valley.

Once reasonably clean and well fed, I dove into the pile of paperwork assembled for me by Captain Hisler and Sergeant Henderson, fully expecting to spend the rest of the day catching up with company administrative matters. This was not really possible, as I also had to take part in the debriefing of Corporal B.'s team, to review the debriefing notes with Lieutenant Robertson, and to add supplementary comments based on my own observations.

Later I met with the XO, the S-3, and the platoon leader to discuss the performance of Corporal B. As usual, the amount of work to be done easily overwhelmed the time available. The last day of 1969 did not carry with it any easing of the pressures. By nightfall we were busily preparing teams for the following morning's insertions and preparing orders for other operations planned for the next few days. Somewhere in the dark hours we took a moment to shake hands all around the Combat Operations Center and to offer all hands best hopes on the arrival of 1970. Despite being rather frazzled, I wound up staying awake until 0200 before sacking out for the three hours of sleep that were possible before another day was due to heave over the horizon.

With the arrival of morning, not to mention the arrival of 1970, I woke to find that the Igor had already assembled the teams and the aviators for the morning briefing. He had threatened to destroy anyone who bothered me or tried to wake me—thereby handing me an additional forty minutes of sleep. Perhaps it upset my system, which had become reasonably attuned to fatigue, or perhaps I was so tired from the previous days and nights in the Ashau that I needed more time to recover. Anyway, for whatever reason, I mushed around the command center like a zombie until some bitter black coffee cleared my head of the cobwebs.

It was fortunate that I had Lieutenant Coffman available, otherwise the whole show might have been two hours late in getting on the move. My achy body and my fuzzy head finally began to really recover when I was strapped into the UH-1H piloted by Major James and we had lifted to an altitude that gave us some chilly, less humid air. The point that needs to be made in all this is that everyone, no matter how hard he tries, cannot expect to function at full capacity, at all times, during combat. Stress precludes restful sleep, and cumulative fatigue is like burning the candle at both ends. With support from men like the Igor it was, of course, no problem at all—things got done on schedule, no matter what.

My own evaluation of my performance that morning made me a better commander. I could see that burnout was possible, and I made every effort to watch my Marines more closely as they continued to live at the harried pace set by our commitments. All of us—even Coffman, with his relentless energy—would need occasional breaks from the pressures if we were to survive.

Our new year opened with a bright day of sunshine and fleecy clouds. Our flight to the Ashau was quickly over, and we got down to the mechanics of making false insertions and real ones too. Not one shot was fired by any team that morning, nor did the helicopters expend any ordnance. If the NVA was nearby—and they were—they surely failed to make their presence known. Once down on the pad at Phu Bai, I shook hands with the door gunners on Major James's helicopter, gave him a bear hug for New Year's, and snapped him a salute as he lifted off to return to his unit compound at Camp Eagle. I was happy to begin a new year on such an auspicious note—no contact and no losses on January 1, 1970.

As I walked to the COC, my body was telling me that a nap would be a healthy investment of time, but my executive officer greeted me with the news that I was going to be a social butterfly instead. My disposition began to darken again.

It turned out that the U.S. Army was the proud possessor of a tradition that revolved around paying formal calls on New Year's Day to the senior officer present. We Marines, who knew nothing of this tradition, were about to take part by my paying such a call on the commanding general of the 101st Airborne Division. Maj. Dan Meskin, commander of the CH-46 helicopter squadron HMM-262, and I were invited because we were the only two Marine commanding officers north of the Hai Vanh Pass—a topographical feature about forty-five miles south that delimited the northernmost portion of the opening to the sea that provided the harbor for the city of Da Nang. Both of us were worn to a frazzle, and neither he nor I cared to make any personal or political hay at some formal function, nor did we enjoy watching other people drink and act up when we had no options other than black coffee.

Of course, since there was no other alternative open, we went anyway.

Dan and I coordinated our arrival at the 101st Airborne Division to place us both on the scene at the precise moment stipulated. If the Army was going to be social, we were not going to let them criticize the Marine Corps representation—us—by arriving late to the affair. Neither of us was particularly neat and tidy, as we suffered equally from possession of tired, worn clothing that had been subjected to the worst beating that any laundry in the world could dispense. From tip of toe to tip of nose we two majors were not the sartorial equals of the better-equipped and better-supported Army folks, and we expected to be the ugly ducklings at this unexpected event. No starch, no spit, no polish, no fakery, just tired Marines trying to do what we were supposed to do, when we were told to do it. The idea made me angry, and I expected to spend my appointed time at the party being polite and hating every minute of it.

Major Meskin and I arrived and presented ourselves to the young lieutenant presiding over the doorway through which a large number of well-appointed and professional-looking Army officers were passing. Instead of a perfunctory and uninvolved greeting, he boisterously welcomed us and said that General Wright had been worried that we might not be able to come at all. He then left his post and escorted us to the area where a reception line had been established to permit the general to shake hands with the commanders as they passed by. We were whisked to the chief of staff, who asked the officers next in line to make a slot for the two of us so that we could immediately reach the general.

Before we had time to register more than mild surprise, we were being warmly and personally wished a Happy New Year by Maj. Gen. John Wright, the commanding general, who boomed out his welcome and engaged us in conversation for a number of minutes. He then turned and passed us to his assistant division commander with some extraordinarily flattering comments about our units and with the admonition that the brigadier was not to permit Dan or me to leave until he found time to talk with us some more. Things were happening quickly to change my attitude about the gathering.

Once away from the reception line, we were further surprised and pleased to be taken directly to the brigade commanders—all

•Official U.S. Marine Corps photo of Lt. Gen. Herman Nickerson, Jr. (1970). Reconnaissance Marines nicknamed him the "Godfather of Long-Range Patrolling."

•Maj. Alex Lee, commanding officer, Third Force Reconnaissance Company, prepares to accompany a team about to patrol in the A Shau Valley in December 1969. *(Courtesy author)*

•Lt. Col. Clovis C. "Buck" Coffman, Jr., operations officer, Third Force Reconnaissance Company. (*Courtesy Colonel Coffman*)

•*Below*: First Sgt. Lonnie B. Henderson receives a decoration from General Nickerson while Major Lee (*foreground*) looks on. (*Courtesy Bruce Norton*)

•*Below right*: Capt. Norman Hisler, executive officer, Third Force Reconnaissance Company. (*Courtesy Bruce Norton*)

•Second Lt. Wayne V. Morris served as adjutant, Third Force Reconnaissance Company, and platoon leader, 3d Platoon.
(*Courtesy Bruce Norton*)

•*Middle left*: A Marine OV-10 Bronco of the type used by Third Force Recon as the mission command aircraft during company reconnaissance operations in August, September, and October 1969.
(*Courtesy Jim Holzman*)

•*Middle right*: The Third Force Recon's living area, Quang Tri Combat Base, in August 1969. Note the sandbags in place on the tin-roofed huts to prevent the roofs from being lifted off during a typhoon.
(*Courtesy Bruce Norton*)

•Gen. Lewis Walt, assistant commandant of the Marine Corps, visits Third Force Recon. Major General Lom of the Army of the Republic of Vietnam and Major Lee are in the foreground.
(*Courtesy Bruce Norton*)

•Cpl. Guillermo Silva poses in the company's living area at Phu Bai in 1970.
(*Courtesy Bruce Norton*)

•*Above right:* Lance Cpl. Charles Sexton, who was awarded a Navy Cross, poses in front of Third Force Recon's Combat Operations Center at Quang Tri base in September 1969.
(*Courtesy Bruce Norton*)

•Sgt. Arthur Garcia, Team Snaky's team leader, rides a Marine Corps CH-46 en route to the A Shau Valley in January 1970.
(*Courtesy Bruce Norton*)

•Third Force Recon's fighting position on the mountaintop known as Zulu Relay, overlooking the A Shau Valley. The terrain dropped nearly vertically to the ridge line dominated by this weapons pit.
(*Courtesy Bill Moss*)

•U.S. Army helicopters from the 2d Squadron of the 18th Air Cavalry make the approach into the Phu Bai airstrip.
(*Courtesy Bill Moss*)

•*Middle left*: Sergeant Garcia is presented with the Vietnamese parachute insignia by Major Lee at a company formation in Phu Bai in January 1970.
(*Courtesy Bruce Norton*)

•*Middle right*: Cpl. Paul Keaveney survived Team Snaky's February 7, 1970, firefight with an NVA battalion. Keaveney suffered four bullet wounds: one in each shoulder, one in the leg, and one in the side. Yet he continued to fight until the unit was relieved, a heroic action for which he was awarded the Silver Star.
(*Courtesy Bruce Norton*)

•Two Marines of Team Snaky leave a CH-46 helicopter in a landing zone in the A Shau Valley in February 1970.
(*Courtesy Guillermo Silva*)

•A lighter moment for Corporal Keaveney as he plays with the company's mascot, Bullet.
(*Courtesy Bill Moss*)

•*Top right*: Marines of Third Force Recon in a CH-46 helicopter of HMM-262 en route to man the radio relay site in the A Shau Valley. Face paint wasn't necessary because the NVA knew Marines were situated on the hilltop.
(*Courtesy Bruce Norton*)

•*Left to right*: Sergeant Henderson, Lieutenant Coffman, Major Lee, and Captain Hisler pose during the celebration of the Marine Corps' birthday in a hangar at the Phu Bai airstrip.
(*Courtesy Bruce Norton*)

•View to the west from the piedmont area that lies just inland from the coastal plains in Northern I Corps. The A Shau Valley lies to the west behind the ridges in the distance.
(*Courtesy Bill Moss*)

•Some Marines of Third Force Recon used C-4 explosive to heat their coffee in the field in 1970. (*Courtesy Bill Moss*)

•*Middle left*: Major Lee (*left*) and Lieutenant Coffman (*center*) enjoy a relaxed moment with their mentor, General Nickerson, in Phu Bai in 1970. (*Courtesy Bruce Norton*)

•*Middle right*: A reconnaissance Marine on break in his night harbor site. (*Courtesy Bill Moss*)

•A member of the company prepares for deployment to Third Force Recon's stationary site, Zulu Relay, in the A Shau Valley. Machine guns were seldom carried on reconnaissance or surveillance patrols, however, because of the weight of the weapon and its ammunition. (*Courtesy Bill Moss*)

•A lone Marine breaks for a cold meal while on patrol.
(*Courtesy Bill Moss*)

•*Top right*: For protection, this reconnaissance Marine wears gloves, his sleeves down, and his collar up as he crosses a stream in the A Shau Valley. His thirty-round magazine is a non–Marine Corps issue item.
(*Courtesy Bruce Norton*)

•Lt. Col. Alex Lee, official U.S. Marine Corps photo, 1974.

•*Below*: Cpl. Teddy Bishop and Sergeant Garcia, pictured in the jungle just five minutes before both men were killed in a fight with a larger NVA force.
(*Courtesy Guillermo Silva*)

full colonels—where we were introduced by the brigadier in a manner that made it clear that we were considered to be important to the 101st Airborne Division. Both Dan and I were amazed. Where we had expected hostility, we encountered respect. Where we had expected to be viewed as outsiders and interlopers, we encountered genuine warmth and camaraderie. Where we had expected to be uncomfortable and uneasy, we quickly came to feel at home. The sense of brotherhood and shared destiny was so strong in that room that it overcame any doubts about the ceremony that might linger in our minds. Clearly, it was a derivative moment of rededication to the profession of soldiering and a reaffirmation of the fact that honorable practitioners of that profession might wear any uniform. The color of your uniform mattered not at all to the men in that room; not at all!

Later on there was a moment of serious intent as the general made a short speech outlining his hopes for 1970—without reference to the troop withdrawals planned for the coming year or the increasing power of the antiwar movement at home. He was positive, intense, and emphatic in his praise for all those in his division and in the other units represented at the party. General Wright took special note of the presence in the room of two Marine commanders and praised highly the work of Major Meskin's squadron, which on numerous occasions had provided lift helicopters for units of the 101st. When he shifted to remarks about Third Force Reconnaissance Company, he heaped accolades on the unit and on the performance of the individual Marines and Navy corpsmen.

General Wright was eloquent and effusive, paying us greater compliments than those that he gave to any unit of his own division. I stood proudly in my faded field uniform, wishing that every man who was serving in Third Force on that January day could have been there to hear this general of the U.S. Army sing their praises. They, of course, would have been touched, as I was, to see how great was the respect for Third Force at that New Year's ceremony.

After the speech and a heartfelt toast—coffee cups and beer cans raised on high—to the new year, a light meal was served. As the snacks were being devoured, the general came across the room to engage me in a more personal conversation. I tried my best to thank him for his kind words and to point out how magnificently we had been supported by the officers and men of the 2d Squadron of the 17th Air Cavalry. The general was quick to point out that he knew about our being harshly judged in Da Nang for flying more with the Army than with the Marines. He also made sure that I understood that he was aware of everything his aviation soldiers did for Third Force and that he fully supported his aviation commander, Col. Vern Bindrup, who would do his best to meet any commitment we might levy on his unit.

In addition to an exchange of deeply held thanks, the general and I became involved in a long and detailed discussion about tactics and techniques used by my Marines. His curiosity was operating at full power, and my answers to his questions grew increasingly detailed. I felt that I was monopolizing his time and tried to beg off, but General Wright was intent on getting his questions answered and would not let me escape. After all, when a two-star general asks a major to continue the conversation, the latter continues at his pleasure.

Aside from operational matters related to our conduct of reconnaissance missions, the general wanted to know all about the survival of Zulu Relay. He seemed to be astounded that they had been out there so long without being successfully assaulted by the NVA. None of his units had ever operated a full-time communications site in enemy territory for more than a few days without being attacked and driven back to the coast. I did my best to describe the site to him and to venture my opinion that it was indeed unlikely that the NVA could launch a successful attack on that piece of thoroughly rotten real estate without massing a major force and taking a great number of casualties. I continued to field his questions until he was urged by his chief of staff to spend some time with his other guests.

Major Meskin and I were bemused. We had shared the view that this whole thing was a waste of time and energy, yet in less than an hour we had learned a pair of leadership lessons: we both were too quick to judge, and, if done right, such a ceremonial act as "calls made and returned" might well assist someone like the general in properly setting the philosophical agenda for the combat commanders serving within his span of influence. Not only did we learn something important, we also had been treated with dignity while enjoying ourselves to the hilt. Our mood was greatly altered by the experience as we took our leave to return to our organizations.

When I returned to Third Force I settled in the COC and tried to convey to Captain Hisler and Lieutenant Coffman the gist of what had happened and my feelings about our relationship with the 101st Airborne. It was a pleasure, also, to forward to the troops at hand in Phu Bai, and those deployed on operational patrols, the general's kind words. I sent them out in message traffic to the field and had them passed down the chain of command for those in garrison.

By mid-afternoon I was again feeling the effects of fatigue. My solution was to stop drinking coffee for an hour or so, after which I dozed off in my chair. This was occasionally my means of dealing with the late-night pressures, and the radio operators and the operations sergeants who manned the various duty sections had all seen me catnap when things were slow. Of course, naps are a luxury that can easily be shattered by events of a predictable nature and those that are utterly unexpected.

I was awakened by one of the communicators who had evidently been shaking me for some time before my eyes finally focused on him and I grunted some form of inquiry as to what he wanted. He was most apologetic and said in a rapid-fire staccato, "Sir. Sorry to bother you. The Igor has gone to take a shower, and we have a problem at Zulu Relay." Reacting as quickly as I could, I came awake with a sinking feeling. I feared the worst for the Marines out on their mountaintop.

Grabbing the proffered handset, I keyed for the short interval that it took to activate the cipher system—which happened to be working that day—and began, "Zulu, Zulu, this is Ancient Scout Six actual. Say nature of problem! Are you taking fire? Over."

For what seemed an excessive amount of time, the loudspeaker for the tactical net remained silent. My mind was busy coming up to speed as it processed all manner of potential disasters that might have befallen the relay or one of the teams operating in the Ashau. Finally I heard the beep tone that announced to me that the cipher system was bringing me a message. A puzzled Marine came up on the net and reported, "Six, this is Zulu. Be advised I have a brown Huey in orbit around my position. They have entered our uncovered net [secondary tactical frequency was not set up for encryption] and have requested permission to land

Silver Eagle on our landing zone. Interrogatory, who the hell is Silver Eagle? Why is he out here? Is he cleared by you to land at our position? Over."

For a moment my sense of relief that the relay was not under fire overcame my surprise, but not for long. Silver Eagle was the call sign for the commanding general of the 101st Airborne Division. Instead of relaxing comfortably in his command post where I had been with him a scant four hours before, General Wright was risking his neck on a single helicopter mission beyond the farthest reaches of the operational area of his division. After the New Year's ceremony he had flown to the Ashau Valley and was asking permission to land his aircraft at a site manned by only twelve Marines.

Breaking from my thoughts, I transmitted, "Zulu! Six! Silver Eagle is head brown man. He is cleared to land if he chooses. Require that his aircraft clear the zone and return to orbit if he visits. Make maximum use of covered positions, as visit may draw fire. Be nice to him, he is a friend!"

Zulu Relay acknowledged my message, and I sat back to ponder. The comparison was disturbing. Despite the fact that Third Force was garrisoned in relatively civilized circumstances at Phu Bai, we seldom received any senior officer visitors. In fact, during the entire time that I was in command of Third Force, no officer above the rank of captain from the personnel, intelligence, or operations staff sections of III MAF ever came north to speak with us at our headquarters. If they wanted to discuss something with me, they sent for me and demanded that I present myself before their desks.

The boss, of course, was different. We did see General Nickerson whenever he could sneak the time needed to make the trip. One time he had arrived with Maj. Gen. Lewis Walt, visiting the war from Marine Corps headquarters, and Major General Lom of the Vietnamese Army in tow. Herman the German was the rare sort of general officer who was attuned to combat, and he loved to see his operational folks up close. It helped everyone's morale to know that General Nickerson was brave as a lion about going out to see his troops whenever he felt like it, wherever they happened to be at the moment.

Not one of the colonels on the various staffs or in the air wing, who so roundly criticized the company, ever came to look at what we were doing. When it came to visits by outsiders, Colonel Polakoff and Major Scott from the SRC were frequently guests at our table. Colonel Layne from the sensor program was also prone to drop in from time to time—even if he did not have a mission for us.

From farther away, we often saw Colonel Gray, but that was different. He was famous for traveling across the face of the world to find out whatever he wanted to know. That he happened to be stationed at Quantico did not enter into that equation at all— he just showed up in Quang Tri or Phu Bai when he felt like it!

It goes without saying that our dangerously placed radio relay site in the NVA's backyard had never been a featured high point on the senior officer's guided tour of the battlefront. That the commanding general of the 101st Airborne thought enough of my Marines to risk his life by flying to the Ashau and spending time on the ridge line at Zulu Relay with some of them endeared him forever to every man in the company. Marines, like troops throughout history, pay honor to any senior officer who demonstrates that he actually cares about their welfare. It was a rare moment for us, one that reflected, again, that out in that Asian war we were really a band of brothers that transcended service boundaries.

After the passage of fifteen or twenty minutes I heard in my headset, "Ancient Scout Six. Be advised that Silver Eagle has departed. Just like Santa, he brought presents. Over." The general had flown to the Ashau to hand out several sundries packs— special packages filled with cigarettes, candy, soap, and other health and comfort items—to the Marines working there that day.

The gesture made by the commanding general of the 101st Airborne Division was not forgotten by my Marines. One day, about two years later, I had the opportunity to repeat the thanks that I had messaged over to his headquarters the day of his impromptu visit to Zulu Relay. In the name of all who had served in Third Force, a few of us who had gathered at my home took the time to call General Wright at his home in Washington and thank him again for his service to us. He expanded on his earlier favorable comments by remarking that once the shooting had stopped in Vietnam, he had been hard-pressed to get the Army to complete the citation for the Valorous Unit Award—VUA—for the company.

That remark caused us to pause and take notice. None of us had ever heard anything at all about a VUA or any other award. General Wright was amazed that we had not received the award and promised to check the matter out at U.S. Army headquarters.

Just two days later he called me and passed the word that the roadblock had been blown; the VUA was on its way to the Marine Corps, signed and sealed by all the appropriate folks. The problem lay in the fact that Headquarters, U.S. Marine Corps, had never been made aware that a Marine unit had been awarded the VUA. To ensure that we were not screwed out of the award, General Wright sent me a personal copy of the documentation via certified mail to my home address. Third Force had been awarded only the second Valorous Unit Award ever given to a Marine unit by the U.S. Army, and we were immensely proud to place that unusual ribbon bar in the appropriate slot on our ribbon decks.

Because of an administrative error this award was not cleared for delivery to the Marine Corps until most of the men who served in the company in 1969/70 had returned to civilian life. We mailed out copies of the citation to everyone we could find, but I would estimate that more than two-thirds of those who did the work that earned this accolade for superior performance never learned of it.

14

SENSORS BY THE
BUSHEL BASKET FULL

Soon after my arrival in the Republic of Vietnam to take command of the company, Third Force Recon became heavily involved with the use of sensor technology. Nobody could have been more surprised by this turn of events than the Marines themselves, the majority of whom had never even heard of sensors. It took an act of faith for them to accept the most simple sensor we had, the Patrol Seismic Intrusion Device, known by its initials as the PSID.

Trained to be self-reliant and to depend on the full use of their own senses, the force reconnaissance Marines were nearly all opposed to adding these newfangled items to their combat load. Of course, they were even more opposed to the whole idea when they learned that we would, on occasion, be the means of implanting the more sophisticated sensors in areas dominated by the NVA. In fact, those who had heard the many rumors about the "MacNamara Trace" along the DMZ were most outspoken in opposing the use of these bits of electronic wizardry. They had heard tales of the losses suffered by the engineers who were installing the specialized gear that that trace included, and they felt that it was a waste of time for a line unit to become involved with such foolishness.

Regardless of the general opinion within the company, we had no choice in the matter. No other unit was working in the areas where we conducted our normal patrols, and aerial delivery was frequently not a realistically accurate means of emplacement. If one of the powerful decision makers in Saigon or Washington wanted a sensor within five feet of a road junction on National

Route 9, putting it there became the job of someone willing to physically go there and stick the fool thing into the ground. In short, a reconnaissance unit, because we had no other forces available for that task and because, even if there had been other forces available, it was still logically a reconnaissance task. The sensor units had no field assets that could be expected to survive outside the edge of the camp wire.

Third Force Marines came to respect the equipment, but they retained a rather unshakable disdain for the troops assigned to man the sensor assembly and sensor readout teams. As the Marines laughingly said, once they had become fans of the use of sensors, "If you want it done right, keep the 'twidgets' out of the field!"

Luckily, or perhaps it wasn't luck at all, sensors of various kinds were no strangers to me, to Buck Coffman, or to Colonel Polakoff. Our section within the development center at Quantico had been assigned the responsibility for almost all sensors in the Marine Corps. Additionally, we were also responsible for "maintaining liaison with the other services" and with the Defense Department regarding sensor equipment and techniques. We had tested all manner of seismic, acoustic, radio-frequency, night-vision, capacitance, miniradar, infrared, magnetic, ground-pressure, and metabolic effluvia detection devices. Some were good, some were useless; the majority had some merit if used properly and some severe drawbacks if improperly or inefficiently employed.

During 1968 we sat through some of the longest and most boring concept briefings ever convened. Until the ideas had been sifted, however, it was a given that the Department of Defense would listen to almost any crackpot who professed to have a way to solve the myriad difficulties associated with finding an enemy or simplifying, for the participants, the way that the war in Vietnam was being waged.

Friction was constant as various constituencies within the government and the civilian research community competed for funding. Tensions were quite high when projects were being presented to decision makers. I remember vividly how, on one occasion, my involvement as a member of a particular sensor committee placed me in a finely appointed, walnut-paneled conference room in Washington, listening carefully to a beautifully documented and well-prepared briefing that ate up most of one busy day in 1968. An outside contractor had had a brainstorm that included a sensor delivery system that was to be contained in special projectiles for the standard infantry issue, 81mm mortar. When the projectile was fired upward by the mortar crew into its selected trajectory, however, bad things began to happen.

As the 81mm projectile was proceeding toward the enemy, a small explosion would eject the steel base plug from the munition and an antenna would deploy. The contractor foresaw the use of dozens of these devices each night by units establishing defensive positions. Sensors of various types could be fitted into this munition for delivery by the mortars into areas through which the enemy might move. The sensor-acquired information on movements could then be evaluated and acted on at the infantry battalion level. Everyone seemed pleased with this concept until I was asked to comment for the Marine Corps. When I suggested, rather calmly, that it was an excellent presentation of a particularly lousy idea, there was some tension around the conference room.

My view to the contrary was that friendly infantrymen, Army or Marine, are generally found in their fighting holes, which would lie beneath the various trajectories of the outgoing mortar projectiles. I offered the strongly held opinion that soldiers or Marines hunkered down in their defensive fighting holes would become rather hostile when dozens of 1.5-pound solid steel base plugs began to rain down on them from above. In fact, I suggested that the poor damned infantrymen had enough to worry about without being whacked on the head by their own people.

The sponsoring service and their contractor were not pleased with my attitude. Their level of disgruntlement was serious, resulting in a call from the most senior officer attending the meeting, Lieutenant General Leavelle of the Air Force, to my general at the development center, Maj. Gen. Alan J. Armstrong, telling him that I was a disruptive influence on the committee. Armstrong's response was roughly, "Good, that's just what I sent him for!"

At Quantico, sensor work could also get exciting in a political manner. At the highest levels of the government, sensor work was directed by an organization known by the unlikely title Defense Communications Planning Group. DCPG had vast amounts of money and great power. They ran roughshod over anyone who opposed the whole idea, and they lavishly supported much valuable research by those, in the service and outside in civilian life, who were positively motivated to use these technical detection means. Occasionally, we at Quantico would find ourselves involved with DCPG in unusual and somewhat politically based fashion. On several occasions we were directed to duplicate tests made by another service when DCPG had doubts about the results presented by that service.

Obviously, this sort of assignment had the potential to create some serious interservice warfare. Had it not been for the rock-solid support of our boss, General Armstrong, we would have been smashed down as upstarts and troublemakers when our test findings did not coincide with those presented by someone with both power and a vested interest in the test results. In 1968 various groups attempted to make their sensor systems preeminent over the competition. The nautical term for this practice many years ago was gun decking, which meant that false gun decks were built on ships to fool onlookers as to the true amount of firepower they possessed.

A twist of fate and the power of DCPG caused me to become involved in the battle for Khe Sanh in 1968. This all began when a Khe Sanh battle photograph appeared on the front page of the *New York Times* in early February of that year. Pictured was a Navy doctor, serving with the 26th Marine Regiment at Khe Sanh, applying his stethoscope to a steel stake implanted in the earth. The caption stated that this doctor was listening to the sound of the North Vietnamese digging tunnels under the combat base for the purpose of blowing it up in the faces of the Marines. Parallels between Khe Sanh and the battle for Petersburg in the Civil War followed, and the lamentations went on and on and on and on.

DCPG may have heard directly from the president—I don't know—but I do know that things began to happen at lightning speed. Before a good deep breath could be drawn again in quiet, I found myself on the far side of the world at Khe Sanh, in the company of three DCPG officers, setting out to prove or disprove the tunneling theory.

Within a day we were fully convinced that we could seismically detect any tunneling effort amid the wild array of seismic inputs from bombs, rockets, artillery bursts, and Marines tramping around in the trenches. Our tests were simple; the device used was an early, preproduction model of our just completed Marine Corps AN/PSR-1, a basic geophone-based seismic detection instrument. The key was the rhythmic nature of any form of tunneling or other digging, as opposed to the more random seismic noise from explosions and troops stamping their feet.

Obviously, the doctor hadn't applied common sense to reach a similar conclusion. Instead, his near panic was communicated by the press to the highest levels of our government and they, in turn, were terrified of the public's reaction. The result was an around-the-world trip for four of us, with a few days under artillery, mortar, and rocket fire thrown in for excitement. We issued our report, stating that tunneling was not taking place, and returned to our normal duties.

Crowning all of our travails at Quantico in the sensor effort was the requirement that we generate, in forty-seven days from the word go, the Marine Corps policy on sensors. That policy was to be properly integrated with Defense Department efforts, as well as all the disparate efforts of the individual services. As an aside, we were also to develop an organizational structure, staffing for that structure, and equipment for that structure. Working from this creation, they then wanted us to present the basic concepts for sensor utilization throughout the Marine Corps. We wrote it, but it was not a pleasurable or rewarding exercise.

Guidance was minimal from headquarters because of limited understanding of the field and the enormous lack of interest in the subject outside the small, understaffed intelligence component there. Wanting to give them something that would be useful and operationally sound, we wrote hundreds of pages. Portions of that policy document and some of the units created by it survived into the era of the Persian Gulf War of 1991.

Without the participation of Colonel Layne and Colonel Gray—two Marines stationed within DCPG—the Marine Corps might have been left out of the sensor world altogether. Both of these officers were the fiercest defenders of the Corps, willing to move mountains to ensure that we got information, equipment, and support for our sensor programs. Therefore, it was no surprise when Colonel Layne, known worldwide as the Bear, arrived at Third Force in 1969 to inform Coffman and me that we would be continuing our involvement with sensors. The Bear was to be our contact for all sensor work in our part of the war. A straight-forward man, he told us that he wanted Third Force to implant them as part of our operational mission.

The Bear was famous for winning arguments by a combination of superior reason and pure intimidation. He was huge, aggressive, and smart as hell. We had no argument, therefore, with him or his ideas, for it was both a professionally sound move and a logical survival tactic to support this man fully. I immediately established sensor involvement as a command policy for Third Force. We would actively become involved in whatever Colonel Layne might request in support of his sensor-employment missions.

It was expected that the Bear, and the people he worked for, would effectively control and manage all of the sensors used in I Corps. As part of that control effort Colonel Layne wanted Third Force to provide him with the capability to obtain credible precision placement of some of his devices. During development tests the Bear had learned that many folks might report precise placement by air or by hand, but the actual locations might well be somewhat less precise than was reported. On the other hand, he knew that if a Third Force Marine told him that the device was eighteen feet from a road junction, on an azimuth of 234 degrees magnetic, he could depend on the truth of that statement. We were the logical folks for the job, and he and I already had a strong working relationship. That relationship fostered a fine, unquestioning interdependence that worked.

Now that we had the job, Buck Coffman quickly developed two methods of making these implants. One, the sensor implantation would piggyback on a team that was already assigned a reconnaissance operation in the appropriate area. The first mission of the team would be to place the sensors; its second goal would be to continue the planned surveillance. This was not often acceptable, as the sound of digging might well be detected by NVA regulars who, the Radio Battalion reported, were pressing more troops into service in the counterreconnaissance role. We felt among ourselves that the pressure was going to go up and that the NVA was always going to be out hunting Third Force

Marines. Any NVA contact at the sensor-implant site would compromise the team, and we would likely find ourselves in a firefight while the team was extracted. That unpleasant result would leave the primary operational mission—reconnaissance—uncompleted.

Our second technique required us to lay on a complete air package, run a special flight to place the sensors, and extract the team as soon as the deed was done. Despite the expense in money, manpower, and matériel, this was the method we preferred. If we had a firefight the NVA troops might think that they had driven away another reconnaissance effort. If no firefight ensued, we hoped that the NVA would conclude that a team had been dropped and it had slipped away into the jungle. We always were in favor of anything that added to the level of tension for the NVA commanders.

Regardless of the method we used, it was presupposed that if we did it right, the enemy might well spend all day in and around the site without concluding that we had been there to conceal sensor surveillance devices.

One of the most effective sensors, both in the air-dropped version and the hand-implanted version, was an acoustic listening device. Third Force deployed many of these devices in the early months of 1970. Once in place, the sensor monitoring teams simply listened to the sounds that the jungle made and searched for sounds made by the NVA passing through that part of the landscape. In the air-dropped version the device looked much like a bomb. It was attached to a parachute that slowed its fall and would snag on trees, thereby suspending the device where it could overhear a wider area. An antenna sticking out the tail of the device permitted burst transmission of the information gathered to an orbiting EC-121 aircraft. Each device was equipped with a booby-trap feature that caused it to blow up if anyone who found it opened the case.

A tape recording that was passed around the intelligence community in 1969 was purported to have been made when two NVA troops found one of these devices and carried it to their leader. That worthy gentleman happened to be the dispatcher controlling the secretive movement of trucks in the Ashau Valley. It was alleged that the man in charge was not interested, and they left the device on the ground where it happily transmitted their conversations into the sky for our eavesdroppers. About five days later a more senior NVA officer noticed the device and asked what it was doing there. Failing to get a satisfactory answer, he directed someone to disassemble the damn thing posthaste. The final transmission was a sharp click that denoted to anyone listening that whoever had received that order had applied himself to the task and was summarily killed.

By whatever mode they were inserted, the sensors provided an invaluable addition to our intelligence-collection efforts. Both acoustic and seismic sensor readouts could be subjected to sophisticated analysis. The results provided an immediate increase in our understanding of enemy capabilities and intentions. Teams in the field were often provided with advance warning of enemy movements, including, in some cases, the direction of that movement. On one occasion sensor data permitted us to alert the relay that the NVA was discussing them and that an assault was possible.

On another occasion we learned from an acoustic sensor that a new NVA reconnaissance unit had entered the Ashau Valley for the purpose of countering our presence. The voices recorded through sensor device corroborated the Radio Battalion communications intercepts on the same subject and gave us additional information on unit strength and areas of operations. With bits and pieces of concrete, verifiable information coming in every day from sensor readout analysis, the Third Force Recon Marines quickly got over their initial reluctance to take part in this new mission.

In fact, to perform the sensor missions correctly, we had to establish another educational package within the company, namely, sensor school. The Igor and I spent untold hours explaining everything we knew about sensors to a rapt audience as we sat in the COC late at night sweating out the teams. The troops wanted to know how the devices worked, why they were being used, and who was going to learn—just what—from their use. Their interest in this rapidly changing scientific field was impressive and rewarding. Lieutenant Coffman and I made every effort to give the Marines the full scoop as we knew it from our time at Quantico. When we were stumped for an answer, we put in a call for the Bear, and he would fly to the Third Force pad and stop off long enough to put out the straight word.

Being able to see at night, even with the rudimentary night-vision equipment of 1969/70, gave us an edge over the NVA that often saved lives on our side. At Quantico, Lieutenant Coffman and I had been responsible for all Marine Corps involvement with night-vision equipment as a side issue of the sensor business. We tested big night scopes and small night scopes and every version in between. All of these image intensifiers helped us see better at night than we could with our unaided eyes. Impressed, we urged headquarters to secure more of this type of equipment for the Marines deployed to the Republic of Vietnam. We were believers, but believers with a sense of caution. We could easily see the value to night-vision technology, but we could also see that total dependence on equipment of this type could get you killed.

Vietnam was a place with weather and other conditions that surpassed most of the considerations of the research engineers. It was wetter than they thought possible; it was hotter than their worst model; and the dust was finer than they had anticipated. Obviously, night-vision devices were delicate instruments that suffered when exposed to these factors, not to mention the rigors of combat use in the jungles and mountains. Despite the possible failures of that equipment, however, Third Force never turned down any opportunity to add more night-vision scopes to our inventory—by legal or illegal means.

This area of sensor-related technology was important because it gave us an edge when it counted and improved our survival rate. In planned ambush contacts and in unplanned night firefights when a team was fighting to stay alive, the night scopes might make the difference between living and dying. Had we been in possession of the night-vision capability displayed by U.S. forces in combat against Iraq in 1991, Third Force Reconnaissance Company might well have been able to take the night away from the NVA.

Small, man-transportable moving-target radars had just come into use in the Marine Corps in 1968, and in 1969 we looked at their potential use in Third Force. I wanted to find a way to repeat a success that I had observed one night in February 1968. During my sensor-related visit to the Khe Sanh siege, I had been permitted to demonstrate a method of coordinating the moving-target radars and the night-vision scopes. Some clear thinkers had devised this particular technique during test work at Quantico.

The radars were set to scan down the finger ridges to detect movement and establish precise range to the moving NVA riflemen. The night-vision scopes—in this case the large AN/TVS-4 scopes on tripods—were situated well away from the radars, in places where they could verify by direct observation that the targets being detected by the radars really were men.

With the two different devices separated by a known distance, and with each providing a precise azimuth to the targets, an extremely accurate fire solution was possible. In fact, on the night in question, we were able to take action against the NVA by requesting an immediate fire for effect by the artillery without any prior ranging fires. Because the information was accurate, the coverage of the moving group of NVA soldiers was total. I suppose that most of those enemy soldiers departed this earth without any idea how the Marines had been able to hit them so suddenly.

Seeking every possible edge, we looked carefully at the possible integration of these two technical detection means by Third Force Marines in the field. It was just not possible, however, to find a way to employ the radars. While I found the moving-target radars to be impressive tools, I could never find a way to successfully integrate their use by the operational teams. The night harbor sites that the teams specifically chose to sleep in were nasty, broken ground where the NVA was unlikely to maneuver and where the team could mount a credible defense if detected. To be useful to the teams, the radars would need to be placed where there was a more sweeping view of open terrain, but the team leaders did not need to increase their vulnerability in order to add the radars.

As we did with everything, we also considered the total weight of all items to be carried in combat. The radars of 1969/70 were not light enough to be a practical item for reconnaissance teams to carry in the field.

Whenever we thought that we had learned all that we were going to learn about remote sensing work, something new would appear to add to the many tasks accomplished by Third Force Marines. For example, one of the teams returned from the Ashau Valley floor with an intelligence coup in the form of six feet of communications cable. This cable, which had evidently been laid by the NVA to provide secure communications between their headquarters in the north and their forces deployed in the Republic of Vietnam, was an impressive find. The NVA obviously thought that by switching to use of the cable, they would keep the U.S. forces from monitoring their operational communications, as the Marines did with their Radio Battalion and the Army did with its similar units.

We quickly completed the report on the team's patrol and sent it up the chain of command, along with the cable sample for evaluation. In the Third Force COC we were convinced that this was an important find, but we had no idea how this would be viewed by those above us in the hierarchy. We need not have worried. Higher elements of the U.S. government took this find with all the seriousness that we could ever have desired. In less than a week we had a visitor.

An Air Force Jeep arrived at the Third Force COC, bringing to us one of those men who have no name. He was of medium build, medium height, an utterly nondescript man who could have blended into almost any crowd of civilians. He introduced himself as a Mr. Green. None of us believed him for so much as two seconds, but that did not matter in the least. His credentials said he was from one of those myriad agencies in Saigon that nobody had ever heard of before. He had arrived to talk to us about the communications cable, however, and we were happy to sit down with him and discuss the next step in this process.

Mr. Green explained that the cable we had cut to obtain our sample was a brand-new, 27-pair multiplex communications link. This type of cable had been manufactured in Hungary for military field use by various countries within the Soviet bloc. That information did not surprise anyone, as we considered it logical that the Russians had supplied the NVA with anything they needed by way of sophisticated communications gear.

On the other hand, we were all amazed and surprised to learn that the first thing he had on his mind was an emphatic request that we stop cutting the cable when we came across it in the future. Mr. Green explained that he had come to us to obtain help in applying an alternative approach to dealing with the cable— he wanted to begin listening to it. Of course, he never offered to tell us how he or his agency (which I assumed to be the National Security Agency) would listen or from where—aircraft, ground, or space platform. In his scheme of things our role was to be limited to hooking up a monitoring unit to the cable. That unit would have a transmitter attached, and once we had turned the device on, it was evidently none of our business who learned what or how things went from there.

When Mr. Green unpacked his equipment it quickly became obvious that we were dealing with the first team. The device was extremely small, remarkably well engineered, and without a single identification mark to betray the country of origin. The case was smooth and almost seamless, without any distinguishing marks other than two wire terminals and an antenna terminal. It looked as if it would be extremely difficult to disassemble, and one would have to destroy the device to get any kind of look at the electronics package inside. Attachment to the 27-pair communications cable was simple: we had simply to loop a fitting around the cable and trail out the connecting wire to a site chosen for hiding the transmitter.

Our only instruction was to turn it on *after* attachment and to leave it in place. We were not able to learn anything at all about the unit, not even some items that I felt were important. Mr. Green would not confirm or deny the presence of an explosive booby-trap feature, nor would he discuss what did, or did not, happen when the unit reached the end of its useful life—an explosion or silent, internal meltdown. We were not even permitted to learn what frequency it used to transmit the data it was stealing from the NVA.

All in all, it was frustrating, but Mr. Green was a smooth, unruffled character who gave away nothing from his side while asking the Third Force Marines to perform yet another unusual mission. Of course, not only would we do it, but we would take great pride in doing it damn well.

In a matter of days we scheduled a team to carry the monitoring device to the Ashau. Since we needed to take another look at the area where the cable had first been seen, we combined a normal surveillance patrol with the mission of attaching the monitoring unit to the cable. On their third day in the field the team reported a good hook, which told us that somebody, somewhere, for reasons we all supported, could now listen in on the NVA. The following morning the Commissar called me on the secure land line from the SRC and told me that a message had been received reporting that our mission had been a success. At that we felt gratified, albeit a bit left out. We need not have wasted any time feeling that it was over. The NVA saw fit to get us involved in short order.

The North Vietnamese Army may have had many illiterate peasants and its own coterie of fools, but there were also some markedly smart soldiers among the communists we met in the Ashau Valley. Intelligent problem solving is something to be respected, even in your enemy. With nothing much more than their bare hands and the fortitude created by necessity, the NVA overcame much of our technological advantage. They often used wire to tie treetops together to thwart aerial observation; they used branches to sweep away the "tea bag" antipersonnel mines dropped by the Air Force along their trails and road nets; they dug up all manner of unexploded U.S. munitions for reuse against us; they listened to the English-language chatter on U.S. radio nets to take advantage of security errors; and they quickly defeated the magnificently designed cable monitor of Mr. Green's agency. We were impressed. How Mr. Green felt about the matter was not revealed to us.

Less than a week after learning that the team had established a good hook, we were visited by another civilian carrying a duplicate device. This was a Mr. Brown, whose credentials matched Mr. Green's, and he asked us to put in another monitoring link. He did not offer any kind of information on whether or not the other one was working or not working. We had to assume from his dour and grumpy manner that it had either failed or had been spotted by some alert NVA soldier passing through the Ashau. We accepted the device on the same terms as the first one and sent it to the valley the next morning with an admonition to the team leader to be particularly careful when he was hiding the transmitter.

Two days later we again had a good-hook report, and within a day or two thereafter we received a confirmation from above of a successful mission. By the end of the week, however, Mr. Brown was back for a repeat performance. I was sure that the NVA had a way to spot the electronic alteration made to their communications cable by the device, but the close-mouthed Mr. Brown would not discuss my theory. He was probably right to ignore my idea because it was flat wrong.

The third monitoring device that was sent to the Ashau became a priority target for later observation. The team leader was ordered to focus his attention on the trail network near the attachment site and to look for any NVA regular who appeared to be involved in checking on the cable. He could not stay and sit on the attachment site like a hen hatching her eggs, but after hooking it up he could withdraw in a careful manner to hills from which the trails could be watched. Three days after the team had reported a good hook, we had our answer.

Our unsophisticated enemy had evidently learned in some way that the cable communications were compromised and had decided to do something about it on a daily basis. All of our technical engineering skills were defeated by a simple bamboo stick and a piece of strap. While watching the trails, the team spotted an NVA support trooper, all dressed in gray, dragging a seven- or eight-foot stick and walking casually along the edge of the trail where the cable lay. On the end of the stick he had a strap that encircled the cable. That bit of strap would permit him to find anything that had been attached to the cable, meanwhile putting some distance between his body and the offending attachment— just in case it happened to be rigged to detonate high order in his face when the strap struck the device.

We reported this bit of common sense–based, intelligent problem solving by the NVA to those above us in the chain. There were no more visits from Mr. Green or Mr. Brown, even though we wanted to see them again to suggest that they design a monitoring head that could be placed beneath the soil on which the cable rested—thereby defeating the way in which the cable was being checked. We never had any further contact with either of our not-so-chatty friends.

Throughout the time that Third Force operated independently we took part in sensor-related missions. Colonel Layne kept us in the game and kept us busy with our small part in the technological war. As the bigger picture unfolded, more and more remote sensing was used to offset the steady reduction in U.S. forces committed to the war in Vietnam.

15

OVERSUPERVISION FROM HIGH PLACES

Everyone who's ever spent a day working in an operational unit is familiar with oversupervision from on high. By the time the United States became engaged in Southeast Asia, technology was evolving that supported increased micromanagement. The war in the Republic of Vietnam was the first war in history that permitted such a wide range of seniors to meddle with minutiae several levels below their station. The stories are legion about the actions of President Johnson, Secretary MacNamara, and a host of others in high places who reached down to chime in regarding even the smallest details. Every man jack in Saigon, Hawaii, and Washington—and all points in between—wanted to have some form of personal impact on the way the working folks in the Republic of Vietnam went about their daily lives in combat.

In a previous tour in combat with 2nd Battalion, 7th Marine Regiment, I had seen the ill effects of this kind of intrusive oversupervision. On one occasion during Operation Stomp, in August 1966, we had used tear gas to encourage some Vietcong troops to abandon a tunnel complex. The resultant uproar of various journalists caused, by rough count, about seven levels of command to waffle and issue pronouncements of one kind or another about our actions and about the judgment of our battalion commander, Lt. Col. Leon Utter. *Time* magazine carried a piece that proclaimed the imminent relief of our boss, as did other members of the opinion-molding press, including the *Washington Post* and the *New York Times*.

Meanwhile, only one senior officer, Col. Oscar Peatross (later lieutenant general), was willing to stand firmly on the side of common sense. He flatly stated that to relieve Utter from command, they would have to relieve him from command of the 7th Marine Regiment. He also pointed out that the tear gas flushed armed men from cover, none of whom could then shoot the Marines who were present, and he liked it that way. We dodged the bullet that time, but the big-brother-is-watching-you status of our lives was not permanently altered.

It was therefore no surprise to me that by the summer of 1969, the high level of interference by those who were conspicuously far from the sound of the guns had become an art form. No unit was ever immune to it, *ever*. Curious battalion commanders could overfly their units and get involved in a fire-team-level maneuver; regimental commanders could overfly the battalions and meddle to their heart's content; and ever higher officers could add their voices to the cacophony. Command became a difficult and ofttimes frustrating occupation, one with dangers inherent to operational decision making that were wholly unrelated to actions by the enemy.

To illustrate a minor example of this complex activity, I will cite an incident that took place during my combat tour in 1966. Cruising around in his helicopter, General Walt was making life difficult for all of us, having bypassed the regimental commander, the battalion commander, the company commander, the platoon leader, and the squad leader in order to control—himself—the positioning of riflemen on the western bank of a small stream. The general had been shouting on everyone's radio net, demanding that ten Marines be deployed to sweep the far bank of the stream as two battalions of the 7th Regiment moved parallel to that waterway.

Shortly after this disruption, the general had his helicopter land outside our command post in order to continue involving himself in squad-level maneuvers during a face-to-face confrontation. Our boss, who was busy maneuvering his battalion, seemed unruffled by the general's approach. General Walt stormed into the battalion command group where I—then in the rank of captain—was serving as operations officer, and began shouting at Colonel Utter.

It seemed that not one person he had spoken to was able to give a precise and satisfactory answer to his question, "How many men do we have on the west bank of the stream?" He did not want to be reassured that our battalion commander was aware of the need for security on the far side of the water, he just wanted to know how many men were there, period!

Since three levels of command lay between us and the squad of Marines on the battalion's flank, we did not have a clue as to the *exact* number of Marines who had crossed to the other side of the water. What we did know was that I had included in the operations order specific mention of the need for the flank company to physically secure the far bank as we maneuvered parallel to the water. My boss expected the commanding officer of Company G, which was operating on that flank, to follow the order he had issued.

The angry general bore down on us, devoting all of his energies to getting to the bottom of this problem. It was a lousy time for a harangue, but we could see it coming. Junior Marines scattered in every direction because General Walt was famous for his quick temper; the stories of a number of injustices inflicted on reasonably competent officers were well known among all of the mid-level officers, such as myself, who were forced to bear this sort of indignity without comment. On this particular day, it appeared that our time had come.

Colonel Utter did not turn a hair! This was a Marine from the old school who happened to be taking part in his third major war. He issued mission-type orders, allowing his subordinates to exercise their intelligence and their initiative. We admired him and served under him with the deepest sense of professional pride. After the general had roared his question again, Colonel Utter calmly answered, "We have fourteen Marines across the water—that is, Sergeant Brownmiller's squad—and they are packing an M-60 machine gun along with them."

All of the bluster and roaring ceased. In fact, a short, pleasant discussion followed, after which the general hurried back to his helicopter and left our area to oversupervise someone else. Another typhoon had blown over us without blowing our heads off. Our mood turned almost giddy.

My boss was busily getting on with the task at hand, as were the rest of us, but I could not help asking him how he knew that fourteen Marines were doing what he had just told the general they were doing. I was also a bit curious as to who the hell

Sergeant Brownmiller was, to be the subject of personal interest by the battalion commander. Did such a man really exist?

Leon Utter leaned back, looked me over from head to toe, laughed a bit, then slapped me on the back, saying, "A. Lee, don't be dumb! You know perfectly well that I don't have any more information than you do about what is going on over there right now. Our job is to maneuver the battalion, not the individual riflemen in some tired sergeant's squad. That job belongs to the sergeant who was put there by his platoon leader. Brownmiller is just a name I made up. General Walt wanted information so he could feel that he was involved, and I made some up and gave it to him. Now he is happy and has gone to bother someone else. That makes me happy. Let's stop worrying about generals and the things that they can find time to fret about. Getting the job done is what's important. Don't ever forget that!"

I took the lesson to heart, and as fate would have it, was likewise faced with a serious case of oversupervision from on high.

As the war was winding down in 1969/70, we found that Third Force Reconnaissance Company was going to be involved in a way that none of us had anticipated. The boundary between the Republic of Vietnam on the south and the Democratic Republic of Vietnam on the north included a strip that was laughingly designated a demilitarized zone. Like several DMZs that had been established in other countries, this area was not demilitarized at all. On our maps, the DMZ was roughly eight thousand meters wide, with the national boundary between the two separate Vietnams in the center. The area lying to the south of the national border, that is, on our side of the line, became a subject of discussion at the various peace conferences that took place between the U.S. and North Vietnamese diplomats. In particular, they sought agreement on just who might or might not be permitted to operate within the limits of the DMZ.

One of the concessions reportedly offered by Secretary of State Kissinger was the removal of major U.S. and South Vietnamese forces from the DMZ. All such forces were to remain south of the red line on the map denoting the four-thousand-meter buffer zone on our side of the border. We did, however, retain the right to insert "squad-size" units north of the red line to preclude surprise attacks from the north and to serve as a presence on the ground.

Third Force was detailed to be the U.S. unit to operate across the invisible red line. The idea made some sense to us, but the method of implementation left a great deal to be desired.

Because we had been operating throughout the DMZ for some time, we had no qualms about the mission. We knew that the NVA would be there in strength, and we knew that no agreement reached on the other side of the world would, in any way, reduce the danger. In fact, with the larger Marine, Army, and South Vietnamese forces being ordered to stay to the south, the danger to the operating teams was greatly increased.

To begin, we merely shifted a portion of our operations to the DMZ and made more detailed notations of the team findings in reports to the SRC in Da Nang. I suppose the data found its way to Washington in the normal manner; once it left my unit, I did not waste time worrying about people twelve thousand miles away reading those reports, nor did I concern myself with all the possible places those reports were being sent. I should have.

Not long after Third Force had increased the number of DMZ reconnaissance patrols, I received a surprise visit from Colonel Polakoff. The Commissar was unashamed to show the world that he loved the Third Force Marines. He visited as often as he could, staying hours on some occasions, only minutes at other times. He was always upbeat and cheerful, and the troops treated him as one of the family. But this time he came with a long face and a somber manner. Despite anything he could do and anything that General Nickerson could do, Third Force was now to be fully and completely oversupervised from *very, very* high places. Those people on the other side of the world that I had so blithely dismissed from my thinking were now going to direct me to do this and to do that on a daily basis. That something close to a zillion command levels lay between my command post and Washington, D.C., did not faze the faceless bureaucrats who wanted to "take control of the situation."

The following day a large truck from the III MAF headquarters in Da Nang arrived with several specialized Marine communicators on board. These Marines were teletype operators and their supporting technicians, the kind of communicators one normally finds far up in the higher command echelons. Placement of Marines of this sort in our unit did not sit well with the Third Force troops. Specialized Marines who dealt with communications gear of this complexity were far different from those who served in the infantry or in reconnaissance units. In the main, they were men who had college time behind them, men who found themselves performing duties in the U.S. Marine Corps more through a quirk of fate than any choice of their own.

Some of these communicators were quick to express disdain for Marines who actually placed a pack on their back and confronted the enemy in the field. Thus, we had an instant powderkeg situation wherein some of my less-civilized Marines might well deal with these outsiders. Worse, it was well known that the greatest propensity for use of illicit drugs was among the educated communicators who often had a bit too much time on their hands. None of us wanted the outsiders, but we had to take them. Making them part of Third Force was not going to be easy.

This bunch turned out to be a remarkably capable detachment, and in just a few hours they had established a real-time teletype linkup between Third Force headquarters in Phu Bai and the command center in Da Nang. Messages initiated from my COC now had the obvious potential for direct and immediate transmission to Da Nang, coupled with immediate, selective retransmission across the thousands of miles to Washington. Just who in the capital city of our nation would need to read an insertion report or an extraction report from Third Force was not made clear. Our impression was that nobody in Da Nang would, or could, answer that question either. While the intelligence staff folks at III MAF implied that this need for real-time communications was a response to a specific White House directive, they would never look me in the eye and say that it was true. It would not have surprised me if the other end of the network terminated in President Nixon's bathroom!

With this new capability to make reports to our superiors came some detailed requirements setting forth what was to be reported and actions that were to follow reports. At first I was directed to send "flash precedence" messages when a force team entered or departed from the DMZ area north of the red line. That sounded simple enough, and we began to do so immediately. Clearly, that was a mistake. Not one thing is truly simple when you are being oversupervised from high places. I should have remembered that.

Next we were informed that our provision of a U.S. presence in the DMZ meant that at least four units must be deployed at all times. That too sounded simple; it did, however, require shifting resources from surveillance of other possible routes of entry used by the NVA to channel forces south into the war. The DMZ was not a tiny area. It contained an enormously complex canyon and trail network, any portion of which was worthy of our continued examination. So far, so good. The level of intrusive interference remained acceptable and had minimal impact on our operations. Sadly, this was only temporary. Those who oversupervise from afar never allow things to remain at the acceptable level; it is a tenet of their existence that they must be disruptive.

During one confusing afternoon in January 1970, a team from Third Force operating in the central DMZ, north of the red line, came into contact with an estimated company of NVA. That meant that on the ground there were about sixty to one hundred NVA soldiers, versus six Third Force Marines: a ten-to-one advantage for the other side. During a brief firefight, the team withdrew to the south, and I directed that they be extracted, their having answered the question, "Are there any NVA units in this part of the DMZ?"

The company intelligence officer debriefed the team, and we made our normal reports of contact, including the special report over the teletype. By dark we had received a rocket from an angry deputy assistant chief of staff for intelligence in the III MAF headquarters. "By what authority did you permit that team to be extracted? Do you know that extracting that team left us with only three elements for presence in the DMZ? Why did you fail to immediately insert another team? You will be relieved for this failure!" Such behavior was not unusual, for this officer had insulted me in this manner on several other occasions, even suggesting that he might physically deal with what he intemperately called my insubordination. It was demeaning, making me coldly angry.

Despite the loud noises, I was less than fully terrorized because this colonel had not had the pleasure of placing me in command, nor was he anywhere in my chain of command. In fact, he had *never* even seen me. I felt confident that he would have a difficult time getting me fired.

An angry calm came over me. This was obviously only the beginning of intrusive oversupervision. Things like this had the potential of getting a great deal worse for us all before the unlikely chance that they would get any better. We were all deeply concerned about this and felt that additional pressure from afar would only complicate our already demanding lives. I called Colonel Polakoff to alert him to the threat I had received and to our opinions on outside interference with operational decisions. I also reported that in the morning, in the normal course of operations, I would send another team into the DMZ.

Third Force Reconnaissance Company did just that. We placed a team into a portion of the DMZ where four major trail networks converged. Doing this took some time, and I returned from mission command at midday to find that new tasks had been levied on us. Beginning immediately, Third Force was to keep a team on standby for immediate insertion into the DMZ in those instances when a deployed team was driven out of the assigned patrol area by enemy action.

With this the oversupervision became onerous. With our operational tempo already high, adding a standby element would increase the pressure on all of the other teams without doing a damn thing toward accomplishment of the missions that needed our attention. We were being had, and there was not one sensible thing we could do to improve the situation.

Shortly thereafter, we heard again from people who lived comfortable lives some thirteen time zones away across the face of the globe. A new message arrived telling me how to organize and operate Third Force Reconnaissance Company in combat. The directive noted that a presence in the DMZ now meant squad-size elements, and therefore, we must cease patrolling with our standard six-man teams and employ eight men on any patrol that might cross into the DMZ. Typical of most of the messages we received from the teletype, it was clear that this order had been written by a civilian who was not comfortable with the military phrasing and acronyms that we all took for granted.

Now the oversupervisors were being intrusive and involving themselves in a way that demonstrated they were not present in the operational theater. We had both operational reasons and reasons based on the laws of physics for the team size that we had chosen. It was a physical fact that a force recon team of six combat-loaded Marines was all that an army UH-1H, with its own four-man crew, could safely lift at one time. In fact, in hot, humid weather the older UH-1E helicopters used by the Marine Corps could not match the performance of the Army's hotel-model Huey. We either had to go shorthanded or employ more than one helicopter when we flew with the Marines.

Third Force was now facing a new level of danger, one that was being forced on us from above without a thought for the operational situation on the ground where we were in Vietnam. Compliance with this directive would mean subjecting two helicopters, with their crews, to possible enemy fire for every insertion, increasing the size of all landing zones accordingly, and calling more attention to every insertion. Because of the danger inherent in landing two helicopters for every insertion, compliance would almost totally rule out the use of false-insertion techniques as well. We knew from experience that once inserted into the DMZ, eight-man teams would be less effective. The larger teams would be harder to hide, more difficult to control, and far harder to safely extract if they came under fire.

Besides the operational aspects, use of the eight-man teams would cause us to virtually run out of troops when this manpower drain was added to our other operational commitments. We challenged this directive by return message to III MAF, but within the hour we were informed that the subject was closed.

It quickly became clear that I was looking at a no-win situation. If I restricted our DMZ insertions to zones large enough for two helicopters to land in together, we would lose flexibility and become more predictable to the enemy. If I used sequential landings in the normally tight landing zones, I would more than double the danger to the helicopters and the Marines who were being inserted. The longer we provided a target in and around an insertion site, the greater was the opportunity for the NVA to pinpoint that site and take ground and/or artillery action. The options grew less and less attractive.

While team size was of extreme importance during insertions, it became an even more critical matter during extractions, with their potential to become long, involved bloodbaths. I was pleased to shed the NVA's blood but did not want to add to the danger faced by my Marines and the Marine and Army aviation crews that were supporting us. Statistically, one out of every two missions to the DMZ ended in a firefight and an unplanned extraction under fire from a hastily selected landing zone. Such a situation could prevent us from using the larger helicopter zones. It was also impractical to make two landings at one site to take out part of the team with the first aircraft while the remaining team members fought for their lives and waited for the second helicopter.

Unplanned contact with the enemy was a natural offshoot of our search for information on their movements. The NVA could always be counted on to be moving troops into and out of the DMZ for purposes related to their own long-term goals. The enemy was quick to maneuver against us; they had heavy weapons to oppose our helicopters; and they had the luxury of their own artillery available in most areas of the DMZ. While the U.S. and Vietnamese forces might well live by the agreements about the DMZ, the other side took no notice at all of the rules of engagement that came down to us from above. All the NVA ever did was take advantage of our national naïveté.

It took about as long to reach a decision on the eight-man team directive as it has taken to discuss it here. I really did not feel that a choice existed. This was combat, and I was the commander on the scene who had life-and-death responsibilities to discharge. An uninformed and unthinking individual had directed that we do something stupid. I chose to answer with a cheery "Aye, aye, sir" and ignore the stupid part while telling him just what he wanted to hear. I had learned my lesson well in 1966 from Leon Utter, and in Third Force Recon in 1970 we never wasted a moment agonizing over the necessary deception of those who wanted to meddle with us.

We began the following morning to report full compliance with the directive.

Every reconnaissance team that deployed from Third Force was carefully documented in the Operations Shop. Lieutenant Coffman was a meticulous record keeper, as was Lieutenant Morris, the officer directly responsible for careful personnel accountability. The two of them collaborated at all times to ensure that we never had to face the possibility of anyone being left behind when things became obscured by the confusion of combat. To fill the extra billets on the new eight-man teams, we created some phantom Marines who had serial numbers, as well as names ranging from Smith, Aguinaldo, Jones, and Mueller to Swenson, Czbrowski, and Plockington.

Then, our reports of DMZ deployments all had eight identifying kill numbers (the first letter of the last name and the last four digits of his serial number) that related to six real Marines and two of the phantoms. We told those oversupervision experts just what they wanted to hear, without adding a jot of additional danger for the men of Third Force Recon and the helicopter crews who served them.

During February and March 1970 we often received additional directives on tactics, equipment, organization, and duration of patrol efforts. These flawed inputs from afar were given due consideration and all the operational weight that they deserved. None! Acceptance of the DMZ surveillance mission by Third Force Reconnaissance Company did not mean that we should stop applying common sense and professional judgment—based on experience—to the problems and dangers we faced. We were doing our best to locate the enemy wherever he might be found and to pass our findings on NVA activities in the DMZ to whoever needed it. We were absolutely unwilling to do stupid things that would get Marines and soldiers killed just to please some oversupervisor.

Third Force had to take care of its own. Nobody else could do that for us, nor were there any folks who clearly had that in mind. Our deceptive practices were those we deemed absolutely essential on the basis of what we knew and what we saw during daily combat operations. We were convinced at the time, and I remain convinced, that we were better qualified to direct the operations in the DMZ by Third Force Reconnaissance Company than anyone residing in Washington, D.C. We did not, in any way, duck our responsibility as we made sure that all of the missions assigned to us were accomplished. And we sought to do so with a minimum cost in blood and treasure.

16

MISSIONS IMPOSSIBLE

Outsiders—who really did not have the foggiest idea what we could or could not do for them—viewed Third Force from many differing perspectives. Some seemed to think that we could slither into Hanoi to whisk General Giap away to his just reward. Others had more modest needs that could not be fulfilled by their own assets, so they turned to us. Still others, like the army officers on the XXIV Corps staff, considered us useless and suggested that we be made command-post guards. When the situation called for it, though, we got missions from all of them whether they liked us, merely approved of us, or actively hated us.

Nobody seemed immune to finding some difficulty that could be solved if they could get a few of those recon guys to do the dirty work. Requests for our services came to us directly from those organizations with whom we worked closely; distant elements brought their pleas to Colonel Polakoff, who usually turned them away with a quiet admonition that Third Force was busy doing things that had a higher priority. On occasion the request would have merit, and he would call me on the electronically encrypted circuit and ask if we could find time to accomplish one thing or another.

The missions ranged from the most mundane to a few rather exotic activities that evolved because of our frequent and close coordination with several of the truly clandestine units who crossed borders on a daily basis. Some missions were easy, some were arduous, some resulted in peals of laughter at the incongruities of life, and, of course, certain missions ended in tragedy and deep personal anguish.

From the engineers would come a request for a couple of divers for a couple of hours. Captain Hisler or the Igor would point out that we did not operate in couples, we operated in teams. We also insisted that we have control of site security, communications, and personnel. This often surprised the requesters, many of whom regarded us as arrogant and unfriendly in the extreme.

When we did support the engineers, it was usually to clear explosives from a bridge or culvert or to search for such explosives. The NVA was never afraid to place underwater mines on bridge pilings deep in areas that were nominally controlled by U.S. or South Vietnamese forces. While they did this frequently, it was our good fortune that the NVA did not have access to sophisticated underwater explosive devices for this work. They depended more on Rube Goldberg–type munitions fashioned from unexploded U.S. projectiles than on items that had been specially designed for underwater use. These cobbled-together devices were sometimes the most dangerous because of their shabby construction, but they were easier to locate.

Once or twice we deployed Third Force teams to assist the engineers in placing explosives on riverbeds or the ocean floor, where they would be detonated either for bridge/pier construction or for channel clearance.

As you would expect, we received a plethora of special missions from the numerous intelligence-gathering elements operating in the Republic of Vietnam. There were calls for prisoner snatch missions and POW recovery missions; and some missions sent us out to confirm or refute any number of assertions made by aerial photo interpreters, staff analysts, or others with strongly held opinions. One of these actually began with a phone call from General Abrams to General Nickerson. A question was asked concerning some shell casings noted by the photo interpreters who were examining possible NVA firing sites in the Ashau Valley. General Nickerson called and requested that we find out immediately whether the casings were old U.S. discards or new NVA cases that might indicate reoccupation of the valley by NVA artillery. We found out, and in short order General Abrams was informed that these were old U.S. 175mm cases; there were no new NVA firing positions in the Ashau Valley.

For the most part, we were sent out to validate or disprove

assessments based on analyses of raw data fed to the intelligence community by widely disparate sources. For example, an aerial observer might report an underwater bridge that would permit the users of a particular trail or road to cross a stream. We would be asked to go look at the bridge, to determine if it was wide and/or strong enough to allow wheeled vehicles to cross, and to destroy it if possible. Those who made these requests seldom considered that the NVA might well be bivouacked nearby in the jungle.

The aviation elements—Marine, Army, and Navy—asked us to perform aircrew recovery missions: that is, we were to determine the fate of the airmen lost when aircraft were shot down. It was U.S. policy that every effort would be made to bring home the men or their remains. This was, of course, a policy that everyone in Third Force supported without reservation, as we had an identical policy concerning recovery of any of our men lost in the jungle: we would not abandon them, no matter whether they were alive or dead.

Recovery missions could take us almost anywhere. We were occasionally asked to violate the artificial boundaries of the war (and we did so without the slightest qualm) by going across the border into Laos, penetrating deep into the DMZ, or beyond, if necessary. We were asked to search in the jungles we knew and in those with which we were not familiar. Because of the nature of the war, and the desire of every airman to get across the beach (or "feet wet," as it was called), we were often involved in underwater searches for crashed aircraft.

All of these searches were necessary because of the rather high survival rate among those who were downed by enemy fire. When aircraft were lost to ground fire or, in the case of those operating across the DMZ, to missile fire, it was not unusual for the pilots to survive. Jet pilots would eject from their stricken aircraft; rotary-wing aviators often were able to autorotate their machines down to a survivable impact with good old terra firma. Others were not so lucky.

All of the various reconnaissance elements in the Vietnam War took part in these aircrew recovery searches at one time or another. Occasionally, we would find the aircrewmen alive and overjoyed to see our camouflaged faces. Cold beers were passed all around after that kind of mission! On less successful missions we would find only the shattered or charred remains of our flying comrades. No one who ever extracted a dead airman from the wreckage of his aircraft will ever forget having taken part in that mission—ever. Some, who had never been on such a mission, said it should be easy, because we did not know these men on a personal basis. Absolute and utter nonsense!

Oddly, one such recovery mission gave us one of the biggest belly laughs that all of us who took part could ever remember experiencing in the war. Late one morning we received a particularly sad call from the operations officer of the 101st Airborne Division. A soldier had been lost, and the Army requested that we come and help them locate him or recover his body. Obviously, we quickly agreed to do whatever we could to help them; after all, the 101st was breaking its back to support us in every way.

Since the soldier had been lost in a river, we organized a two-team package, with an extra pair of radiomen along for the ride. In fact, the two radiomen who asked me for permission to come along were from the attached radio teletype element.

For some reason, I felt that it might be good for these outsiders who lived with us to see some real work in the field. They were permitted to tag along for the purpose of manning the two tactical radios that would keep us in contact with the COC. Because I was going along myself, I felt that I could provide these two neophytes with some valuable insight into who and what we Third Force Marines really were.

Shortly after we had gathered all the necessary gear for the mission, two U.S. Army UH-1H helicopters arrived with two supporting Cobras. The captain leading the flight briefed us on the mission. A transportation element of the 101st had been landing their aircraft on a sandbar at a large bend in a river to the north of Phu Bai in order to wash them. On this particular day, while scrubbing a helicopter with rags and brushes, one of the crewmen stepped back to look at his handiwork and fell backwards when the sand shifted beneath his feet. He slipped off the bar into deep water—roughly ten feet—where the river was busily cutting away the sandbar. The soldier, who had been wearing his flak jacket, instantly disappeared from view and was not seen again by his flight crew.

When we arrived it had been nearly three hours since the soldier had drowned. It was our job to see where he had become entangled under the water and bring his body out for return to his family in the United States. If we could find him.

We were assured by the Army captain who had fetched us from our COC that the security situation was one of zero risk, thus raising my suspicions immediately. In my experience, anyone who felt that way about any area in the Republic of Vietnam was destined to fall suddenly and fatally on his own sword. After I told him just that, we went forward with our mission. He flew us to the site and landed us on the sandbar, after which he lifted off with his two UH-1H helicopters to overfly the river search mission while controlling the Cobras who were milling about overhead.

I selected one team to dig in on the sandbar, for security, while the other team, including myself as an add-on diver, was designated to conduct the search for the soldier's body. The two extra radiomen were to stay with the security element and to remain widely separated in case of an attack by indirect fire weapons such as mortars, rockets, or artillery. That way, at least one radio would likely survive to keep us in contact with our COC if such an event took place. When we were ready to begin the mission, we had eight Marines scratching shallow fighting holes in the sandbar and seven more Marines with SCUBA tanks and all the requisite underwater gear looking for the lost soldier.

Those of us performing the search were roped together at an interval that permitted each of us to touch the fingertips of the Marine on either side. This would ensure that we physically touched every nook and cranny on the river bottom. On the first pass we anchored the search on the south bank, where the current most probably would have carried the body. Off we went in the murky water, rubbing our hands along every crevice and feeling each submerged snag for the telltale feel of a sodden flight suit or dead flesh.

It was slow work. Visibility was virtually nil, and the initial search produced no body, nor did we find any of the normal items of equipment that the missing man might have been carrying on his person.

When we had traversed as far down the river as I felt was logical for a body search, we surfaced and signaled to the helicopter overhead. The crew dropped a previously installed length of climbing line, and we linked to it in order to be towed back upstream. Arrival at the sandbar was uneventful. Then off we went again to cover another portion of the river's deeper channel. During the next two hours we repeated this arduous process three times, all without finding a trace of the missing man. We were all growing dangerously tired, and everyone was deep into his second set of diving tanks.

With the air supply available for continued bottom search work dwindling toward zero, it was time to call it quits. Despite our 100 percent effort to recover the body, it appeared that the river had won. As we began the fourth and last pass downstream—still tied securely together—I noted that the Cobras were no longer visible, thought about aborting, but did not do so because of the hour and the false sense of security that near exhaustion brings.

The fourth pass down the river was also uneventful, and again the helicopter dropped the line and we began the towing process to traverse the fifteen hundred or two thousand meters back to the sandbar. My SCUBA tanks were on reserve about that time, and I suppose everyone else was breathing from the bottom of the air supply that the twin-72 tanks provided.

When I found myself in waist-deep water, I began to stand up. At that precise moment the NVA opened fire on the sandbar from the north bank of the river. Down we all went; back in went the mouthpieces for survival. The little air that I had left seemed far preferable to poking my head above water to get it shot off by some irate NVA soldier. While under the water we could hear the firing, but we could not tell how the fight was going.

Shortly thereafter, it became obvious that when the small amount of air left in my tanks was exhausted, I would have to leave the water, find my way to my web gear and rifle, and get into the fight. At this time, the humor of the situation almost destroyed me. Here I was, sucking on empty tanks, dressed only in a swimsuit, preparing to stick my nose into a firefight. I laughed out loud at my stupid situation, but laughing is not something one should do underwater. The entry of water into my mask, my nose, and my breathing passages resulted in a no-turning-back decision to move. Having already untied myself from the other Marines, I was ready to make the leap from underwater creature to land mammal.

The actual movement ashore was more of a floundering as I divested myself of my tanks and crashed out of the water—

coughing, spluttering, and laughing like a complete fool. Up I lunged onto the sandbar. After taking five or six rapid strides from the water, I jumped into a depression where I landed on top of one of the most frightened Marines I have ever encountered. It was one of the straphanger radiomen who just knew, when my wet and loudly profane body piled down on him, that he had been killed by an NVA soldier who had dropped out of the sky. He went pasty faced and nearly fainted.

The whole thing gave me a case of hysterical laughter—very likely a result of oxygen deprivation—which rendered me nearly useless as a contributor to the fight that was going on around me. This was a damn serious turn of events, yet there I lay, half-naked, laughing like a madman. What an example of courage and fortitude I must have been as I snorted and guffawed my way into my fighting gear and got my rifle in hand to do whatever it is that laughing hyenas do in firefights.

After a time that seemed eternal—perhaps it was thirty seconds to a minute—I got my head back into the game at hand. AK-47 fire was coming from the northern bank of the river, but it was not concentrated. Nor did a heavy machine gun seem to be present. My Marines were returning fire with a methodical precision that gave me the assurance that they were not rattled.

Pushing the pale radioman aside, I used the radio in the hole with us to make a switchblade report of enemy contact to the company COC. Within thirty seconds, Coffman was on the net to "Roger" my report and ask what I needed, and when. My first request was for Cobra gunships, my second for the blues. I gave the Igor an abbreviated version of what had just happened, and he responded, "Grog, it serves you right. You ought to wear more clothes if you are going to go outside to play!"

Being fired upon does not always mean you are going to die, even though most untrained outsiders might have been convinced that the end was near. Sometimes the NVA would fire and fire, with all of the rounds passing overhead. Sometimes all we would see was ricochets as the NVA fired a few magazines into the river in front of us. I chivied the radioman to get his rifle working, and he and I began to fire systematically on the bases of the larger trees and shrubs on the riverbank. We did this for two reasons. The first was to improve the morale of the frightened radioman, and the second was to put down aimed fire in areas where the

NVA might be hidden. Firing back went a long way toward improving my morale as well.

Before too long the NVA fire slackened. They were leaving. Two heavily laden Cobras from the Aerial Rocket Artillery arrived and began to beat the northern bank of the river to pieces with antipersonnel rockets from their double racks. We gave a muted cheer as the gunships poured their ordnance upon the jungle where we hoped the NVA soldiers were hiding.

It was time to go back to Phu Bai. Our briefer, who believed that the risk of NVA intervention during the body search was zero, came to get us with his two UH-1H helicopters. He seemed to be fully at ease when it came to landing his helicopter on the sandbar where we had just been receiving fire. Perhaps the whole thing was beyond his understanding, or perhaps he was just another brave man who landed there because we asked him to. Our reloading for return to Phu Bai was quick and the takeoff uneventful. Not one round was fired at the helicopters.

Coming back from an unsuccessful mission is crushingly depressing. Thirteen sad Marines from Third Force, plus two outsiders, all sat with long faces and aching hearts. Success was our creed, and we had gone to the aid of a fellow American and had failed to find him alive or dead. Although it may have been a stupid blunder on his part to fall into the river, we were still heartbroken that one more American would be posted as missing. We held inside the sorrowful knowledge that there would *never* be any final resolution for the family of the lost soldier. Each of us silently feared such a fate, and it weighed heavily on all of the men crouched in the helicopters as they returned to Phu Bai.

Of course, with the trademark resilience of their age, the troops soon set aside, for the moment, the serious aspect of what we had just experienced. Instead of brooding, those who had been there began to tell and retell, with gestures and sound effects, the tale of my sudden appearance in the life of the terrified communications Marine. That young man, who had just passed through his very first rite of passage, felt that after his initial shock at being jumped on by a wild, semi-naked madman with a diving mask on his face, he had conducted himself like a true combat Marine. I agreed with that and made sure that everyone knew that he had performed well under fire. We all laughed and laughed—covering in the normal human manner another painful day in our lives.

Third Force Recon continued to take part in an array of unusual mission assignments. One in particular began rather innocuously. Late one afternoon I returned to the COC in Phu Bai from a two-hour stint over the Ashau Valley. With Chuck James as pilot, we had been transporting team leaders on their overflight of those areas where their teams would begin patrolling the following day. Buck Coffman handed me a canteen cup full of cold, dark, and repulsively stale coffee and asked, "Well, boss, do you feel like becoming a commando?" Thinking that he was joking, I brushed the question aside and began to discuss the operations planned for the next morning.

Lieutenant Coffman chuckled and persisted, telling me that somewhere in the deepest recesses of the intelligence community a request had been generated for our assistance in a full-blown combat raid against an NVA weapons storage site. Since storage sites are likely to be guarded by rather surly and well-prepared detachments of regular infantry troops, I offered that this was a mission better suited for an infantry battalion, not a reconnaissance company that was accustomed to operating in six-man teams.

I immediately got on the electronically encrypted circuit with Colonel Polakoff, and he gave me the lowdown on the effort that we quickly dubbed Mission Impossible. The entire project revolved around one young NVA second lieutenant who had changed sides. Having opted to leave the communists behind, one of the enemy's small unit leaders—who may have just been tired of living in the jungle and being bombed—appeared ready to provide our side with a worthy target. Our newfound friend wanted to tell us all about a significant arms cache that was used by the NVA to store weapons of all kinds before they were distributed to the Vietcong units.

Officers from the North Vietnamese forces who changed sides were rare, and all of his handlers instantly began to cast about for someone who would accept a helicopter assault into, and destruction of, that weapons cache. Obviously, if the staff-weenies could get someone to do just that, enormous credit would be theirs. With that would come a round of medals for every staff officer who happened to reach out and touch the mission as it was being massaged in the headquarters. Of course, they failed to consider that their scheme could easily result in the deaths of many Marines if the information was part of a preplanned trap.

As the Commissar filled me in, he did not suggest that Third Force take the mission, nor did he counsel refusal. As a true professional, he did me the honor of telling me straight out what he did and did not know. While, as it turned out, he was under great pressure in the SRC to get us to accept Mission Impossible, we were not subjected to any pressure at all.

I did learn that an infantry force would not be sent, as all three of the 1st Marine Division's regiments were already up to their ears in missions, and they were not interested in looking for trouble. I also learned that the Reconnaissance Battalion of the 1st Marine Division had chosen to pass on Mission Impossible, citing the level of their security commitment to patrol actions within the artillery's covering fan. That, of course, was certainly true and was in specific keeping with their assigned mission within the Marine Corps structure.

Our sister unit, First Force Reconnaissance Company, was based in the Da Nang tactical area, which itself was some forty-five miles south of our location. Despite the fact that the target of the mission lay southwest of Da Nang, and it would have been a logical expectation for the mission to fall to an element operating out of Da Nang, First Force was not prepared to accept any role in Mission Impossible.

Time was short, and we were the ones who were now being asked to pull this thing off. The mission was not an intelligence-gathering effort. It would mean a deep deployment raid against a potentially well-defended weapons storage and distribution site, far outside the support range of friendly fires. For those who viewed force reconnaissance as strictly a data-collection element, it would be logical to refuse the mission as an inappropriate use of the unit. Those who professed to believe in the commando theory for force recon companies would jump at the chance. Since my views were not wedded to either camp, it was my job to mull over what was presented and make a logical and realistic decision to accept or reject the mission.

The NVA officer who had defected spun a fine tale. He provided long and detailed information on the movement of supplies and equipment from the north into the Republic of Vietnam. He had come south from Hanoi on a train; he had ridden a truck from

Vinh over the Mu Gia Pass to Tchepone, Laos; and he had walked south and east from there to the Ashau Valley. His was not an unusual tale: in fact, it was a well-known and previously documented one. While the Commissar and I let pass the chance to shout in their faces that we already had that sort of movement information, some of it dating back to about 1962, the intelligence types who debriefed the young NVA officer were all atwitter. In their view it was a simple case of belief in the source of the information, followed by an immediate unquestioning response by some combat unit.

Well, they found that everyone was either busy, uninterested, unwilling, or skeptical. Third Force was busy, and we were famous skeptics, but nobody could nominate us for the uninterested or the unwilling group.

I told Colonel Polakoff that Third Force would consider Mission Impossible if General Nickerson wanted us to do it and if we were given three things. First, we must have a full and complete briefing on the defector's story, not just the highlights. Second, we must have whatever we decided we needed in the way of support without all the normal hassle and arguments that wasted our limited time. Third, the defector and one person from the intelligence community who believed in this man must accompany us on the mission.

Colonel Polakoff gave me his word that he would do his best to make sure that the three conditions were met if General Nickerson approved the mission and gave it a "go." It was also strongly suggested that I send this mission out under the command of someone other than myself. The Commissar was actually teasing me about my having been on patrol in the Ashau one day when General Nickerson called to speak to me directly. The implication was clear that it had better not happen again.

Within hours we had the defector's information and an open account for air support for the mission. Additionally, the defector was to accompany the Third Force Marines, along with an officer from the exploitation branch of the intelligence staff who was fluent in Vietnamese. Obviously, the senior folks in the headquarters staff had enough influence to keep this thing rolling along at an incredibly rapid clip. I felt that within hours we would receive a formal order, over the general's name, to make this thing happen. Planning began.

From the defector's information we learned that the target was an enormous cache of arms and ammunition stowed in a cave that occurred naturally in a limestone formation in a valley about seventy miles southwest of the city of Da Nang. According to the NVA second lieutenant, the cave was always filled to capacity with explosives and rockets as well as massive quantities of small arms weapons and ammunition. He reported that matériel arrived in the early morning hours, man-packed in by the transportation troops that had walked south from Tchepone, through the Laotian valleys and the Ashau Valley.

The issuance of weapons and ammunition to the Vietcong units, and movement of these items out of the stockpile, would take place at night. Daylight activity would be at an absolute minimum to reduce possible aerial observation of their movements. The NVA defector reported that only an understrength platoon of fourteen to twenty NVA infantrymen was based at the cave as security against any attack. The logical time to mount a raid, then, was in the middle of the day, long after the delivery troops had withdrawn to sleep the daylight hours away and long before any distribution troops could be expected to arrive. Midday also was advantageous because of the heat and humidity that would serve to make the defenders lethargic and stupid.

I selected Lieutenant Robertson, the company intelligence officer, to create our raid force. He was to choose seventeen Marines besides himself who would be organized into a strike force for Mission Impossible. He had one fictitious member detailed to the force. That phantom would be replaced by Ancient Scout Six—myself—as raid commander after we were airborne on the way to pre-assault staging at the 7th Marine regimental command post at the An Hoa Combat Base. Joining the mission at the last minute would place me beyond the reach of the telephones over which I might be denied the chance to lead my Marines on the mission.

I chose to go because I deemed it the only honorable course of action. In my personal philosophy I saw it the duty of a unit commander to lead from the front, not from the sandbagged safety of the COC. The men of Third Force had earned the right to see their commander subjected to the same dangers they faced on a daily basis, and they had every right to expect that this treacherous mission would be led by their boss.

Our Mission Impossible raid team was quickly formed. It was a formidable array of talent: a total of nineteen Marines and one NVA on the ground. The company gunnery sergeant would walk point with one of the company's most experienced team leaders as his backup. The NVA defector and his handler would follow next, and I would walk as the number five man, with my radioman in the sixth slot. Every slot back to the number twenty man—tail-end Charlie—was filled by carefully selected, highly experienced, and fiercely combative Marines who were ready for any contingency. We took two corpsmen along both because they were strong fighters and because we might well need their professional services if things worked out in the NVA's favor out in the target area.

Lieutenant Robertson did a superb job of putting the raid force together, and we got down to specific details quickly. There were equipment lists to develop, tactics to be practiced, and immediate action drills to be created and practiced until moves became second nature. We were serious men preparing for a perilous, and possibly fatal, activity. If prior planning and preparation prevents what is known throughout the Marine Corps as "piss-poor performance," we were going to do everything necessary to avoid falling short of full readiness for the job at hand.

Robertson went to Da Nang, ostensibly as the raid commander, to check personally with the SRC and other sources for the latest information that might affect the mission. He returned quickly with the word that the mission was a go, scheduled for the next day. This put us all into a virtual frenzy of checking, rechecking, and then rechecking again every item selected for inclusion on the raid. While normal operations were going on around us, our focus was on the cave and on our plan for destroying every item so laboriously carried there by the NVA. Beneath it all still lay our basic skeptical view that the defector might be lying through his teeth and that when we landed we might run into a rock-hard ambush.

By first light on raid day everyone had his gear ready. The morning hours were given over to tactical planning and rehearsals of every aspect of the mission that we could anticipate. Since this mission would need a long-range helicopter, we would be using the CH-53 instead of the smaller aircraft used by the Army and Marines for reconnaissance support. We even practiced deployment on landing, using a chalked outline of a CH-53 passenger cabin as our start position. We were ready.

The CH-53 arrived precisely on time and eighteen heavily laden Marines and corpsmen filed in quickly and took their seats. We were to pick up the NVA defector and his handler in Da Nang during a brief stop, after which we would proceed to the An Hoa Combat Base. There we would refuel all of the helicopters and conduct the final, face-to-face briefings of all hands that we demanded. Directly addressing everyone's questions before the mission would go a long way toward eliminating as many chances for misunderstandings as possible.

Touchdown in Da Nang was only momentary as the NVA defector and the accompanying Marine lieutenant scrambled aboard the racketing CH-53, taking seats next to me in the rear of the aircraft. Since we were all fully camouflaged and covered from head to toe with all of the vast array of equipment needed for jungle operations, I suppose we scared the Marine lieutenant half to death. His effect on us was far different. He made us laugh so hard that our sides ached. He was pretty, he was cute, and he was neat and tidy in the extreme. This officer had clearly never seen a day's field duty since he was in the three-day war for second lieutenants at The Basic School in Quantico. The young officer was equipped with a web belt, a canteen, and a standard-issue .45-caliber M-1911A1 pistol—nothing else. His field gear was unsuitable for the mission, but we were already on the move, and he would have to make do with what he had.

This boy was a joke, but not a very funny one. His clean-shaven white face gleamed out over a white T-shirt peeking out of the neck of his utility uniform. His sleeves were rolled carefully one turn above the elbow, thereby ensuring that he would obtain the maximum number of cuts and abrasions on his forearms—all of which would fester and become infected in a matter of hours. All in all, this officer, upon whom our lives might depend before the day had passed into history, needed some guidance. I began to jot down notes for his edification.

As the CH-53 completed its climb out from Da Nang and settled on course for An Hoa, I finished scribbling in my notebook and, because of the overwhelming noise level, hand signaled my radioman to join me from across the cabin. Lurch, as he was known because of his enormous height and mildly cadaverous features, was normally the noncommissioned officer in charge of the company SCUBA equipment—when he wasn't plying his trade as a radio operator in the field. On my hand signal Lurch crossed the aircraft cabin and knelt down to see what I wanted. He had to lean well down to hear me, while pointing at the shiny Marine lieutenant, shout in his ear, "On my signal, paint him up!"

Our new arrival appeared to be nearly catatonic with terror as he gazed fixedly across the cabin at the large, ugly assembly of force recon Marines sitting hunched in the undersized nylon seats, all of whom were staring at him in a way that did *not* appear friendly. I tore my notes from the notebook and handed them to him. He momentarily ignored the papers in his hand, but Lurch reached out a huge paw and slapped his leg, pointing at the slips of paper and indicating that he was to read them right then.

The note was short and to the point, telling the lieutenant who I was and that he would now became "tactical" with the help of Lurch, who would paint his face and show him how to hide his white T-shirt. It also noted that he had best be sure about the NVA defector, as that worthy individual would walk near the point with his personal Marine lieutenant immediately behind him—followed by myself with a horde of other Marines who might just shoot both of them if we were being led into an ambush. He seemed to understand fully. His hands shook while Lurch carefully applied face paint and rolled down the lieutenant's sleeves, buttoning them tightly at the wrist.

The man was clearly out of his element and seemed dazed as we roared south toward the An Hoa Combat Base. While I was deeply concerned that our interpreter might not be functional, the NVA defector was as stoic as a statue, keeping his eyes wide open and his mouth firmly shut.

After a quick flight (the CH-53 helicopter was much faster than the aircraft we were accustomed to using), we arrived at the An Hoa Combat Base, where we found the Cobras ready and waiting for things to get under way. Once the CH-53 had landed and shut down its two engines, we enjoyed the moment of relative quiet as we filed off the aircraft to stand well clear during fueling. Lurch quickly unfolded an antenna, and he immediately established a communications link with the SRC back in Da Nang. I revealed my presence as raid commander to the Commissar, who did not seem surprised to hear my voice instead of Robertson's rasping out of the electronic encryption device.

Polakoff told me that the mission was on a momentary hold due to weather. The aerial observer who was scheduled to control the fixed-wing attacks that would precede our landing reported 80 percent cloud cover over the target area. That was surely bad news, as weather tended to worsen in the late afternoon. Even worse, the colonel told me that heavy weather was moving in from the southwest, with both wind and rain predicted. Our formal briefing in the morning had been for clear weather over the target, with little chance of interference from storm fronts for three to four days. I was astounded to hear of this new development and was nearly out of line in my anger when I asked him, "Where the hell was all this weather when we got our briefing data from meteorology this morning?"

He had no answer, and I felt stupid for being snotty with him out of frustration. After all, the Commissar did not issue weather forecasts. I made a mental note to apologize later—on the supposition that I would live that long.

Since we were on hold for the moment, we had time for a detailed briefing with all of the helicopter pilots, some immediate action drills that included the NVA defector and his handler, and some tactical formation practice. We waited, sweating out an almost four-hour delay, with the tension so high that it could be heard in the timbre of everyone's voice. My Marines were impatient. They bitched and grumbled. We sat.

Far to the southwest an aviator grew impatient too. He called in the air strikes that were supposed to be followed by our Mission Impossible team bent on killing the NVA platoon guarding the weapons storage site. At the precise moment, relative to the overall plan, when we were supposed to be on the ground blowing up the NVA's cache of rockets and other weaponry, the jets dropped their ordnance in the rough vicinity of the target cave and went home. The aerial observer announced that his evaluation of the strike was "100 over 100" (a rating that translated to 100 percent coverage of the target and 100 percent destruction of that target).

Why the aerial observer was not subject to the same order to wait that we obeyed, and why he called the air strikes without the assault element being present, was never explained to us by anyone from either the air wing or III MAF headquarters. As far as I know, he acted unilaterally, and his actions did not result in a reprimand of any kind.

No matter what strike evaluation he announced, it was a bald-faced lie. He had already stated on the radio that he had no visual confirmation from the air of the cave entrance and had instructed the jets to attack an area in the valley where the cave was reportedly located. When the jets pulled off after their last napalm drop, the aerial observer announced that the weather had closed in, and he too departed for home. We now had no role to play and no reason to stand around, our bodies festooned with the tools of our trade.

I broke the news to my Marines. They were so fully prepared for the hard and dangerous task ahead that it took some time to convince them that we were about to fly back to Phu Bai without doing anything. We all felt somehow cheated out of the opportunity to show our detractors just how damn good we really were at carrying out an assignment on short notice, one that others had found to be too difficult or too dangerous or both.

The CH-53 pilot fired up his turbines, the Cobras lifted off to return to Marble Mountain, and we started our flight back to Phu Bai. Only the interpreter seemed pleased: every sign of fear and tension was gone from his dark green, black, and loam-colored face. The NVA defector never changed expression; his stoic acceptance of the vicissitudes of life seemed appropriate to the situation.

Most of the extra missions that Third Force Reconnaissance Company took on during the time we served in Northern I Corps were dangerous. Some were boring, humdrum affairs that really did not require much in the way of skill or courage. Others were just stupid and wasteful. No mission was as frustrating and demoralizing as Mission Impossible, however. The troops were convinced that we had been lied to—on purpose—from start to finish. Nothing I had to offer could alter that perception.

17

BOMB DAMAGE ASSESSMENT

This chapter title is partially misleading, for I am using it to make a point regarding the psychological stress under which the members of Third Force Recon functioned. Clearly, no scientific studies of the stress levels inherent to long-range reconnaissance patrolling are gathering dust in the national archives—only anecdotal information based on what we saw as we lived it. Some men reacted stoically at the time and appear to have remained unaffected and undamaged as the years have rolled by. Others who were "sore afraid" in the war theater also show no evidence of long-term psychological effects.

A few have reported that over the years they had all the classic symptoms of post-traumatic stress disorder—nightmares, reliving terrifying times in a daydream state, and an inability to resolve their own innermost feelings about their time in combat in the Republic of Vietnam. Worse, the men who suffered evident psychological damage question the reasonableness of their own survival. That is sad to contemplate because they all, each and every one, deserved to survive.

We lived in a bullet war, not one wherein enemy artillery or air bombardment—with their accompanying fragmentation effects—would play any major factor in our lives. Third Force casualties were seldom the horrible maimings that one sees so frequently in the regular infantry. Reconnaissance Marines did not lose limbs to traumatic amputation by mines and booby traps as did line infantrymen. The men who lost their nearest and dearest friends did not see them shredded into hamburger, nor did they pile them into body bags by the handful. Although their experience of the war was thus altered to the good, in a manner that I find difficult to explain, it appeared to me that the troops were made even more vulnerable to anguish by the nature of the war we were fighting.

Third Force did live through several periods of incoming rocket and artillery fire while we lived at both Quang Tri and Phu Bai, suffering a number of men seriously wounded and some considerable damage in the process. But these were limited attacks, and we all knew that despite the rounds impacting in our living area, the NVA was not after us; they wanted the airfield and the headquarters complexes.

The mines that resulted in tragic maiming wounds were planted by NVA troops in locations where they would do the most damage to Americans on the move. They were called, in the jargon of the time, "surprise firing devices." They came in various sizes and shapes, and they evoked great fear in the infantry. Their awful destruction of young, vital men—converting them in an instant to ruined hunks of humanity—would produce wounds that would require months and years of repair before the maimed could ever reach even a tiny portion of their former abilities. While we saw almost none of that sort of massive injury to friends and comrades, we did see it occasionally, and the men of the company were deeply affected by what they saw.

What we did see, all too frequently, was the death or grave wounding of one or more of our comrades by rifle and machine-gun fire. To us it was always akin to a death in the immediate family. We had no psychological support that would match that found in larger formations. We were not shielded from the agony by large numbers of fellow participants, nor were we ever separated from the individual by distance. The losses were personal, heartbreaking, and deeply felt from one end of our small band of brothers to the other.

Each time a man was killed, we not only felt the loss of an honorable friend and comrade, we also had to face the reality of our own situation head-on. In Third Force we had no illusions about catching the million-dollar wound that would take us quickly home to friends and family. We would either survive our war unscathed or find that being hit at all was terminal. Obviously, the thought of being captured was equally frightening to consider, as we knew full well that torture and execution would be the fate of any member of Third Force who fell into the hands of the NVA.

Oddly, it was not the reality of our own chances for survival that seemed to have the greatest effect on the men of Third Force. The effects of our own weaponry on the NVA soldiers appeared to have an even greater psychological impact on them. Often after sitting in on the debriefing of a team that had done a bomb damage assessment, I would sense that they needed to talk it out in greater detail. Lieutenant Coffman and I would gather them into the COC at night and let them try to get the gruesome descriptions out verbally instead of in their nightmares. Fear was not easy for them to articulate, and, in most cases, it was not mentioned as they described what they had just experienced.

In reality, you cannot be prepared for what you will encounter when you go into the field with a team that is doing a bomb damage assessment of a B-52 strike. These bombing missions, known by their code name as Arc Lights, were delivered to specific locations in I Corps because of decisions made far up the chain of command. Ordering Third Force to assess the effects was a logical extension of the duties of our commanding general. He was being supported by massive strikes into his operating area delivered by B-52 bombers based at Anderson Air Force Base on Guam. In response to that support it made sense for those of us in the business of data collection to provide the bombers with something in the way of a report on the results of their effort.

Logic is nice, but it does not reduce the psychological impact that these assessments had on some of the Marines and corpsmen of Third Force Recon. Conducting such an assessment exposed the men to piles of arms, legs, heads, and torsos. Entrails would be dangling from the shattered tree stumps, and the stench of human debris was overpowering. Some described dropping into a crater to take cover from incoming fire, only to lie face-to-face with half a man's head, the eyes blown free of the sockets. Others kept telling and retelling their story about intestines looped around a tree trunk. The tales went on and on, and the impact of these events was clearly extensive. No one visited a successful B-52 strike and returned unaffected. No one.

Using the B-52 bombers effectively in the Vietnam War required a great deal of expense, a massive base of support, complex control measures, and real targets. Sadly, targets were often only phantasmagoric, and the bombs fell thunderingly to earth—to no real purpose. Assessing an unsuccessful strike was just another dangerous walk in the sun, one that might be interrupted at any moment by the NVA's equivalent force that was also there taking a look to see just what had happened. A successful Arc Light, however, was a different matter.

Many people have praised the B-52 efforts, while many have damned them as useless batterings of the earth's crust. I belong to the former group. At Khe Sanh in 1968 I saw just how this weapon of massive destruction could be made to work for us in a war that was often characterized by rifle-versus-rifle engagements taking place at a range of a few feet, deep within the jungle. I view the use of these heavy bombers as both viable as a means of attacking targets and vitally important because of their terror-inducing potential. The mere possibility that one of these strikes might fall across their units should have been enough to cut the restful sleep of the NVA field commanders to an absolute minimum.

The whole situation reminded me of the mythological hammer of Thor, only this time it was the mortals who got the chance to select where that crushing hammer would fall. My only reservation with regard to the Arc Light strikes was the matter of security, which was often either lousy or nonexistent.

Americans are miserable performers when it comes to something called operational security, and because of that, many of the long, arduous B-52 missions flown the three thousand miles from Guam to the skies over I Corps were wasted. Poor security often permitted the enemy to know when and where the Arc Light would fall. NVA forces that had been located and selected for destruction by this potent weapon simply moved out of the beaten zone in time to avoid being pulverized. It was shameful to think of the effort in manpower, the strain on the machines of war, and the bottomless pit of money required to mount even one mission, much less the dozens flown each month. All that effort was often squandered by security failings.

Normally, Third Force would receive a warning order from the SRC for all Arc Light assessments. That warning order, which was generated in Saigon, or perhaps even higher in the cabin, would arrive two days before the time scheduled for the first bomb impact. The warning order contained the scheduled time of aircraft arrival on target, the coordinates of the strike, and the request of an on-ground assessment. We were not the only ones who got warning orders. The damn things went everywhere in a wide-ranging, world-class distribution that gave nearly everyone the word.

For example, in 1968 I happened to be in Frankfurt, West Germany, waiting out a mechanical delay that was holding up my flight east. Since I was traveling under a red passport and toting a blatantly obvious locked official U.S. government leather bag of goodies, I received more than the normal courtesy-type attention from the flight crew. As we waited in the terminal, the commercial captain showed me a sheaf of NOTAMS (notice to airmen) that he was required to read before leaving eastbound. He laughed and said to me, "Going to be a real hot time along the DMZ out in Vietnam on the thirteenth. There are three Arc Lights cleared for that night."

I was amazed by the statement and asked to see the NOTAMS. Sure enough, the times and the giveaway altitude and course data were listed in such a way that any spy with a lick of sense could use them as a starting point to warn his communist masters that NVA units in the DMZ ought to move before the thirteenth arrived.

Warning commercial aviation to steer clear of particular altitudes and courses was just one of the many ways that Arc Lights were compromised. Sometimes spies within the Army of the Republic of Vietnam just passed the word north. By whatever method security failed, the results were the same: the NVA was permitted to leap clear of the descending hammer of Thor.

As if operational security failures weren't bad enough, regular security with regard to Arc Lights was also as porous as a sieve. Targets were proposed by many elements—Third Force included—of the data-collection and analysis organizations of the American and Vietnamese forces. Any suggested targets were, of course, forwarded to the Vietnamese for clearance, despite the knowledge that many Vietnamese military headquarters had information leaks to the other side that rivaled the Johnstown flood for volume. Approved target lists were often posted in the various headquarters that had an interest in the area being struck. All in all, it was similar to our own dilemma in Third Force: namely, trying to be secretive about where something important would be happening, but at the same time, telling everyone when and where it would be taking place.

The security of the Arc Light targeting was also compromised by radio nets over which pre-strike warnings were broadcast in the clear. These warnings, which were not-so-subtle announcements of heavy artillery missions, were made in good faith, with the aim of saving lives on our side by cautioning airmen to avoid being in the wrong place at the wrong time. Sadly, those who directed that they be broadcast never seemed to consider that the NVA monitored most of our frequencies every day.

Despite occasional evidence to the contrary, the NVA was intelligently led by men who remained alive because they studied their enemy. It would take no stroke of genius for them to decode a heavy artillery warning that was followed by a range and a bearing from a particular site such as Dong Ha or "Camp Carroll." By combining the locale wherein the warning was issued and the time when the danger would begin, a listener would have a rather good chance of reaching a valid conclusion as to the target area that was about to be struck. A savvy NVA regular who was able to put two and two together in his mind would move his unit without waiting for any other verification of danger. And move they did.

We in Third Force had some success in submitting what we considered priority targets for Arc Light strikes, but those submissions were often defeated by the later movement of the target unit—just prior to arrival of the B-52 bombers.

Last in security-related problems came our friends the Russians. Year after year a so-called Russian fishing trawler was stationed on the high seas just off the landing strip at Anderson Air Force Base on Guam. Observers on board could easily count the B-52 aircraft as they lifted off for the long mission to Vietnam. With appropriate magnification those same watchmen could verify the external ordnance load hanging from the wing-mounted weapons on the B-52. From that spy ship came a stream of electronic traffic that made it painfully clear that every Arc Light was the subject of at least six hours' notice flashed to the NVA on the ground.

Regardless of those wasted missions (and there were many), successful ones were amazing to witness. We used a seven-man team on bomb damage assessments because the team took no field packs with rations or sleeping gear for an overnight stay. We carried merely a fighting load of ammunition, grenades, and smoke and tear gas. Four men were designated as security, and they would be the fighting part of the team, as opposed to being the assessment portion. Three men were designated as the data collectors, and they carried cameras, notebooks, and plastic bags to bring home anything of particular interest.

On one Arc Light assessment that I remember quite clearly, even twenty-five years later, we dropped out of the sky in a UH-1H just as the dirt was falling into the holes made by the first impacts. Not two kilometers away the remaining sticks of bombs were still hammering the earth as we piled out of the helicopter and took cover in a huge, hot, smelly crater that was roughly forty-five seconds old. The first sensory impact was the amazingly intense sound of the other bombs exploding to the west of us. Even though some distance lay between our crater and the new ones being ripped out of the ground, the noise was stunning. The overlapping explosions made thinking difficult, and we all felt a bit dazed by the intensity of the reverberations.

Once bombs stopped falling and the sound overload had passed, we were absolutely overwhelmed by the stench. Some of the acrid, penetrating smells were given off by the explosives; some were the result of the obliteration of the jungle itself; and still others rose from the various human body parts that were lying in and under the churned earth. The combination of the aromas mixed with our own smells of sweat and fear provided an olfactory overload that returns to my consciousness every time the thought of a B-52 comes to mind.

Nothing on earth prepared the novices for their first moments among the bomb craters.

Visually we were assaulted with sights that need not be set forth here or anywhere in any further detail. Even the recovery of the bodies of pilots and aircrewmen from burned-out air crashes or from days-old underwater crashes does not compare with walking among the victims of an Arc Light. We looked, we estimated how many men might have been there when the bombs fell, and we took the sights and our personal feelings away with us.

The men of Third Force were tough and capable, yet nothing could have prepared them mentally or emotionally for what they would see and smell while checking out the B-52 strikes.

Everyone got his turn at bomb damage assessment missions; it was another of the various missions that were assigned to whichever team was available and reasonably fresh. While this was just another aspect of the pressure under which the men of Third Force labored, it is possible that these missions contributed to the problems of those few men in the company who suffered psychologically after their return home.

18

ALL BUT ONE

Any war that is conducted as haphazardly as was the shabby one we fought in the Republic of Vietnam is bound to become a personnel disaster. Third Force Reconnaissance Company was no exception, and we never had a moment when the manpower needs of the company were met to my satisfaction. At the heart of the problem lay the national policy of our country, at the time, to rotate men into combat as lonely, unattached individuals, not as part of any cohesive military elements.

After initial deployment, none of the combat units ever received replacements as teams, squads, sections, platoons, companies, or battalions. Instead, as slots were emptied by combat losses, sickness, emergency leave, rotation home, or the simple inability of some to function effectively, confused and frightened new men came into the units, one at a time. We had absolutely no spare time to devote to creating a spirit of teamwork and cohesiveness, yet we were forced to divert time and energy from prosecution of the war to incorporating and motivating new arrivals—all the time.

A second reason behind our personnel difficulties was the scarcity of men with the right temperament, skills, and professional knowledge for force reconnaissance work. Not every man can be expected to perform satisfactorily in a unit like Third Force. In a perfect world, Third Force would have been receiving men with regular infantry experience followed by two to three years of entry skill schooling and reconnaissance operational training. We did not. Only the personnel dragons know for sure what really happened to all of the men trained and sent to the Far

East by Second Force Reconnaissance Company. I do know that we saw very few of them, despite our having received in the mail detailed lists of who was being sent from Camp Lejeune to the war in Southeast Asia.

Searching out men who would rise to the challenge we offered was not always bad. In fact, Hisler, Coffman, and I often chuckled that being forced to create our own force reconnaissance Marines gave us the chance to build them without the bad habits and snotty attitudes that others might pass on to them in training. We did have one problem, however; a serious one that had to be dealt with as a matter of policy, pride, and professionalism.

Reconnaissance Marines are, by nature, aggressively self-confident. They frequently have to be to survive. Some members within the reconnaissance community play upon that nature and inculcate an attitude of violent hostility toward anyone who is not a so-called real recon Marine. They label *anyone* who does not wear all the badges and know all the songs useless. In vulgar terms these Marines will sneer at their *real* mission in life—namely, support of the infantry—and say, "If you ain't recon, you ain't shit!"

Obviously, we had to stamp out that kind of mental garbage instantly among the replacement drafts and volunteers who came to us. That complex task fell to Captain Hisler, both because of his fantastic fund of professional knowledge and because he was able to look the big talkers in the eye and point out that he was not badge heavy. Did they dare call him useless?

Hisler's point was made quickly and without restraint among those who demonstrated the slightest hot-dog attitude. A few Marines failed to understand that this was a serious matter. They shipped out, and almost overnight the problem vanished. Now we could work to establish teamwork among the Marines and corpsmen who would learn that they were part of something far larger than themselves. Badges came to mean exactly and precisely what they should mean: the wearer had been fortunate enough to go to a school that specialized in some skill or another.

Making necessary decisions regarding personnel took time and concentration. Combat is always fought according to decisions made with limited information, and it was unfortunate that we had as much fog in the manpower world as we had in the more frequently described fog of war. We got good Marines and a few great ones; we got good officers, adequate officers, and one who was a disaster.

The worst personnel decision I ever made in my life took place one routine afternoon in December 1969 when an officer replacement was dispatched from the personnel office at III MAF headquarters for duty with Third Force. He was a first lieutenant who purportedly had performed without serious difficulty as a member of an infantry unit and who now wanted to be part of the reconnaissance community.

Actually, he was somewhat wished upon us. According to a lieutenant colonel in the personnel business, this particular officer was a protégé of the commanding general, 1st Marine Division, who thought him well suited for the adventure of reconnaissance and wanted Lieutenant M. to broaden his experience through service in Third Force.

During the initial interview, I looked, I listened, and I grew uneasy with this officer who was a bit too polished—almost too good to be true. It was obvious to me on a gut-feeling basis that I did not want him for the company, yet there was nothing specific on which to deny him his opportunity. I just sat there with a deep-seated urge to toss him on the next truck headed back to where he came from. Regrettably, I did not listen to my inner voices. I permitted him to become, for a very short time, a member of the company, for which I am ashamed.

Lieutenant M. looked the part of a Marine officer, being recruiting-poster handsome. He was also bright, providing professional-sounding responses to my questions and offering short examples of his experience-to-date in the war. His manners, likewise, were conspicuously on display when he talked to me. As a result of the meeting, I assigned Lieutenant M. to command one of the platoons.

As soon as I was through with him, Lieutenant M. became the personal property of Buck Coffman, who was to train him in the reconnaissance indoctrination program that we used to get every newly accepted Marine in the company up to speed. Whenever Coffman was not pushing him, Captain Hisler was teaching him all of the internal policies of Third Force, in an attempt to turn him quickly into a productive member of the command.

Neither Hisler nor Coffman took to the man. Both shared initial reservations about the long-term value of Lieutenant M. that they brought to my attention with increasing concern. Part of the problem related to his mannerisms in speech that reflected a certain arrogance and a definite attitude of superiority. I listened to both Lieutenant Coffman and Captain Hisler, evaluated their views, and balanced those views against the dire shortage of officers. My decision to let him stay in the company seemed, at the time, to be the correct one. It definitely was not.

Everyone who has ever served as an enlisted man—and I have—knows and hates the kind of officer who talks down to his juniors. Some officers do it out of simple ignorance; others do it maliciously, based on a misplaced feeling that they are somehow superior, upper-class beings. A small minority of officers do it because they specifically hate those they perceive to be the inferior lower classes serving beneath them in the military hierarchy. For this type of officer, enlisted men are neither respected as men nor honored for their professional contributions. Behind a facade of utterly false concern for their troops, these officers often rise to startling levels in rank.

Shortly after Lieutenant M. had settled in as a platoon leader, I obliquely learned from some of the team leaders that he was considered pretty snotty for an unproven officer. The remarks attributed to him were those of one who actively disliked, as inferiors, those he was obligated by his station in life to lead. Faced with a potentially disruptive situation, I sat down with Lieutenant M. and discussed his leadership style and the substance of what was acceptable to me in junior officers. I suggested that if he was one of those officers who could not respect those who served with him, then he had better plan on leaving for assignment elsewhere.

Being a quick study, Lieutenant M. was able to feign full understanding of my anger and to offer a heartfelt apology for starting out in a manner that displeased me and demeaned anyone in Third Force. His well-crafted words persuaded me to give him what he asked for: an opportunity to demonstrate his capabilities—or lack thereof—before I made the final decision as to whether or not he would be relieved of his duties and sent packing to the III MAF headquarters in Da Nang.

Being both smart and physically fit for the task at hand, Lieutenant M. did not fail Third Force Reconnaissance Company in training. He did not fail the company in matters of adherence to the policies delineated for him by Captain Hisler. He was intellectually capable of complying with those he did support and finessing, for a time, those that he disliked. Where Lieutenant M. did fail utterly, however, was under the pressures of combat.

Manning the radio relay site was dangerous work. Those assigned there could not hide, nor could they move away should a superior enemy force come to destroy them. Regardless, the site was manned day after day, week after week, month after month—in times of quiet and under fire as well. While we might change the radio call sign of the relay from time to time, we knew that the NVA was not taken in by the deception.

In order to reach a final decision with regard to Lieutenant M., I wanted to see how he performed when given a difficult task. I told the operations officer to send him out to the relay site as officer-in-charge when the next replacement cycle took place. Coffman selected a coterie of proven performers to go with Lieutenant M., a group that included Staff Sergeant Williams, who was detailed to back the officer up. Among the experienced junior Marines chosen were several who had already earned our full trust and confidence as dependable fighting men.

The relay party was briefed, inspected, and on the appointed day—January 3, 1970—they were flown west to the eastern edge of the Ashau Valley to relieve the wet and weary marines on that bleak hilltop. Eleven Marines accompanied Lieutenant M. on his first operational combat assignment as a member of Third Force Reconnaissance Company.

Our mountain in the Ashau, many, many long miles from the nearest friendly unit—an Army artillery fire base called Bastogne—was an ugly, eerie spot that could cause the hair to rise on your neck. Zulu Relay was situated on a tiny pinnacle with razor-sharp ridges leading up to it. The mountain was nearly a vertical cliff on the western side and almost as steep on its eastern face. Only two approaches existed along the ridge line, and neither of those would support an assault force more than one-man wide. The Marines, dug into the hillside, could cover those ridge lines with both heavy and light machine-gun fire, Claymore mines, and the concentrated fire of their own weapons.

We all knew that the site could be taken by determined NVA forces. Nevertheless, we planned to make it as difficult as possible for them to make the assault. Each succeeding element sent to the site improved the defenses by adding to the mines implanted on every conceivable avenue of approach. Zulu Relay was going to be a tough nut to crack if the NVA decided to come calling.

It was to this site that I dispatched Lieutenant M., fully expecting him to do his duty. In the normal course of a detail to Zulu, hundreds of messages would be retransmitted, hours would be spent in silent standby on the radio, awaiting team reports from farther afield, and many more hours would be filled with boredom and waiting, waiting, waiting—the normal state of most wars. It was my hope that Lieutenant M. would come to know and respect the men sent to the mountaintop with him. It was also my hope that he would be capable of effective leadership during an attack should the need to defend the relay site arise.

It was Zulu Relay's job to facilitate communications with the teams deployed even deeper into terrain dominated by the NVA. Many of the patrol areas in the Ashau Valley and to the north toward the old Khe Sanh Combat Base and National Route 9 were totally blind to radio signals from our COC at Phu Bai— near National Route 1—on the coast. The teams in the deep areas depended on Zulu Relay for their lives, and every Marine on the mountain knew that quite well.

Two or three days passed. There appeared to be no change operationally with Lieutenant M. on site: the relay communicators continued to do their job. Everything seemed normal. This came to an abrupt end on the fourth night, when the weather turned particularly nasty. That evening the darkness brought heavy rainsqualls, with high winds along the coast hammering the rain against our billeting area, bringing with it periods of near-zero visibility. The same darkness and rain descended on the Marines at Zulu Relay as they crouched in their fighting holes.

When I was in the Third Force COC it was easy for me to spend the evening hours close to the communicators who manned the bank of radios—hour after hour after hour—that connected us to the teams, to the SRC in Da Nang, and to all the other organizations who wanted to talk to us. I lived there. My cot—as was Lieutenant Coffman's—was behind a plywood wall, and the Igor and I could be yanked awake in seconds if we were needed.

On this particular night we both were in the COC listening to the radio traffic and discussing matters with team leaders and other Marines who felt the need to talk over ideas and to seek professional guidance. Ten to twelve men were sitting on the briefing benches and on the deck in front of the operational map when the Marine monitoring the primary tactical net called out, "Switchblade, heavy fire, ground attack, Zulu Relay!" We all felt a chill pass through us. This was the worst possible time for such a thing to happen. The weather was very much in favor of the NVA and might keep us from influencing the action at all.

The COC operator turned in his seat and reported to me that while the radio operator on Zulu Relay had been transmitting, he could hear the familiar sound of a Russian 12.7mm heavy machine gun firing and the crackle of a heavy volume of small arms fire in the background. He also reported that Zulu Relay had now gone silent. That meant trouble with a capital T.

There was much to do, and everything had to be done quickly. Every radioman and every clerk knew what he was required to do next. First, our main tactical radio net was switched to loudspeaker so Coffman and I could hear what was going on without waiting for the operator to pass the word. Simultaneously, the secondary tactical frequency was activated by a standby operator who called out to Zulu Relay to establish communications, if possible, with a different radio operator at the site. On other nets the SRC in Da Nang was alerted to the situation, and the COC of the 101st Airborne Division was sent an initial report, as was the watch officer in the aviation COC of the 2d Squadron of the 17th Air Cavalry.

Flash precedence messages went to the artillery, who might be asked to fire the 175mm guns from fire base Bastogne in support of Zulu Relay. Those guns could just barely reach, with limited accuracy, that portion of the Ashau, but the support might be attempted, and the gunners deserved a warning. Our liaison officer with the Vietnamese was informed that the Third Force relay site was under attack. DASC was notified of the possibility of air support requirements for a U.S. unit in a survival situation. All of this took place without an order from anyone. It was a tribute to the organizational skill and professionalism of Lieutenant Coffman; he could make an operations center run like a Swiss watch.

Internal tension is a relative condition. We had been tense, of course, as we waited for reports from deployed teams that they were still safe and in their night harbor sites. At the word switch-blade, however, the tension shot up and adrenaline began to pump through us all. Every man in the place had his own private thoughts about our men on Zulu Relay.

Suddenly, we got something to build our hopes upon. The operator on the secondary tactical frequency reported traffic: not intelligible traffic, just sounds and occasional words that told him that Zulu Relay was still there. Someone was trying to reach the COC by radio. Those who were in the COC as observers moved back to give us room at the main map station. We heard a steady background drone as the various operators made the situation known to all and sundry.

At the primary radio the transmissions of our inquiries began. "Zulu, Zulu, Zulu, this is Ancient Scout Three. Sitrep, over," said Coffman into the handset. He received no reply. Other than background static, the loudspeakers were silent. The twelve men out there in the dark and rain, so far away, were in mortal danger, and we had no information with which to make decisions.

While Lieutenant Coffman did his job as the operations officer, I got on the radio with Colonel Polakoff in the SRC. He was quick to reassure me that whatever we needed from Da Nang would be forthcoming. I offered my opinion that Zulu would hold out, surmising that they had lost some antennas in the firefight, not that they had been overrun. Polakoff had been to Zulu Relay, and he agreed that the antennas were quite vulnerable and the Marines highly capable of hanging tough.

He also told me that an unusual atmospheric condition had permitted the SRC to overhear a portion of the transmission from Zulu Relay. Earlier in the evening they had been listening to my primary tactical frequency and had been able to read nearly every transmission from the relay to our COC on the coast.

This was amazing, as we were already operating at roughly twice the rated range for the AN/PRC-25 radios. We had to use specially configured antennas and every other communicator's trick to get the transmission ranges we were habitually using. For the AN/PRC-25 radio transmissions to reach Da Nang directly from the relay site seemed impossible. When we first manned Zulu Relay our tests indicated that communications with the coast at Phu Bai were a chancy matter, and we never considered direct links with Da Nang.

It took a curious lance corporal in the SRC to find out that if conditions were right, the SRC could listen in on our network in the Ashau without need of our rehashing reports. This was both good and bad. Any commander prefers to learn what is happening in his unit before some staff person far away gets the word to his superiors. As long as the Commissar was there in the SRC, I had no concern on that score, but others in the III MAF intelligence and operations sections could be expected to be far less supportive, and they were virtually next door to the SRC. Regardless, because of the conditions of the moment, I now knew that our crisis would be monitored on a real-time basis by Colonel Polakoff, plus some others from whom I could expect only scathing criticism of Third Force.

Immediately after talking with the Commissar I used the land line to speak with Colonel Bindrup of the Air Cavalry. As the commanding officer of all of the U.S. Army helicopter assets we had been using, Colonel Bindrup would have the final say on any attempt to evacuate or reinforce Zulu Relay by air. Since no other way existed to get there, short of a ten-day walk in the jungle, keeping Colonel Bindrup aware of the situation seemed the correct action at the time. Had some other colonel answered my call I might well have been tongue-lashed for suggesting a possible airlift at 0200 with thirty-five knots of rain-filled wind slashing across the coastal plains.

Not Colonel Bindrup; he came straight to the point. "A. Lee, I understand. I'll give you Chuck James with four Slicks and two Cobras. That is all the lift you can manage out there in this kind of weather, and I don't have enough pilots who are capable of flying in this crap. You know what is needed. I pass the decision to go or not to you—as of now. My pilots will arrive knowing that you will be the overall commander if you decide to extract or reinforce. I expect that we will lose two or three of the aircraft, but we won't let those men die out there in the Ashau for any lack of balls at this end! The helicopters will take off in ten minutes for staging on your lift pad. Good luck! If you need anything, anything at all, just call me."

I was stunned. Aviators were, in my experience, mostly naysayers, and it was heartening to have such an immediate decision that illustrated the direct and utterly total support of Colonel Bindrup for Third Force Reconnaissance Company. He had just handed me complete command and total authority over six of his aircraft and twenty of his most skilled men. He knew that the risk level was enormous. Only experienced pilots like Major James could fly effectively on instruments. The younger pilots would be forced to hug up close and fly by watching the lead helicopter's anticollision lights as the major threaded his way through the fog and clouds among the peaks surrounding the Ashau.

I could now order a reinforcement, a fighting extraction, the establishment of an alternate relay site (one was always under consideration from the first day that Zulu had been manned), or I could do nothing after weighing the possible cost in men and matériel. As I briefed Coffman and Hisler on the telephone conversation and possible courses of action, the thrum of helicopters in the hover-taxi mode resounded through the COC. Our birds were staged and ready, and shortly thereafter, the sleepy-eyed Army aircrews slipped into the COC to wait out events with the men of Third Force.

As the Army aviators from the Commancheros settled in, the number of onlookers had grown to more than twenty Marines and a couple of corpsmen. They were paying rapt attention to every action—no matter how minute—of those of us at the main map station. Every man who came in made it clear that he wanted to go along if we launched to extract or reinforce Zulu Relay. "Doc" Norton, then a second-class corpsman (now a retired Marine major), and the rest of Team Snaky were up front and, as a team, were the first to volunteer to head west to the Ashau with me.

No matter what war you find yourself involved in, radios can play tricks on you, tricks that do not show up in the manuals. There were frustrating times when we could shout farther than we could transmit. On rare occasions we could listen to a taxicab dispatcher in Jacksonville, Florida, while we sat in a bunker in the Republic of Vietnam. No matter what you anticipate, your radio set may not see fit to accommodate your wishes.

On this particular night our luck held, and the radios all performed outside of their design envelope, giving us range and power beyond any reasonable expectation. Despite the rain and the rushing winds howling in from the South China Sea, we had equipment that was doing its best to please us. What we needed now was someone on Zulu Relay to be able to talk to us. While Lieutenant Coffman continued to call on the primary tactical frequency, the operator on the secondary frequency was showing the initiative that sets great communicators apart from those who merely can talk on radios. He was busy getting information.

We all shared the fear that Zulu might have been overrun by some version of a wild-eyed, screaming Asian horde. But for those of us who had been there, we conjectured that enemy fire or the fierce wind had taken away the tall, long-reaching RC-292 antennas, and the tubular whip antennas that remained just did not provide the transmission range to reach us. In my bones, I knew that Zulu could be taken, but only over an extended period of time.

As the competing theories were being examined, the secondary radio operator began to experiment. He reported that he was hearing static-choked fragments of words and shifts in the background noises that indicated someone was trying to talk on his frequency. He knew that Zulu could hear the COC's transmissions, even if its antennas had been blown away, because they were being beamed out by special directional antennas with a remarkably strong signal aimed directly at the relay site.

As I listened he began to say, "Zulu, Zulu, this is Ancient Scout on two. We think you lost antennas. If you hear me, key twice, over." As quick as a wink, the background noise made two distant alterations and the communicator said, "Sir, I am in comm with Zulu."

While that was a bit of an overstatement, we began the laborious process of authenticating who was sending. He sent, "Zulu, Ancient Scout. Key the last two digits of your own kill number, over." We knew every operator's kill number and we knew, from the simple routine of the previous night, precisely who would likely be on the secondary tactical net trying to call us. The operator who was supposedly receiving our signals was either an NVA soldier or a Marine who should key back to us five times, then one time, to reflect the last digits in his kill number, a 5, and a 1. When five separate and distinct alterations in the background came back to us, followed after a long pause by a single break, we knew that Marines were still holding their position on that dark, miserable mountaintop.

Now it was time to get some real information, information that we could use to make rational decisions. To do that we had to use a system of statements and microphone key responses that was similar to the "one blink for yes, two blinks for no" technique used to communicate with victims of stroke who cannot make their responses known in any other way. It was not easy, but we did learn that we were right: the antennas were down because of a heavy attack by the NVA. We also learned that as far as the communicator knew, there were at least four casualties, condition unknown. While this laborious dialogue continued, I decided to refrain from launching the helicopters, although I did order the formation of a sixteen-man reaction force to accompany me should I choose to fly to the Ashau to extract or reinforce the Zulu Relay.

Much clamor ensued as everyone seemed intent on being chosen to go. I detailed Captain Hisler to sort out who was going, with the admonition that he was not going, nor was Coffman. Marines dove out of the COC to get their gear and reappeared in moments in full fighting rig, ready to go. My gear was always packed and ready, so to leave for the Ashau would have entailed only putting on my harness and shouldering my pack with a radio set already attached. Regardless of my own view as to my readiness, a communicator dashed into my living area and quickly changed the battery on my AN/PRC-25, just to be sure I was using the freshest one available. Final decisions had not been made, but we were locked and cocked.

Suddenly the loudspeaker for the primary tactical frequency came alive with a loud, unintelligible string of unconnected gibberish. It was in English, but seemed to be in no cogent form. When the babbling stopped, Coffman growled in his most menacing fashion, "Zulu, this is Ancient Scout Three, actual. Get hold of yourself. Request immediate situation report, over." As soon as he released the key on his handset, the voice returned. The words made no sense, but the whine of a coward who was puking with terror was unmistakable.

Coffman turned to me and snarled, "That's that fucking pretty-boy Lieutenant M. The no-good bastard!" I agreed with his cogent summation.

Third Force Reconnaissance Company had an officer in the process of falling apart when every man on the relay site—and every deployed team operating beyond the relay—could die as a direct result of his cowardice. I had never before experienced so much pure, uncut fury welling up within me. Keeping himself in check must have cost Lieutenant Coffman great pain too. He looked stricken at the thought that a man who was purported to be a brother officer would disgrace himself so completely, when so many lives were in the balance.

Carefully managing his voice, Coffman tried over and over and over to calm the whining Lieutenant M. During breaks in the babble he suggested deep-breathing efforts; he suggested that Lieutenant M. sit down with his head between his knees; and he constantly asked in the most direct and forceful manner that Lieutenant M. hand the radio handset over to someone else. There was little or no change in the behavior, but at least we knew that Zulu Relay was still there and that whatever else had happened, there had been enough of a lull in the fighting to allow them to replace the downed RC-292 antenna.

Zulu could now talk to us, but the problem was they had an incoherent man in charge, and he had the handset. Over the secondary tactical frequency Coffman said, "Zulu, this is the Three. Get somebody to coldcock that jerk and get him off the radio. Now! Do you copy? Over." From out on the mountaintop so many miles away the lance corporal communicator keyed to us the response for "Yes."

While things had now been set in motion to rectify the situation, it would be some time before it would happen. For survivability, the two communications sites on Zulu Relay for the primary and secondary tactical frequencies had been placed as far apart as the position would allow. To go from one to the other in the dark, during an attack in the middle of a torrential rainstorm, could easily be a fatal move for the communicator who had just been handed that job. All we could do was wait.

They were not waiting in Da Nang. As soon as Zulu got its big antenna back into operation, the SRC could, and did, receive the voice transmissions directly. Whatever atmospheric conditions permitted this in the first place had not changed in the last hour. It was, by then, what is often referred to in the Marine Corps as zero-dark-thirty, or way past the middle of the night. No matter. With Third Force having a major enemy contact at the relay site, the straphangers began to assemble, hovering over the Commissar like so many vultures. He had people from the operations section, the plans section, the intelligence section, and even the personnel section badgering him for information and giving him free advice.

Some officers from the operations section, who had knowledge of how to do it, called me on the unsecure land line. Directly over a line that any NVA regular with two straight pins could tap, they would begin with, "What the hell is going on out in the Ashau? I understand that you have only twelve Marines out there. Do you think that they can hold?"

Now Lieutenant M. began stringing real words together. Words that we could understand, even if we did not want to understand them. He transmitted in the clear, "You have to save me! We can't hold! We're all going to die! You have to do something! You have to save me!" When he used the word me, indicating that he was the most important person present at the Zulu Relay site, he sealed his fate with us forever. His duty was to take care of the Marines placed in his charge, not to sweat his own fate. Again, he ignored Coffman's flint-hard voice and sent for all the world to monitor, "Save me! We can't hold! There are only ten of us. You have to come help me!"

That caused the listeners in Da Nang to get their fingers busy again on the phone sets, and I was told later that I refused some twelve calls from senior officers who had hopes of interjecting their utterly uninformed opinions into my decision-making process. Colonel Polakoff had done his best to keep the overseers off my back, but he had little success with those senior to him in the colonel business.

The mood among the listening men in the COC was initially that of complete shock. Nothing in their experience had prepared them for this, and they held back a bit at first. Then the muttering began. In minutes there was a consensus that Lieutenant M. should be shot. Meanwhile, I was mildly concerned that just such an event was about to take place out in the dark on Zulu Relay. After all, there was ample precedent in Northern I Corps where news of officers and noncommissioned officers being fragged (albeit for vastly different reasons) was unsuccessfully hushed up by those commands where such an event had taken place.

Because I was fully convinced that those who voted "death" were right, I had to force myself to acknowledge that I had a problem. I did not have the luxury of agreeing with their hastily pronounced sentence. My oath of office forced me to try to keep that from happening. I made the relief of Lieutenant M. for cowardice under fire a formal event by officially issuing the appropriate order verbally, followed by putting it into writing for inclusion in the COC log. My orders to Buck Coffman were to keep trying to get the failed officer off the net while I handled some of the calls from Da Nang.

Lieutenant Coffman snarled into the handset, "You are through. You have been relieved by Ancient Scout Six. Get off the net! Put somebody on who can talk. Gimme Chickee Trumbo. Now, you asshole!" After several repetitions of the above message—and variations thereon during the ensuing half hour—things changed out in the Ashau Valley. The whining stopped. The pleas for rescue stopped. Sanity returned. I do not know exactly what happened at the radio, and I never asked directly because it might have been necessary to take some action against various people for assaulting an officer or some other chargeable offense. I do know that suddenly the babbling Lieutenant M. stopped talking to us, and we were treated to a professional Marine's interpretation of the situation.

Cpl. Chickee Trumbo came up on the net and transmitted to the COC, "Igor, this is Chickee. We had some big trouble. None now. The Oscar 2 [Lieutenant M.] is WIA, got some frag in arm. He can't come to the radio just now. NVA hit us with rockets and mortars, about twenty-five bursts on position. Four whiskey [wounded], zero kilo [dead]. Echo six [Staff Sergeant Williams] worst hit, head wound, all others are non-evac. Echo six holding on, can wait for morning lift. Zulu can hold, we are doing fine. Do not worry. Weather impossible for lift, do not send helicopters. Zulu will hold! Over."

Air rushed out of us all as the tension was eased. At last we knew something about what was happening. What we knew was that once again a calm, capable, and decent young Marine had stepped into the breach and performed as a Marine should perform under fire. He was cheered by everyone there, all of us wishing he could hear our shout of relief and encouragement.

The remaining hours of darkness passed with no further attacks on Zulu's position. Reports streamed in from the relay commander—one tired, but capable, corporal. All of the men and machines poised under my control for possible dispatch to the Ashau, and possible death, remained ready to go on five-minute standby, with the aircrews and my Third Force Marines asleep in groups of two and three on, and under, the briefing benches. Those who an hour or two before had faced probable death, snored steadily while the rest of us cranked up another day's operations in addition to preparing for an unplanned exchange of the element dispatched to man Zulu Relay. Somehow we did get all the planning done by first light, but everyone knew that this was not over yet. Tempers were short.

Corporal Trumbo carefully affirmed that he would not shoot the former member of the company, Lieutenant M.—at least not at the moment. In the COC, 1st Lt. Clovis Clyde Coffman, Jr., would not so affirm. In fact, he flatly told me that as the operations officer, it was his duty to shoot the hapless fool. Nothing seemed to affect the resolute Igor, and I was concerned because Coffman knew I was 100 percent in favor of executing the coward, and he used that knowledge against me. There are some moments during the exercise of command that give the commander less-than-positive feedback. This was one of those moments.

I sent Captain Hisler with the lift helicopters that went out to the Ashau at first light, taking advantage of an early morning break in the weather. I would not send Coffman and did not want to leave while he was still angry enough to throw all our careers away over one incompetent. By noon it was all going to be history, one way or the other. I did not want our history to be influenced any further by an officer who was unfit to carry the title Marine. My own fury was equal to or greater than Coffman's, just a bit more under control. To this day, Coffman still holds me accountable for Lieutenant M.'s survival, saying, "A. Lee, if you hadn't got in my way, I would have shot the bastard, and you know it."

When the exchange of personnel on Zulu Relay had been completed by Captain Hisler, Lieutenant M., along with two lightly wounded Marines and eight who were not wounded, was delivered to the Third Force Reconnaissance Company landing pad. Staff Sergeant Williams had been taken directly to the medical pad where he was turned over to the U.S. Army for treatment. I met the returning Marines on the ramp.

Placing myself solidly between Coffman and Lieutenant M., I hugged Chickee Trumbo then turned to Lieutenant M. and announced his relief from all duties in Third Force for cowardice in the face of the enemy. I gave him one hour to get the fragment wounds in his arm treated and to assemble his gear for immediate departure, in disgrace, for Da Nang. I ordered Captain Hisler to disarm Lieutenant M. and to stay with him until he was turned over to the personnel people in III MAF headquarters who had sent this man to us.

Administrative matters can strangle you if you let them get the upper hand. To avoid later hassles over this disgusting event, I went to my living area and drafted an officer's fitness report on Lieutenant M. It was a cold and bitter exposition wherein I tried to carefully lay out the facts behind his relief and my opinions regarding his unsuitableness for further service in the Marine Corps. A derogatory report must be signed by the officer reported on, and I afforded Lieutenant M. a short moment wherein I directed that he sign the report. He was told explicitly, without the slightest reliance on profanity, of my views on his shortcomings as a man and as a Marine.

Lieutenant M. was then dispatched south in the company of Captain Hisler. The captain carried with him the fitness report, planning to turn it in at III MAF for the mandatory review at higher levels. He did just that, and we forced Lieutenant M. from our minds. An Article 32 investigation (a military equivalent of the district attorney's case preparation before indictment) and a general court-martial for cowardice in the face of the enemy could have been requested, but we had no time for that. We had another day's missions to get under way, wounded Marines to patch up, and the need to force that difficult night from our minds as quickly as possible.

I lament the epilogue to this story. Roughly eighteen months after the events briefly described above, Lieutenant M. was selected for the rank of captain in the Marine Corps. I was stationed at headquarters in Washington when I learned about it, and I went ballistic. I furiously, and repeatedly, raised with the president of the selection board and three other general officers the issue of the report of cowardice I had submitted on Lieutenant M. To my absolute horror, I learned that Lieutenant M. had somehow removed the report from the system, thereby erasing forever the only documentation of his conduct under fire. With an otherwise acceptable record, he had been selected for promotion.

In the interest of brevity, suffice it to say that the complaints raised by Captain Hisler, Lieutenant Coffman, and me were eventually sufficient to lead Lieutenant M. to conclude that his failure would not remain under the rug and that his future did not lie with further service in the military. Finally convinced that we meant business, he resigned his commission and departed from the Marine Corps.

Third Force Reconnaissance Company shall not forget Lieutenant M., nor shall we ever forgive him. His self-centeredness proved that he cared nothing at all for the Marines with whom he served, nor was he willing to live up to his oath as an officer. His whine made him anathema to all those other young men who, when tired, scared, hurt, and unsure, tried to the best of their ability to perform honorably while facing the enemy. Lieutenant M. made a mockery of the acts of decent men who performed the impressive feat of mastering their fears for the sake of the other Marines whose lives depended upon them.

Lieutenant M. was the only member of Third Force Reconnaissance Company who was openly a coward. Of the roughly two hundred men who served (some for the entire time and others for shorter periods) in the company during 1969/70, all but one served with honor.

19

THE BOSS IS DOWN

One clear, sunny day in late February 1970 I found myself on the ground in the Ashau Valley at a place known on the map as Tabat. Being on the ground in the Ashau was not a new and completely unnatural experience for me; being there in an unplanned fashion, however, with no coherent fighting plan, was enough to ruin my disposition and render me mildly testy. In fact, I was mad enough to spit tacks! My arrival at that spot had been precipitated by an unbelievable combination of events and stupidity. While it may sound like the normal confusion of combat actions, a cogent thread did wind through all of the events that concluded with the downing at Tabat of one Marine CH-46 helicopter in which I happened to be sitting when it suddenly plunged to the ground.

The CH-46 helicopter was not our favorite choice for mission command, but we used them from time to time when the scheduling gods in the 1st Marine Aircraft Wing sent orders to Marine Medium Helicopter Squadron 262 at Phu Bai to support our mission. Squadron HMM-262 was the last remaining element of a far larger Marine aviation force that had been operating out of the Phu Bai airstrip earlier in the war. It had been commanded by Maj. Dan Mesken for most of its service in our area of operations. Major Mesken was an extraordinarily capable aviator, an energetic and resourceful officer who sought to provide effective and dependable support exactly when, where, and how we needed it.

As the commanding officer of HMM-262, Mesken frequently flew the Third Force insertion and extraction missions himself. He and most of his pilots were cooperative. Whenever possible, we avoided flying with the other pilots—his executive officer, for one—who disliked or disapproved of us because the uncooperative ones could not be counted on. For example, they would suddenly develop radio problems or stability-control problems as a potentially hot landing zone came into view.

While the first event that dumped me on the ground in the Ashau started in some office in Da Nang when HMM-262 was assigned to lift us that morning, the second came from far, far away. This period in the Vietnam War was characterized by withdrawal of units and a steady reduction in operations by the majority of U.S. forces across the entire country. Consequently, many previously invisible officers came out of the woodwork in 1970 to get a combat tour under their belts, for promotional purposes, before the American participation in the war came to an end. Some of those officers, who had not yet served in Vietnam, would have happily stayed where they were, but Headquarters, United States Marine Corps, was carefully cleaning house. Orders were cut, sending many inexperienced and untested officers who had not yet come west to the Republic of Vietnam to get their feet wet.

Out of the blue, one such officer with the rank of lieutenant colonel came to take over HMM-262. Dan Mesken went home, and any hint of friendly cooperation between the helicopter squadron and ourselves came to an end. This guy was not going to take any orders, recommendations, directions, information, opinions, or suggestions from a "damn grunt major." He made it clear that we lesser mortals within the ground component of the Marine Corps were fortunate to take our orders from senior officers like himself.

In my experience around aviators in the rotary-wing community—both Marine and Army—it was not unusual for a newly arrived senior officer to fly as copilot for a number of missions with experienced junior officers who could bring him up to speed in a safe and sane manner. I was told by friends in the fixed-wing community—both attack and fighter types—that it was not odd for a first lieutenant with a large number of successful missions behind him to have as his wingman a lieutenant colonel who had only recently arrived in the combat theater.

To take such a commonsense period in which to become familiar with his unit's operations was not part of this particular officer's plan, though. The day he arrived, the new helicopter boss was all over his people, letting them know that he was in command and that they would henceforth do things based purely on rank, not missions flown. When the 1st Marine Aircraft Wing order came down to the squadron for a day's mission with Third Force, the commanding officer penned in his name as aircraft commander for the mission command CH-46.

Some days, my luck was subject to question.

Things began to turn to garbage at daylight, with the situation getting worse as the day progressed. We had three teams to insert and one to extract. Everyone at Third Force Recon was ready—inspected half to death, fed, watered, weapons test-fired, anxiety levels at full throttle—but nothing happened on schedule. Just after first light the AH-1 Cobras arrived from Marble Mountain, and their crews sauntered into our COC to drink coffee and wait for the lift birds to show up. This should not have been a difficult task for HMM-262, as their aircraft were located on the Phu Bai airstrip less than five hundred meters away.

Nothing happened. Since they did not seem to want to call us, we called them on the wire line. Igor Coffman began swearing in "Gurkhali," Spanish, and English when he was told that they were "working on it." It seems that two aircraft out of the three scheduled for our mission needed some tweaking, and the other CH-46 had been unilaterally committed by the commanding officer to operations south of Da Nang. We waited and waited—both worried and agitated—as the optimum insertion time passed and midday approached.

Finally, the CH-46 twin-rotor sounds announced the move of the aircraft to our landing pad. We were significantly concerned when it was confirmed that we were getting just two helicopters, not three. But we did have two CH-46s parked on our lift pad; it was time to get on with the mission.

Once I had all the proper people assembled in the COC, I made a few short remarks about the mission and turned the briefing over to the operations officer. Lieutenant Coffman did not get five sentences into his briefing before the new lieutenant colonel from the CH-46 squadron interjected that he differed with the plan as presented and that he was the "overall commander," being senior in rank to myself and/or anyone else he could see in the room. If the team operating in the mountains had not been out of rations and ready to come home, I would have canceled the mission at that moment.

Being conciliatory is not my strong suit, but somehow we found our way through the remainder of the briefing without my resorting to insults. Lieutenant Coffman and I worked out, with the lieutenant colonel demanding the right to "decide," an alternative insertion and extraction plan for the two lift helicopters. That plan, which we had to accept despite my violent objections, specified that the mission command aircraft would insert one team and extract the single team that we were picking up near Tabat.

As we filed out in the hot afternoon sun to board the helicopters, I exchanged a look with the aviator first lieutenant—an experienced pilot with whom we had flown on numerous occasions—assigned to fly as the new man's copilot. After giving me a tiny shoulder shrug that indicated his personal frustration and his inability to help, he looked away nervously.

Once we were loaded up, takeoff went without incident. The four aircraft flew westward toward the Ashau in what we ground Marines call a column and the aviators call line astern. I was in the back of the lieutenant colonel's helicopter, attached to the aircraft with a gunner's belt and free to lean out either side. I could look out the crew chief's hatch on the right and through the gunner's window on the left. Regardless of my desires, it was clear to me, from the new commander's attitude, that I was not going to get much, if any, say in anything that was about to happen on this mission. It was an unsettling thought.

Despite being angry, I was determined to make sure that none of my Marines could be left behind through some stupid blunder by someone who was bullying his way through his first day of combat operations. As we passed the Zulu Relay site I transmitted the code words that would get the team on the ground ready to come home. While it was late in the day, I could only hope that they were safe and their location remained undetected by any nearby NVA troops.

Before we could get around to extracting the waiting team, we had to deliver the three teams into their insertion zones. HMM-262's commanding officer had summarily vetoed the use of any deception landings, so we all kept our fingers crossed as the insertions began. Luckily, all three selected zones were in the rounded, grassy hills where almost any competent helicopter pilot should be at ease. Two teams were set in place by the other lift aircraft, after which that helicopter was promptly detached and ordered to head east toward the coast and the relative safety of Phu Bai. Our aircraft settled in on a long, low ridge line, and the team debarked quickly without receiving fire in the landing zone.

Now it was time for the last and most difficult act of the show to begin. Insertions could often be made without interference; extractions were more dicey. Although the teams always did their best to move into their assigned extraction sites without being detected by the NVA, by the end of any given patrol, a team might well be under severe pressure from NVA units placed on their trail by radio direction finding equipment or by Bru tribesmen forced to serve as trackers. Additionally, the success of Third Force operations had caused the NVA to deploy several company-size infantry units to operate in the Ashau Valley in a counterreconnaissance role. Often in 1969/70 we encountered carefully coordinated hunts by the NVA who literally placed a bounty on our heads.

As our helicopters—now only three in number—approached Tabat, I alerted the team on the ground that we were on the way and asked the pilot to vector the Cobras down low for a close look. He gave me a not-to-worry remark and ignored my request. As the old, unused Tabat airstrip came into view, we were descending three abreast, with a Cobra on each side at the same altitude as our CH-46. My immediate protest was ignored, and I was told to get off the intercom. Our approach was long and steady, with no deception of any kind. The Cobras were not sent down into the treetops to wagon wheel over the landing zone in preparation to deliver suppressive fires. In fact, none of the normal procedures were going to be followed. Instead, we were just going to blithely land on an old airstrip, load some passengers, and fly away.

My blood pressure was rising. Landing techniques that may well be ideal on a stateside base could be suicidal in the Ashau Valley. After all, the valley belonged to the NVA; we merely skulked around in it watching where they went and reporting that fact up the command chain. During our approach I could see that the crew chief was as uncomfortable and tense as I was. He and I looked down on the starboard side of the helicopter and watched the jungle come toward us.

On touchdown at the Tabat strip the CH-46 was hover-taxied a short distance from point of first impact, moving into an area close to some tall trees on the east side of the strip. The pilot rotated the aircraft ninety degrees until the rear cargo door faced the jungle, thus preventing the machine gunners on the helicopter from providing covering fire for the boarding team. Until that maneuver, the fates had been good to us. The landing strip contained neither a reception committee nor an NVA machine gun positioned to fire on that exact spot. The Third Force team came quickly up the ramp, and each man dropped by one of the open windows where he made ready to fire his weapon if we were engaged. This was an experienced team, and they were obviously concerned about getting out of there quickly.

We were taken under fire by the NVA at precisely the moment I reported on the intercom that all six Marines were aboard for lift-off. It was our bad luck that the fire came from in front of the aircraft. Had the pilot properly positioned the aircraft, his gunner or crew chief could have immediately returned fire with the hard-hitting .50-caliber machine guns. He had not done so. Only Plexiglas separated him from the spray of bullets.

Had he properly set up his Cobra gunships, they could have suppressed the fire quickly once they spotted the source of the enemy's tracers. He had not done so. The Cobras had only just begun to get down into the trees where they could bring fire to bear.

Had this officer had the balls he kept talking about, he would have flown us out of there, straight ahead in the most expeditious manner. He did not.

Instead, he lifted quickly and began backing the helicopter away from the fire, trying to turn to a new heading before he began his run toward safety. As we lifted and started to move rearward, the rear rotor was quickly thrust into the trees, where it made tremendous whacking sounds. From the NVA we took hits somewhere in the body of the aircraft and somewhere in the radio system; the intercom went dead. The noises were incredible.

Thoughts went through my mind of the horrible period of time in 1966/67 when a design flaw in the Boeing-Vertol CH-46 helicopters caused some of them to simply shake themselves to death, killing all aboard. Meanwhile, our own wounded helicopter began to shudder and shake violently. Luckily—despite his lack of common sense—the pilot was proficient at his trade, and he was somehow able to control the unstable helicopter as he lifted and flew to the south over one short stand of scrub brush before crunching it down in a heap a stone's throw from the site used earlier by the team to wait for their extraction.

We hit hard. Immediately after impact—while the air filled with loud sounds and lots of debris and dust flew everywhere—everyone in the back of the helicopter shared the same thought: Fire! As the engine noise died and the damaged rotor heads stopped, I sent the team out the rear cargo door and departed with them as fast as possible. As I went, I took a moment to note that the Marine flight crewmen were also moving quickly to get out on the ground. All of them appeared unhurt, and they were in the process of unbelting as we dove outside.

Having been fortunate enough to have escaped from the crash without being engulfed in an aircraft fire, we quickly set up to defend against the expected arrival of a ground attack. The team leader was not a happy Marine, but he was up to the challenge. We quickly fanned out to establish a makeshift defensive perimeter to protect the downed aircraft and its crew. As we spread out I could see that both pilots and the enlisted Marines were out of the aircraft and safely clear should there be an explosion or fire. I immediately ordered the flying Marines to get down and get to the center of our defensive perimeter.

After the noise and confusion of the initial firing and the crash landing, there was an eerie silence.

Survival in a helicopter downing was not as unusual as one would normally think. Many helicopters received nonmortal damage and were plunked down by quick-thinking pilots who lived to fly again another day. Having made extensive daily use of helicopters over the previous months, I had already experienced several such events. The most exciting unplanned landing prior to this one took place when a U.S. Army UH-1H that I was riding from Da Nang to Phu Bai took a 12.7-mm projectile directly through the turbine. Our pilots had tried to autorotate that one to earth and were about 60 percent successful. The UH-1H helicopter had been badly damaged when it hit, but everyone on board lived through the sudden descent and unpleasant contact with the hardpacked sand under a foot or two of water on the beach side of the surf line. While two or three of the passengers were broken up a bit from the impact, all of us counted our blessings at being alive.

That experience came to my mind as I gathered my thoughts and prepared to fight for my life when the NVA arrived. In the UH-1H incident, we had been on an open, uninhabited coastal beach where rescue was only a matter of an hour or two, and any enemy action would probably be by poorly trained local force guerrillas. In the Ashau Valley, where the NVA was king, things were far different. It was clear that being downed meant that we were in critical trouble.

Had the helicopter been strike damaged—that is, wrecked beyond salvage or repair—we would quickly have faded into the jungle and left the NVA to pick over the carcass. But this CH-46 was a candidate for quick repair, either right where it was camped or at Phu Bai, after being lifted out by an Army CH-64 sky crane. Thus, our hands were tied, and we had to stay with the helicopter as long as we could. Defendable terrain did not exist for us in the open where the aircraft sat, but we could fight from a nearby stand of large trees.

When this happened, I reentered the realm of rank-has-its-say. That is, the lieutenant colonel began to give me guff about my assumption of command while he was senior to me. Now that we were on the ground, I told him to shut his face, or something close to that, and to get moving to recover quickly whatever they needed off the helicopter because the defensive perimeter was moving to the tree line. He made some inane remark about me being out of line before turning to issue orders to his enlisted Marine flight crewmen who were sent to the aircraft. To my utter disgust and burning rage, they returned with an enormous coffee thermos and a case of field rations that had been strapped down in the rear of the aircraft.

The fault did not lie in any way with the young Marines. They had followed their orders and brought what their commander asked them to get. He had merely failed to consider the critical necessity that we recover the defensive armament from the CH-46, and they returned *without* the .50-caliber machine guns. Wasting no time negotiating with this man, I told him to ditch the thermos while I sent two of my reconnaissance Marines for the machine guns and all the ammo they could carry out. When the fight started, I planned to fire the guns dry and then destroy them, rather than leave them for the NVA to enjoy.

Amid all this mindless chaos some good fortune still remained in my allotted share. First, I had six top-quality fighting men with me from Third Force, men who would not flinch if things happened to get really bad in the next few moments. Second, the Cobras were right overhead. Both AH-1s were busily hammering away on the area from which the fire had been received. Third, the flight leader of the Cobras had working communications and had passed the word of our downing through aviation channels. Fourth, I had my own radio and the two radios of the team, all of which could reach Zulu Relay with messages for retransmission to the COC at Phu Bai. Last, we were all alive, and so far we had no seriously injured Marines to carry if we were forced by NVA pressure to run for our lives. As we moved into the tree line and began to examine the defensive potential of that location, my spirits rose.

The team had, of course, immediately called Zulu Relay after getting clear of the helicopter. To amplify their report I used my radio to call Zulu as well, telling them that we were down, that we had no casualties, that we needed lift for all hands, and that we would appreciate some company in the form of jet fighters with cluster bombs attached thereto. Lieutenant Coffman sent me an immediate reply: part professional, dealing with the request for airlift and air strikes, and part personal, wherein he chided me about being a "magnet ass" who always drew more than my share of fire.

There we were, midafternoon on a reasonably pleasant day, settled into a tight perimeter in our tree line. We did not possess the initiative; we had to wait for the NVA to decide what they would do next. All the while, we did our best to retain a sense of humor about the absurd set of events that had brought us to this challenging situation. At least I felt a certain amount of irony about our being stranded at Tabat, a place that was probably a major NVA assembly and staging area. Tucking such thoughts away, I assigned the rather shamefaced copilot and the enlisted aviation Marines to positions along the perimeter. The lieutenant colonel was politely told to go where he would not interfere with me when the shooting started.

Our fate was now completely in the hands of others. That

included the NVA on the Ashau Valley floor near us, the Marines on the coast in the Third Force COC, and still others far to the south in Da Nang where the decision makers lived.

While I was being unceremoniously dumped in the Ashau Valley, things in the Third Force Reconnaissance Company COC began to shift gears. I have been told that when the Cobras reported that the CH-46 was down in the zone, Zulu Relay passed that on immediately to Coffman. The Igor stepped outside and rang the big incoming bell that was used to wake up all hands during a rocket or artillery attack. The resounding clatter brought everyone who did not happen to be deployed in the bush to the door of the COC where Coffman announced, "The boss is down! We will go get him, alive or dead. Get your fighting gear and stand by here for the word to go. Move!"

That galvanized everyone. Shouting and cursing Marines were running in every direction as those who had, moments before, been sleeping or reading or doing some other off-cycle activity got ready to go collect my living or dead body. Within minutes every single man who was not needed to run the COC communications or perform some other required action had put on his go-to-war face, strapped on his fighting load, and reported to the COC to volunteer to go the Ashau. To this day, the feelings of honor and pride that I had when I was told about that demonstration of their personal loyalty to me cannot be adequately described to anyone who was not there. My Marines stood ready to come for me, no matter the cost in blood or pain.

In the Ashau, we waited. There was nothing else to do at our end of the gameboard. The Cobras departed with their ordnance depleted. The jets were still on their way from the scramble pad at Da Nang, and the NVA had not yet shown themselves. Since any activity other than waiting would entail moving away from the helicopter, we could not in good conscience do anything that would influence the action. I concentrated on keeping the people in the small perimeter down and silent. Not a hard task for the six Marines of the team we had come to extract; a hard lesson in field craft for the aviation Marines.

Once we were more or less settled in place for the fight we expected to have with the NVA, the lieutenant colonel decided to interject his comments as he listened to the message traffic I was generating for relay by Zulu to the COC and beyond to Colonel

Polakoff in the SRC. Now we were in my element, and I quickly and quietly explained that he could keep his mouth shut and hope that we might come out of this alive, or he could keep yapping and possibly die in the next few minutes. At last—at long last—he evidently took me to be a serious man, and he sat down to check his .38 pistol, his flares, and his survival radio. We shifted the perimeter to take advantage of some larger trees and kept on with our watchful waiting. Now it was just a matter of who would come along first, the NVA or the recovery folks.

From the airfield in Da Nang the 1st Marine Aircraft Wing had launched two heavily laden F-4 aircraft to help cover us and placed two more F-4s on the alert pad. At their end, it was business as usual. Meanwhile, DASC generated a request to the Army for gunship and aerial crane support. To make it all come together in a timely fashion, it would be necessary to use the Army's Cobras because all the Marine AH-1 helicopters had been moved south to Marble Mountain, a long, long, flight from where we were camping out at Tabat in the Ashau. The flying cranes were local, being based at Camp Eagle and operating frequently from the Phu Bai strip. All of this was fairly routine for the aviation elements; helicopters were frequently finding themselves parked in the outlying areas as a result of enemy action or operational difficulties.

As far as the aviation world was concerned, the problem was a CH-46 on the ground; the presence of Third Force Reconnaissance Company Marines was merely incidental to the aircraft recovery effort. This narrow mind-set was the normal state of things as we knew it. We had grown more than fully accustomed to being noted by a few of the more surly aviation Marines as having less worth than their flying machines. One lieutenant colonel from the wing operations section had spat at me during an argument in November 1969, "Major, one lousy recon team is not worth the possible loss of one of our helicopters."

Despite knowing that a few bad apples held that negative attitude, we worked cooperatively with these people every day, and in most cases, operational efforts proceeded with professional dispatch. The aviation community wanted to get their CH-46 back, and they quickly got busy solving that problem. But matters that are routine for one portion of the Marine Corps—in this case, the aviation component—are filled with fuss and feathers when encountered by others—in this case Third Force Reconnaissance Company. Whereas the aviators were accustomed to recovering seriously misplaced aircraft, Third Force Marines were not attuned to the concept of having their commanding officer misplaced in the middle of someone else's jungle.

Back in Phu Bai things were far from routine. The Third Force Marines were involved in a minor internal war over who was going to go to the Ashau and who was not going to get in on the recovery effort. Lieutenant Coffman, who was overworked unmercifully almost as a matter of policy, was short of temper on the best of days, and I understand that he was thoroughly pissed to find that some idiot had dumped his boss in the middle of the NVA's jungle. I am told that some who pressed him too hard got the back of his hand and the rough side of his tongue, in about five languages. Regardless, he quickly selected those who would be going and led them off to the flight line where he intended to acquire a means of transportation from the assets of HMM-262.

In the Ashau where we waited, gauging the rate of movement of the sun toward the western ridges against the anticipated arrival of some help, we were jubilant to see a single CH-46 and two F-4s arrive overhead within minutes of one another. The lift helicopter was joined within fifteen minutes by four Cobras of the Aerial Rocket Artillery, armed with double pods of the 2.75-inch folding fin rockets. As soon as the Cobras set up the protective wagon wheel over us, the CH-46 landed and sixteen Third Force Marines piled out and swiftly reinforced our meager perimeter. With dust from the lifting helicopter filling our eyes, ears, noses, and mouths, the Igor and I hugged and pounded each other on the back. Now if the NVA decided to attack, either to kill us or to destroy the aircraft, we had the combat power necessary to make it an extravagantly expensive adventure.

Within the hour, the Army arrived—in force. First, they requested permission to bring in a reinforced platoon of the 101st, some engineers, and an aircraft recovery team that would work with the sky crane. Once the Army platoon was on the ground and briefed, we were ready to go home. Using the helicopters that had brought the rifle platoon, we lifted off for the second time that day from the Tabat strip and flew back to Phu Bai without event. Our luck had been superior. No wounded and no dead Marines made the trip—only giddily happy Marines who had cheated death again.

My welcome back from the down, presumed dead category was beyond my wildest imaginings. I was hugged, patted, squeezed, pounded, and roared at by so many Marines that my ears rang and my rib cage and shoulders felt like I had just played for sixty minutes as a linebacker at the NFL level. In addition to the Third Force Marines, some of the Army aircrewmen who flew for the Commancheros added their voices to the tumult. I was deeply touched. The men of Third Force were, in one sense, members of my family. As family, they treated my safe return as something of great value to the clan. I felt that I had been singularly blessed to serve with such openly caring men.

As for the lieutenant colonel who commanded HMM-262, I never saw his face again. Shortly after our extremely bad day together, he and his unit departed Phu Bai for the Marble Mountain helicopter base, and he disappeared from my life forever.

20

TRACKING A REGIMENT

One of the largest and most complex operations conducted by Third Force Reconnaissance Company in late February 1970 clearly and comprehensively illustrates the effective and appropriate use of force reconnaissance. In that action-filled ten-day period we sought out, located, and tracked across some fifty miles the movements of a regiment-size unit of the NVA. We received a simple mission-type order, with no frills. This order drew our attention closely to a specific intelligence need enunciated by the commanding general, who wanted to know if this was a viable threat to his forces and where in his operational area that threat might be employed by the NVA. Answering those questions produced what was close to a textbook case of the application of force reconnaissance operational theory as developed by those who had gone before, modified by what I had learned from experience in Northern I Corps.

The mission began with a report known as a URS. The letters stand for usually reliable source. For reasons known only to the highest levels of the intelligence community, this term had been coined years before to stand for a number of collection sources that had to be hidden from those who used the information. In fact, most URS reports were generated by Marines serving in the Radio Battalion: Marines who spoke Vietnamese with great fluency and spent their days and nights listening to the enemy chatter away on his radios. Almost every Marine—corporal or above—who had more than six months of experience knew that a URS was from the Radio Battalion, but we all cheerfully played the game, never admitting that the charade did nothing to conceal the pertinent facts.

The Marine Corps was listening to the NVA, and they knew it. Their operational radio nets were not protected from anyone who chose to tune in and listen. We often referred to the radio frequency 36.00 on the VHF radios as "NVA Common." The NVA units we faced did not possess the sophisticated equipment needed to electronically encode their transmissions; if they did have the Soviet version of our electronic ciphers, they did not put any of the gear to use in our area. Thus, for the Marines of Radio Battalion it became a cat-and-mouse game, with our patient listeners trying to learn of intended actions from NVA communications and their messages being cloaked in various forms of codes, hand ciphers, and/or obscure references. The superiority of American technology was clearly evident.

Despite that technical advantage, however, we still had many radio nets, like the Third Force primary tactical net, which transmitted in the clear because of the great distances involved. Obviously, when errors were made on nets of that type the NVA listeners could glean massive amounts of valuable information. Sometimes the fault lay with Marine radiomen who got excited and let security slip by them in the heat of combat operations. At other times, many of the culprits were officers who were using the radio themselves to speed things up or to get right to the heart of some matter on a personal basis. Almost everyone who ever served in Vietnam did stumble at one time or another while communicating by radio, and it was only commonsensical to realize that the NVA would always be prepared to profit from our errors.

Radio Battalion was a most unusual unit. They lived separate lives behind barbed wire, far from the regular line units. Very few infantry or reconnaissance Marines ever personally knew any of the men who served in that battalion. What we did know was that they were incredibly good at what they did for us. Even fewer Marines knew that the Radio Battalion had had an element deployed in the Ashau Valley area two years before the first conventional Marine units arrived in Da Nang. Then-Major Gray placed a team of listeners on Tiger Mountain in 1963 to collect information on North Vietnamese activities in the north and the movement of men and matériel into the Republic of South Vietnam. Major Gray was basically the creator of the Radio Battalion and had become personally familiar with the Ashau Valley when some of my Third Force Recon Marines were still wearing braces.

When the URS report came to us that day in late February 1970, it indicated that a major unit was moving southward. It did not name the unit, nor did it contain any specific time schedule or route of advance. The whole report was probably based on a solid bit of intuition on the part of one of the listeners, followed by selective analysis of particular nets used by the NVA. No matter how it was done, this report put us on alert for new adventures. We would hardly be alone, however. Air assets, ground assets, and sensor assets were all brought into the game; Third Force was only a small portion of the overall picture. We would play a larger role than those other elements because we had responsibility for the Ashau Valley and the routes leading into and out of it.

With the arrival of the URS from the SRC came General Nickerson's terse order directing Third Force to find the NVA unit and tell him where it was going, in what strength, and with what weaponry. We now had a mission for which we needed a broad-brush operational plan. We needed to tie what we were already committed to do in the Ashau Valley to a patterned search for the new threat. Working through the night, we created one.

Our intelligence officer opened our session with a detailed analysis of the road and trail network that we had to examine in our operational area. Some of the routes were concealed; they did not appear on any U.S. maps because they had been located by Third Force teams on patrol or lifted from captured NVA maps. Concealed routes and the known network of trails, lines of streams, and roads gave the NVA significant flexibility in making their travel plans.

Another option that was available to them, of course, was to stay outside the boundary of the Republic of Vietnam altogether. They need not cross the border at all if they chose to move south within Laos. If they did that, they would very likely be spotted by the trail watchers deployed by Special Operations Group's Command and Control, North (known simply as CCN). Staying in Laos for the southern movement would indicate that their objective lay to the south of the III MAF area, perhaps in II Corps, where they might menace Pleiku or Dalat before turning east toward the coast along National Route 19. If the NVA entered the Ashau, it would mean that they had no plans for II Corps and that they were bound for the coastal enclaves guarded by forces of III MAF.

Lieutenant Robertson had, through careful analysis, come up with seven primary routes eastward toward the coast through the Ashau and four other possible routes that he considered viable if the unit split up into battalion-size or smaller elements. Fragmenting forces was not unusual for the NVA, who could scatter to the winds while you watched, then reassemble to attack some place where one would least appreciate the attention. The operations officer and I were convinced that Robertson was correct in his selection of routes, and we began to formulate a reconnaissance plan to give us a look at traffic on those routes, starting immediately.

The first order of business was to shift already deployed teams to areas where they could examine some of the trails of interest to this mission. We had six teams working in the Ashau, and by shifting assigned zones it would be possible to put four of them in place to begin checking out the suspect trails by the next afternoon. The orders were drafted and sent to the teams via the Zulu Relay. Specific requests were made, assigning the team leaders the task of going to the trail edges and searching for footprints that might indicate the movement of a large force.

Normally, the teams kept well off of the trails, staying, instead, at a distance where observation of enemy movements without unacceptable risk was possible. Being close to a road or trail would always increase the risk of unnecessary and unplanned contact with superior forces. Planned or not, being right next to a trail had significant disadvantages when six men might meet six hundred—with no warning.

Second on our agenda was the expansion of the Third Force commitment to the Ashau and the reduction of reconnaissance efforts that might detract from the high-priority mission. By morning we had completed our planning; both orders and people were flying out to the Ashau Valley. We needed all manner of support, and the wires between Phu Bai and Da Nang were burning up with requests for photography, side-looking radar coverage, and sensor-implantation flights.

These needs, as well as many additional ones, were attuned to assisting Third Force Recon in locating the moving NVA force before our enemy could mass his troops against one of the coastal enclaves. This was a significant worry because, by 1970, it was not unusual for the NVA to use terror tactics against civilian targets, probably because the resulting bloodshed and gore would further weaken the resolve of the local village and hamlet governments. As that resolve withered, it appeared that the war was going further against us, and the constancy of the U.S. Congress likewise shrank.

In support of the government of the Republic of Vietnam, U.S. Army and Marine Corps troops—now found in ever-diminishing numbers in Northern I Corps, including Third Force—were ordered to turn the NVA force from a threat to life and limb into a target for our superior firepower. If Third Force missed finding the moving NVA, they could easily turn up on the outskirts of any of the coastal cities. Nobody wanted that to happen until long after our aircraft, artillery, and ground forces had been given the opportunity to chew the enemy's force to bits.

Third, Third Force Marines had to execute flawlessly their mission of searching for the NVA force. No reconnaissance plan has merit if the enemy can overrun or even detect one of the searching teams, thereby being warned away from the routes that are being placed under observation. Once fully on their guard, with knowledge of our presence close to their intended route of movement, the NVA could quickly alter their plan, either fading back into Laos or slipping away to an alternate route.

We never for a moment felt that the NVA leadership was unaware that Third Force operated in the Ashau Valley. What was important was keeping them from learning that we had committed 90-plus percent of our effort against the movement of this one particular unit as it shifted southward from across the various sacrosanct boundaries that gave the NVA an utterly incomprehensible and unacceptable—to us—sanctuary from harm.

This was a lousy war, fought with lousy rules. I did not want to lose a team in the process of setting up the search, nor did I want to lose contact with the NVA troops if we were lucky enough to find them as they moved. If a team was discovered and overcome, we knew the NVA was both flexible enough and smart enough to understand what was afoot. They would disengage and vanish, only to return to fight another day.

Fourth, we had to do a lot of waiting. Once the teams were

shifted to this work from other locations, and after the new deployments were completed, we waited impatiently for the games to begin. A vast array of information-collecting agencies fed us reports and rumors, but without a sighting, all we had was a pile of papers and some wispy rumors to feed on as we sweated out the hours. Good reconnaissance work takes time. Once the teams are given their missions, it is painfully hard to stay off their backs while they do the job that they have been assigned to accomplish.

After two taxingly long days of worry and fretting, we had what might be the necessary first clues. Two teams working a route structure that entered the Ashau along a road net on the southern flank of Tiger Mountain reported that the two main trails had evidence of heavy foot traffic during the night. The footprints were those of well-shod—mostly booted—military men, not sandal-wearing guerrillas. This meant regular NVA infantrymen.

The teams also reported wheel tracks, a finding that could mean the hard-hitting 12.7mm machine guns, 82mm or 120mm mortars, or all three. Throughout the war the NVA used bicycles to move weaponry: sometimes a single bicycle, sometimes several bicycles lashed together to move howitzer components or other heavy items. If a regiment was moving, it was logical that it would be hauling mortars and large machine guns along.

This first small bit of information gave us great hopes for a successful operation. Things were coming to a boil faster than our most optimistic evaluations had ever indicated. Now we could focus our effort. Again there was a time of chaos as we shifted gears and moved to confirm the presence of this threat moving from Laos into the Ashau.

Lieutenant Robertson continued to perform magnificently. He used the reports of heavily traveled trails to develop an analysis of the possible courses of action open to the NVA commander. With this analysis in hand we could create a plan that would place a Third Force team astride every known route open to the enemy, including those that led toward the coastal cities we hoped to protect from surprise. All afternoon we were in the air with two complete packages of lift helicopters and supporting Cobras—U.S. Army assets—as we extracted and reinserted teams in operational areas where the NVA might happen to appear. To avoid compromise of our activities, we had to use areas that were well to the west and to the south of what we presumed was the daylight hiding place now inhabited by the NVA units that had been moving the previous night.

The technique we used to establish our overall surveillance was not unlike the following-from-in-front method used to shadow someone who is afoot on the streets of a city. There, you lead with four to six men and follow with only one or two. As each intersection is reached, one man peels off down each available road, thereby ensuring that the subject is never given a route of movement that is not solidly in the saddle between two of your men. Those men from your team who find that they have started down unused routes return to the surveillance and move ahead of the subject to repeat the maneuver again and again as the watching continues. In the Ashau Valley, we prepared to do much the same thing by placing teams well ahead of the enemy unit, along all the possible routes of movement that the NVA might choose to use.

The Marines in Third Force Recon's COC were gleeful as we filed report after report outlining our deployment and our suggestions for preparations that should be made by support agencies. Colonel Polakoff and his staff were also kept busy for hours as we relayed a steady stream of ideas to him for tactics that might be valuable while the NVA unit was boxed in by my watchers. We recommended that the Air Force prepare for three to five B-52 Arc Light missions. The precise target locations would be forwarded later, after we had more complete data. We also asked for AC-130 gunship support at night. Since we seldom used USAF tactical air, we confined our comments to a request for use of aircraft from Thailand, as they became available.

We suggested to the Marine air wing that they prepare A-6 aircraft for RABFAC-offset-bombing missions that might be requested by the deployed teams. We asked for the specific commitment of F-4 aircraft for close air support of the teams, and we alerted them to the expected need for AH-1 Cobras support.

For the 101st Airborne Division we provided possible routes to the coast that might be blocked by ground forces and areas along those routes for which artillery interdiction fires should be planned.

All in all, we made a large number of waves in a short space of time. Later, I received a great deal of criticism from some quarters about being pushy, arrogant, and demanding during the course of this mission. Fulfillment of that overall mission, however, was the driving force behind all of our actions. By dark the third day, we were ready for the NVA to come to us.

In the COC we waited and waited, ready to orchestrate a response once the enemy force was reported. The NVA units customarily moved at night, and we expected them to begin doing so by midnight. Nothing happened. The NVA did not appear to be moving on any trail or road that we had under surveillance. The hours passed slowly; we slept little, if at all, and we drank dark coffee and thought dark thoughts. We received no encouragement from the SRC; they had no new information from the usually reliable sources. Not even the interception capabilities of Radio Battalion could confirm or deny the presence of the NVA regiment in the Ashau where Third Force Recon's Marines were searching.

Well before light we were again conducting an analysis of the routes available to the NVA, searching for some error in our previous examination of the options open to the enemy. Captain Hisler, who was an experienced hunter, was certain that we were 100 percent correct in our team positioning; he advocated no change whatsoever. He strongly defended the view that the NVA had seen and heard the air activity of the day before and had gone to ground. He suggested that we merely wait them out while they tried to hide four thousand or so men in a jungle that was being watched every minute of every hour by teams of tired and angry Third Force Marines. After much discussion I accepted Captain Hisler's suggestion and issued the order to hold tight with what we had.

Despite the interference by the deputy G-2 and deputy G-3 from III MAF—who suggested that we restructure our search techniques—we settled in to wait the NVA out. I reported to the SRC, who forwarded my view to General Nickerson, that the NVA regiment was real, it was out there, and we would hold our positions in the hope that the enemy would make an error. The Commissar let me know that the general had no complaint with my assessment of the situation and that he was going to continue to leave the tactical operation of my company to me. All he wanted was information, and he expected Third Force to get it for him.

Late in the day, as the light began to fade, we sensed that the operation was finally going to go our way. Two teams reported hearing voices and the sounds of wood being chopped. The commotion was coming from the area that we suspected the NVA had chosen to hide in after their movement out of Laos into the Ashau. The immediate question was whether the woodchoppers were the ever-present trail security people that the NVA always had scattered throughout the valley, or were they a portion of an NVA regimental bivouac. To find out, we had to risk detection. A team was ordered to maneuver, before dawn, to a vantage point from which it might be possible to obtain a sighting of the woodchoppers. Third Force Marines had done this, on occasion, to check out the trail security elements, but nobody had tried to snuggle up tight with an NVA regiment before.

At around 0200 the enemy began to move again. Three teams could now report hearing the voices of troops on the move. One team actually saw the NVA flashlights and lanterns being used under the jungle canopy. We now had solid confirmation that a large element was moving from the northern end of the valley in a southeasterly direction along one of the main trails that had been cut just below the ridge lines of the hills that made up the western side of the Ashau Valley.

We also knew the thrust of their movement. If the NVA commander continued on his present course, he would come to two good roads that led eastward to the coast. Because the two roads left the Ashau Valley via widely separated breaks in the valley's western wall, coming together as one road some fifteen miles closer to the coast, the NVA commander could use one, the other, or both as he deemed appropriate. We prepared to monitor both main roads and four minor trail nets that he could use to move to the east as well. Additionally, we stationed observers over routes that led to the south and to the west, in case the NVA suddenly shifted their unit movement away from the most plausible course.

Passing this report on to the SRC meant that, eventually, the Army of the Republic of Vietnam would also be informed. We knew that the potential for a leak of our reports to the NVA existed within the Vietnamese Army headquarters, both locally (via tactical radio) and via high-frequency radio to the NVA high command in Hanoi. Stories about communists who had skillfully infiltrated the military of Vietnam were common among the U.S. forces, and we worried that all of our work would go for nothing if the NVA received a warning from some spy. It was obvious that we had to make the information available, but it created a nagging sense of exposure, one that would not go away.

War always surprises. Right in the middle of the next day, a team in the far western edge of the Ashau Valley stumbled onto some extremely valuable intelligence information. When these Third Force Marines crossed a wide trail that passed beneath the triple canopy, far from the prying eyes of the aerial cameras, they noted on that trail clear evidence of the recent transit of many booted, regular fighting men of the North Vietnamese Army. Amid the boot tracks were the thin-wheel tracks of bicycles or carts that accompanied the unit. On receipt of this sudden surprise, we generated and sent out all of the necessary flash precedence messages and reconvened in the COC to review what we were doing.

Using Lieutenant Robertson's road and trail analysis, we could see that it would be a simple matter for this newly discovered NVA unit to join forces with the one we had located on the eastern side of the Ashau Valley. Without a physical sighting we could not begin to surmise just how large a force could be assembled, but this was obviously a significant threat.

We decided to take two actions immediately, both of which rebounded to greatly alter the execution of this mission. I chose to strike immediately after dark with A-6 aircraft, using the RABFAC-offset-bombing beacon, and to call for an Arc Light by B-52s from Guam. Getting the A-6 strikes was easy; the B-52 strike was *not*, but that was a problem for the Commissar to handle.

In addition to bringing fire to bear, I decided to send the Igor with a team to the western Ashau. He would land in and examine an area where the western NVA force might have bivouacked. He was to search for any details that could help us determine the size and composition of that force. It would be a quick and dirty look at the evidence, but the time for stealthy approaches was passing quickly. We needed hard evidence, and it would take a daring and resourceful man to gather it and survive. Coffman was the obvious choice.

Not long after full dark the A-6 aircraft began striking the NVA on the eastern side of the Ashau. The area they targeted was heavily forested and offered a perfect place to hide large numbers of men from aerial observation and/or photographic detection. If our enemy was going to move on the two roads we were expecting him to take toward the coast, he would be somewhere in that portion of the jungle. To give him something to sweat over, we dropped a number of strings of bombs across the forested area and across the junction where the two roads left the Ashau for the coast.

While this was taking place, Colonel Polakoff called and handed me control of a B-52 Arc Light. Six aircraft were airborne for their six-hour flight from Guam. Three of them would be assigned to Third Force if we could define the "box" we wanted hammered. That was not an easy task. We wanted to hit the NVA forces hiding along the eastern edge of the Ashau, but Third Force had teams in all the nearby hills, and the Arc Light is truly an *area* weapon. With a bit of careful map work in the COC we created a target box that covered all of the southern edge of the anticipated NVA bivouac area and the road junction to the immediate south—without jeopardizing any of the deployed teams with 750-pound bombs.

Our Arc Light would arrive at 0400 and make kindling of a lot of jungle. A strong message for the NVA even if it did not happen to land upon them.

Once we knew that an Arc Light would be made available, we shifted the A-6 offset bombing to the control of the westernmost team in the Ashau. The team leader came up with two areas he wanted to strike. As luck would have it, that was the precise moment that the team's UHF radio, the one needed to talk to the A-6 aircraft, failed. Formal procedures for use of the RABFAC require that the pilots be in direct contact with the Marines on the ground. We had a target; now we had to find a way around the problem caused by the busted radio.

If we admitted to failed communications, the aircraft would go home or go bomb some other place that had nothing to do with Third Force. One way or the other they were going to empty their bomb racks. Faced with this radio failure, and the lack of UHF radios on Zulu Relay, we found a creative solution. Since UHF is a line-of-sight radio, we could talk easily from Phu Bai to the aircraft at twenty-six thousand feet over the Ashau. So I did. When the flight leader called and announced that he was inbound, I would pass all the requisite information as to target altitude, beacon altitude, and the essential grid references to him on UHF, and the COC radio operators would alert the team via Zulu Relay. Once agreement had been reached on headings and such, the mission would be run.

The flight leader would announce that he and his wingman were armed and ready on the inbound leg, and that it was time to "ident the beacon." As soon as he said that, I would give him a cheery "Roger" on the radio, then shout to the radio operator on the tactical net, "Ident the beacon." He would call the relay, who would pass the message on to the team on the ground. Forty or more miles to the west the team leader would get the word and press the ident button on the RABFAC. The flight leader would "Roger" the identification of the beacon, and his computer would take over for the bombing run. With his wings free of bombs, the flight leader would then pleasantly announce that he was returning to base.

It was devious, but it worked. Had we not bent the rules a bit, we would not have hit the enemy. We dropped bombs on an area that appeared logical for the western NVA force to be using as a hideout prior to resuming their movement later in the night.

It turned out that we had some success on both sides of the Ashau. Teams in the valley who could see the bombs bursting reported that there were clearly secondary explosions and fires in both of the areas where the A-6 bomb concentrations fell. None of our teams suffered any casualties from the offset bombing, and we seemed to be on the right track to hurt the NVA before they hurt anyone else.

Later, within one or two minutes of the scheduled hour, the Arc Light strike arrived as advertised. The aircraft were somewhere above thirty thousand feet, and no one from either side heard them or saw them in the night sky. Every team was alerted to the arrival, but nothing prepares you for the sight and the sound of an Arc Light. Bombs poured out of the darkness and chopped a swath through the jungle that probably remains as a scar to this day. Whether the Arc Light strike landed on the NVA commander and his staff we shall never know. What we do know is that anyone who was within five miles of that spot was treated to an awesome fright and the realization that the bombs could easily have landed on them. That was a message I was happy to send the NVA—anytime.

At dawn we were ready to insert the Igor and a team to take a look at the area where the A-6 bombs had fallen in the western Ashau. We needed to find out something about this unexpected force that Radio Battalion had no data on; footprints and wheel tracks were not going to be enough. I did not intend to do a similar mission in the area to the east, as we already knew a bit more about the NVA who had moved in there. Also, we logically assumed that the Arc Light might have scattered hundreds of NVA soldiers across miles of the Ashau Valley floor, making reconnaissance penetration unacceptably risky.

Sending the operations officer into the jungle to gather information on an NVA force of unknown size and strength was not a normal reconnaissance mission, and the tension was high for all hands. Coffman expected a fight and, as he confided in me, he expected it to be savage. We kept the banter and teasing to a minimum as everyone was inspected and reinspected in the predawn gloom. I was pleased to learn that Lieutenant Coffman was to fly into the Ashau with Chief Warrant Officer Kiersley of the Commancheros. Kiersley flew with us often and was one of the best pilots available in the 2d Squadron of the 17th Cavalry. On a number of occasions he performed tricks superbly with the UH-1H helicopter, getting it down between and beneath large trees, among other feats of skill. With the lift helicopter were four Cobras and my mission command UH-1H flown by Major James. Before the tension had time to eat any of us up, we were ready for liftoff.

Flying to the Ashau that morning, I began to ponder what we were going to do when it came time to leave Vietnam. Third Force Reconnaissance Company would soon be closed out as part of the withdrawal of U.S. forces from the war. Here we were, daring to pit our tiny force against vastly superior NVA regular army units, units that were rearmed and remanned over and over and over, no matter how many times they were defeated within the Republic of Vietnam. It was hard to remain focused on the task at hand as I considered the daring and the bravery that I saw daily in my Marines, especially when I contrasted their dedication and performance under great stress with what I knew to be the attitude at home in the United States toward men such as these.

As we flew along I could look across great stretches of dark and forbidding jungle from my seat in the sky. The sadness nearly destroyed me. Sitting in that brown helicopter while almost every Marine I cared about was sweating out his survival, I felt the pain that goes with wasting things that are dear to you. The Third Force Marines mattered to me, and I knew clearly that nothing we could do that day, or any other day, would matter in the long run.

I was soon brought back to the reality of the task at hand by our arrival over the western Ashau. As we circled, I was carefully checking my map to determine if we were in the Republic of Vietnam or Laos. No mapmaker had happened that way before our arrival to paint the appropriate colors that would delineate national boundaries, so we just called the area below "Vietnam" and got on with the mission. Our requested fixed-wing support was still en route when the escort Cobras began to circle over the landing zone, and Kiersley dropped his helicopter earthward to deliver the Igor into the jungle.

For insertion, Coffman chose a small, rounded hillock that was just south of the trail that the NVA had reportedly been using. The area had been hit hard by the bombs dropped by the A-6 aircraft, and the team was delivered without incident to one of the craters. After fifteen seconds the UH-1H climbed out of the zone and began a lazy circle well out of our way to the west.

Immediately upon landing, Lieutenant Coffman confirmed that the bombs had been in the right place: parts of the previous residents and parts of their weapons and gear were scattered all over the place. He and the team began searching carefully through the mess for clues as to the unit identification and size, but their search was short-lived. The NVA troops who had not been on the hill when it was blasted from the air reacted violently to the team's presence amid the remains of their comrades.

Just as the search was being expanded to about fifty meters from the top of the high ground, heavy machine-gun fire was received from two directions. The team members returned fire, and Major James directed the Cobras to suppress the enemy weapons. The four AH-1 Cobras, working at treetop height, quickly subdued the initial fire, but the NVA refused to stay quiet for very long. These were disciplined troops who could conduct fire and maneuver: despite the fire from the air, they were going to go after the team and do their best to destroy it.

While the enemy fire continued off and on, the team reassembled in the original bomb crater where it had landed twenty minutes before. Because the Cobras were using a lot of ammunition, Major James called Camp Eagle and requested that more Cobras be scrambled on an emergency basis to assist in extracting the team. Unfortunately, we did not have the luxury of the forty minutes that it would take for those aircraft to reach our position. Because of their numbers and their proximity to the team, the NVA had the initiative, and they began to exploit it to the fullest.

From the ground, Lieutenant Coffman reported troops moving against them from three sides. The fire was still moderate, but more weapons were being used as time passed. So far, there were no Marine casualties. This was not going to last, though, and it was evident that we had a serious problem on our hands.

The severity of the danger was not lost on Kiersley either. He radioed that he wanted to extract the team immediately before things got any worse. Citing the level of fire and the expected arrival of the fixed-wing aircraft within the next ten minutes, Major James told him to remain in orbit where he was. Kiersley protested, pointing out that ten minutes might be too long for survival of the team and that since he had put them on the ground, he was going to go get them, now that they needed help.

With that transmission Kiersley began to set up for his approach to re-land at the bomb crater where the team was fighting for its life. Just as the UH-1H began its descent, the fixed-wing aircraft arrived overhead, and Lieutenant Coffman announced that the NVA regulars had maneuvered to well inside fifty meters from the team's position in the crater. The F-4 aircraft could not easily drop the bombs or napalm they were carrying if the enemy was closer than fifty meters to friendly troops, so it was necessary to hold the fixed-wing aircraft off the target until we either got the team out or forced the NVA farther back.

Major James accepted the inevitable and told Kiersley to press on with his approach. The Cobras came right down on top of the NVA. Major James flew our UH-1H down behind the one flown by Kiersley, admonishing the door gunners to hold fire until they could see individual NVA soldiers to shoot. All of the helicopters were down as low as the trees would permit, exchanging unpleasantries with the NVA while the lift helicopter landed on the crater's edge. Kiersley balanced the aircraft on one skid on the edge of the crater, and each team member crawled under the UH-1H, climbed on the skid, and leapt into the cabin. Once on board, the

Marines lay prone, firing down the hill toward the rapidly approaching NVA troops.

In Major James's aircraft, as in Kiersley's helicopter, the door gunners fired great sweeping bursts of bullets as we and the Cobras swept around the team and the stationary UH-1H. As Lieutenant Coffman—the last man to leave the crater—scrambled into the cabin, enemy soldiers charged the position. They came at the helicopter from the front and from the left side, running hard and firing steadily. On the left side the door gunner and the Marines could fire back, and they did, with telling efficiency.

With Coffman aboard Kiersley lifted his bullet-riddled UH-1H off the ground, pulling up and gently to the right in order to permit everyone on board to fire on the NVA troops as they reached the crater's edge. Flying with the skill of a man far more experienced, Kiersley flashed out of the crater and over the heads of the NVA infantrymen—with the skids in the grass—holding his rate of climb down, opting instead for speed across the ground.

Once it was certain that Kiersley was not going to crash and was now clear of the hill, Major James called the Cobras off their wagon wheel, and we all flew to the east at treetop height while the F-4s came down the slide to bomb and napalm the hillock a few scant seconds after our gaggle of aircraft had cleared out of the way. Coverage of and effect on the target was, in the vernacular of the time, 100 over 100. That hill was turned into an inferno.

On the way back to Phu Bai, Major James continued to have a conversation with Kiersley, calmly chatting with him to keep his mind on his flying and off the danger he had just faced. When we landed at the Third Force pad in Phu Bai, the magnificent young warrant officer had to be lifted from his seat and assisted to the COC. He had been so frightened by the experience of having live NVA troops charging him at twenty-five meters that he had broken out in hives from the back of his neck around to his cheeks, which swelled until his eyes were virtually swollen shut. Kiersley was through flying for that day, and he rode back to Camp Eagle in the cabin of another UH-1H flown by one of his friends. His helicopter was declared unflyable because of battle damage, and it was left on our pad for the repair crews to patch up.

We were greatly cheered upon our return to the COC by the news that two separate aerial observers had spotted evidence of the NVA unit operating in the eastern portion of the Ashau, and they were engaged in systematically pounding the area with antipersonnel cluster bombs and napalm. While we digested that news, the debriefing of Lieutenant Coffman and the team revealed that we had landed them in an area that had been a headquarters bivouac. The A-6 bombs had landed on the NVA, scattering maps and overlays of the Ashau about. Several of those maps had been carefully brought out with the team, who reported that some of the dead appeared to be field-grade officers of the NVA.

Although this was not definitive information, under the circumstances I considered it amazing that they had found the time to collect anything of intelligence value. Fighting with odds of twenty-plus to one does not leave a seven-man unit much time for trash pickup.

Late that night as we dozed in the COC, we had reports from three separate teams of the sound of movement on trails leading toward Laos. The teams to the east of the valley could detect no indications of movement. It appeared that the thrust to the south or to the coast by that particular NVA force was over for the moment. Of course, they could return to safe havens and prepare to do it all over again.

Maybe their commander died in the attempt, perhaps not. If he lived, I always wondered if he knew why he had been subjected to the aerial pounding that he received. Maybe he did, for in the next month the NVA's counterreconnaissance efforts were tripled. The Radio Battalion told us that three battalions of infantry, supported by radio direction finding units and Brunative trackers, had been specifically detailed to close with and destroy any of the Third Force teams that could be located.

Units like Third Force never killed any NVA regiments. Never. But if used properly, we did have the ability to make their lives miserable by tracing them down for those who had the ability to bring real firepower to the table.

As a final note to this narrative, I would like to speak to the memory of Kiersley, who earned two Silver Stars while flying for Third Force Reconnaissance Company. One of those decorations, downgraded from a recommended Distinguished Service Cross, was for the action described in this chapter, the other for an equally brave performance during an extraction under fire.

Later in 1970 an Army OH-6A that was conducting low-level reconnaissance was shot down by antiaircraft fire. The aircrew survived the crash, which took place in the jungle near the Laotian border, just south of National Route 9 and the famous battle site at Khe Sanh. Kiersley was launched with Cobra cover to fly the crew to safety and had them on board his helicopter when additional heavy antiaircraft fire was received from the ground. As Kiersley's UH-1H lifted off and turned to avoid the fire, one of the supporting Cobras turned the wrong way, and seconds later, the two helicopters collided head-on. All on board both aircraft were killed.

We Marines of Third Force will never forget that brave and decent young flying soldier who believed that regardless of the danger involved, it was his duty to extract Lieutenant Coffman and the men of that team because he was the one who had inserted them in the first place.

21

THERE ARE NO TRUCKS
IN THE ASHAU

Certain moments in life can serve to clarify your views and focus your mind in a way that you never thought possible. For those of us in Third Force Reconnaissance Company, one of those defining moments came in February 1970, when I was told directly to my face by Col. Oliver C. Patton of the U.S. Army that my Marines were liars.

This event was one small result of the shifting responsibilities among the various U.S. military command structures within Northern I Corps. For most of the war I Corps was Marine country. Yet, in 1970, the U.S. Army had fairly large forces deployed in that portion of the Republic of Vietnam, including the 101st Airborne Division at Camp Eagle near Phu Bai and a mechanized unit operating farther up the coast near the old 3d Marine Division area north of Dong Ha. As is usually the case when Army and Marine elements are working in close proximity, friction occurred. We also experienced the normal distrust—based on the perceived possibility of unfavorable treatment—present in Army units when they learn that they might actually find themselves under the command of a senior Marine.

A corps-level headquarters staff, designated as XXIV Corps, was created to coordinate the U.S. Army units and to serve as a buffer between the Marine general officer and the Army unit commanders. It was not unreasonable for this to happen, just unnecessary. When it was initiated I dredged up an old memory from 1958 concerning command structures when the Marines were ordered by President Eisenhower to place the Sixth Fleet Landing Force ashore in Lebanon. In that instance, the U.S. Army flew in a general officer immediately after the landing to ensure that the few soldiers who were initially deployed did not fall prey to the potentially evil effects of working for Marines. The historical precedent caused me to chuckle at the time, but shortly after XXIV Corps was up and running, the impact on our efficiency was far from humorous.

Regardless of why they had been placed there, or the history behind their arrival, this new staff did have a long-term mission. XXIV Corps was expected to assume the overall command of all U.S. forces in I Corps once the Marine units completed the scheduled force reductions. This had a direct impact on Third Force for two reasons. First, it added one more headquarters with which we had to establish and maintain liaison at all times—another manpower drain on our officer and communicator assets. Second, we had to add this new unit to our list of those to whom we made available the information we uncovered during our operational patrols in the mountains and along the DMZ.

When confronted with this new headquarters as it was first being established, I recommended to Colonel Polakoff that his SRC should handle liaison and report-passing duties. He agreed. Regardless of our views, however, the commanding general of XXIV Corps, Major General Zais, made it clear to the Commissar that he wanted his people to deal directly with my unit. In fact, he demanded that he be given operational control over Third Force, but that was nonnegotiable with General Nickerson.

Since my opinion had been overridden by those with more rank, I tried to make the best of an increasingly bad situation and decided to cooperate as completely as possible. To that end I sent an excellent liaison officer and went, personally, to brief the intelligence types on the XXIV Corps staff as to what Third Force Recon was and what we were doing in the way of information gathering.

We got a chilly, arrogant reception in response to our good-faith efforts. I was clearly not welcome. The general would not see me, Colonel Patton would not see me, and none of the various other minor satraps were willing to waste their valuable time discussing combat operations with a lowly major, even if that officer was a unit commander who had been working their area of interest for several months. Getting along, as professionals should, was obviously impossible. The interlude was personally insulting, and it was evident to everyone from myself to Lance Corporal Arguello—who drove my Jeep—that we were being summarily dismissed as nonpersons by arrogant, self-centered headquarters staff.

One afternoon I received a message that none other than Colonel Patton himself demanded that I appear in his office, immediately. I was not of a mind to challenge his right to ask me to stop by for a chat, but trying to treat this event as other than an imperious command from someone who should have extended the professional courtesy that was proper in our relationship was not easy. In a state of moderate apprehension, expecting bad things to happen, I went off to see what was on his mind.

When I arrived at the headquarters I had a few minutes of discussion with the assigned Third Force liaison officer. His comments were not at all reassuring. It was his opinion that we were the subject of an unsubtle character-assassination vendetta within the headquarters. He had overheard some nasty and unsupportable allegations being made against my company by senior officers while he was eating near them in the officers' mess. It seems that Third Force was characterized as being manned by liars and incompetents. He could not begin to halt such serious allegations with his single silver bar of first lieutenancy; the accusers were eagle-wearing colonels.

We were being viewed as "misfits" and "bums" because we were not part of the more conventional force structure. Actually, we were not really in bad company, as these critical officers held the same arrogant disdain for all members of the U.S. Army Special Forces, the U.S. Army Rangers, and even the Special Operations Group's CCN soldiers. My liaison officer was thoroughly shaken to find such an unprofessional attitude during a real shooting war with real men dying daily in the dark, stinking jungles. Nothing I could say on the subject at the time seemed to do anything to abate his frustration or his fury. Not that I blamed him, for I too was furious.

At the appointed hour I presented myself at the office of Colonel Patton and was permitted to sit and wait for more than an hour. I took it for what it was, a calculated insult to a busy combat commander who did not really have the free time to park his ass on a plastic chair and wait. None of the leaders I ever came to admire during my formative years seemed to respond very well to insults or affronts. Neither did I! My temper was approaching volcanic levels after wasting more than sixty slowly passing minutes outside the colonel's office.

Once ushered into the inner sanctum, there were no signs of courtesy or professional decency. Instead, I was left standing at attention, like some new eighteen-year-old recruit, and treated to a harangue. Colonel Patton opened with the comment, "I have been reviewing the reports of your people from the Ashau, and I find them to be pure fabrication. Your people are lying to you about what they see in the Ashau, and you are forwarding those lies as intelligence reports to higher headquarters."

Without taking time to catch his breath, he went on and on and on and on. He did not believe that NVA forces of battalion or regimental size were moving through the Ashau Valley. He did not believe major trail networks had been carved out under the trees, with the tops of the trees tied together to block aerial observation and/or photography. He did not believe that communications cables had been installed on the valley floor. He did not believe that anything reported by Third Force Reconnaissance Company was true, offering the opinion that my Marines were building up phony reports of NVA unit movement and body counts after fictitious firefights.

He did believe, and baldly stated so, that we were reporting such things solely to collect medals. Since both the lack of decorations for my Marines and the stupidity of body counts were bitterly sore subjects with me, I very nearly lost my self-control at that point.

Eventually the yammering came to an end. Colonel Patton finally concluded his tirade with, "This crap about trucks in the Ashau proves my point. Major, there are no trucks in the Ashau! Your people are lying when they report vehicles on those roads. You are lying when you report that information as if it were valid. It is crap, and you know it. If the NVA was using the Ashau Valley for truck movements, I would know about it from the sources available to me because of my position in this headquarters. There are *no* trucks in the Ashau Valley, and I do not want to ever read any more garbage from you about hearing trucks being started and run on the roads in the Ashau Valley. Is that clear?"

I provided him with the requisite, "Yes, sir. That is clear." Then I requested permission to speak.

When he assented, I offered, "Sir, there are two things I must say in response to your comments. First, in Third Force Reconnaissance Company we do not refer to the men as people, we call them Marines. We call them that because they are brave and honorable members of the United States Marine Corps who are being asked to accept, as normal, risks that are so far outside the norm that it would be ridiculous to try to explain it to you. Second, I have personally been on patrol in various parts of the Ashau Valley, and I have heard trucks there, and I have seen their tread marks in the mud as well. That does not matter, though. If my Marines report hearing trucks, then there are trucks in the Ashau. My Marines do not lie. I will stake my life on that fact."

His only response was more of the same, with further references to his sources being superior to the reports fabricated by my "glory-hunting people."

Because I could foresee only trouble if I stayed any longer, I requested permission to depart for my unit. Colonel Patton denied me the opportunity to leave and treated me to a discourse on the waste inherent in creating small units like Third Force where "junior people" obtained too much latitude in their actions. He was a hard-case opponent of any specialized unit, and nothing would alter that set-in-concrete attitude.

Trying a new tactic, I attempted to point out that I knew his sources, and I suspected that the primary organizations producing intelligence data that he was citing were the Air Force reports of reconnaissance overflights and the reports made by the unit flying the U.S. Army Mohawk aircraft equipped with various sensor devices that would locate moving vehicles. My objections with regard to the validity of these two sources were ignored, although I tried to explain that the Air Force called it "visual reconnaissance" when they flew at four thousand feet—traveling at an airspeed of four hundred knots per hour—over the Ashau. The irony of viewing much of anything at that speed and altitude escaped my tormentor completely.

With regard to the Mohawk I offered only one objection—the established flight schedule. The night reconnaissance flight of the Mohawks that worked the Ashau Valley area took off *every* night at around 2300, flew the assigned mission, and all aircraft were parked on the ramp by 0100 to 0130. I suggested it was preposterous to imagine that the NVA did not have the flight schedule posted in every dispatch shack between here and the Mu Gia Pass in the Democratic Republic of Vietnam, better known as North Vietnam. All the NVA truckers had to do to vanish from the Mohawk detection equipment, which relied primarily on vehicular movement, was to park for an hour or so until the mission had gone home for the night.

That "slur" on the security of Army aviation infuriated the colonel, and I was thrown out of his office with the admonition that I had better "watch my mouth" if I wanted to avoid being relieved of duty and placed on charges. On that cheerful note, I left.

When I got back to the COC in Phu Bai we had a formal and rather serious meeting during which I carefully briefed Captain Hisler, Lieutenant Coffman, Lieutenant Robertson, Sergeant Henderson, and Sergeant Billedoux. If Colonel Patton merely bided his time, General Nickerson would rotate home in due course, and I might then be vulnerable to the expected machinations directed toward my relief from command. I wanted the five key men in the company to fully understand what we faced. It was also important for them to know specifically that I intended to make no changes in how we reported what the teams found in the Ashau, or anywhere else for that matter.

If those staff officers of XXIV Corps who were hostile to me and to my unit did get me relieved, I wanted every Marine in the company to know what had been said about them. I also felt they ought to know that as long as I was still the commanding officer, no outside character assassin, no matter what his rank, would ever get away with calling Marines of Third Force liars. Not as long as they continued to report truthfully to me exactly what they saw and what they heard.

While the information on my meeting with the newly established headquarters was being passed throughout Third Force in a carefully controlled and disciplined manner by Captain Hisler, I got the Commissar on the secure voice circuit for a discussion. He too had crossed swords with Colonel Patton in a bitter confrontation, not to mention his conflict with the XXIV Corps chief of staff and General Zais as well. We discussed Colonel Patton and his attitude and jointly surmised that it might not be long before that worthy gentleman would be moving up in the hierarchy to new levels of responsibility where he could surely chop the two of us off at the pockets.

Swallowing our frustration, we agreed that there was no reason to involve General Nickerson, who had enough on his mind without being forced to act as referee between warring officer factions. I was encouraged when Colonel Polakoff almost made a formal order out of telling me to do what I had already planned to do, that is, report what we saw, where we saw it, and when we saw it—without any lies or embellishment.

When it was time for the evening briefing of the teams scheduled to deploy to the field the next morning, the Marines were, to a man, somber and intensely bitter at the thought that anyone sitting on a staff in an office building so far from the reality of the Ashau Valley would label them liars. Many in the COC—including the Igor, who was so angry he was sputtering profanity—openly stated their feelings of betrayal and rage. Third Force Marines were not fools. They knew full well that we all were living on borrowed time when we operated long-range patrols far from any form of friendly assistance. This was pointedly more true than ever now that the NVA was steadily increasing their counterreconnaissance efforts. Had those men been unappreciated mercenary soldiers, they would have walked out that day, perhaps firing a few rounds in the direction of their accuser as they left.

Being Marines with a dangerous and unrewarding job to do, they bitched and grumbled mightily about the unfairness of life in general and military life in particular, then got on with preparations for another mission. Even today I can still feel the warm sense of pride I had deep in my heart as many of the young Marines and corpsmen tried to tell me, in their own way, to remember that they would never let the company down—no matter how many staff officers with overly heavy collars chose to crap on us from above. They knew that all of us were damaged forever by the cheap shot leveled at the company and all the men who served in it. In their own fashion they wanted to show me that they were mad and that they cared.

Life in combat slips and shudders along from one crisis to another, and one cannot dwell on the messy parts of yesterday. We continued to work in the far reaches of the assigned operational areas while the NVA accommodated us by providing targets for observation, for attack—when prudent—and for avoidance—when necessary. Third Force teams were involved in a series of contacts with superior NVA forces, and casualties were sustained. When any of the fine young men were killed or wounded it served to drain, almost to the bottom, the emotional capital available to individuals and the unit as a whole. Our small size and our personal closeness magnified the pain of each loss: there were no strangers in Third Force whose loss might go unremarked.

NVA forces seemed to be everywhere. Their trucks were heard on the floor of the Ashau Valley by three separate teams. The reports were filed with the SRC in Da Nang, including the descriptions of truck noises, just as they were reported to our COC by the Marines on the ground. We waited for the expected angry reaction from XXIV Corps, but it did not come to pass. In fact, nothing happened as the days passed slowly into history.

Roughly two weeks after Colonel Patton had made us acutely aware that he held Third Force in great contempt, we got an opportunity to get partially even. Cpl. Joseph DeSaro, known as "Joey the Cool," gave us the chance to strike back at Colonel Patton and all those in the XXIV Corps headquarters who shared his opinions. We did get to rub his nose in the dirt a little bit.

Joey the Cool walked, talked, and acted like a B-movie version of a New Jersey street hood. His accent was thickly Italian, and he used the jargon of the underworld as part of his normal banter. Despite the posturing, Joey was an absolutely steady professional when it came to running things in the field. His energy was formidable. A veteran of numerous firefights in the DMZ and the Ashau, Corporal DeSaro was both brave and aggressive but also smart enough to temper his bravado with the common sense and cautiousness needed for survival.

Because Corporal DeSaro was so rock solid overall, I was surprised to be awakened early one morning to learn that he was requesting to leave his assigned operational area on the morning of extraction. No purpose was stated. I could only speculate that he had spotted something that might yield some desired intelligence information. Trusting his judgment, I issued the order permitting him to cross the border of his assigned area, an extension of two thousand meters. Flash messages went to various air headquarters adding the new coordinates to those that they could not bomb without my permission.

While all this was taking place, we took time in the COC to examine the possibilities. Corporal DeSaro had been on an active mission in the central Ashau for the past five days. He had made contact with a superior NVA force on several occasions, exchanging fire and sneaking away, supposedly undetected. I was convinced that his team was being subjected to sophisticated radio direction-finding techniques: the NVA seemed to be able to close with him far too easily after his team had slipped away.

Joey the Cool seemed to be unfazed by the state of things in the Ashau, choosing, on the fourth night of the mission, to spend considerable time on the radio calling for and controlling an offset-bombing mission using the RABFAC. After the offset-bombing runs were completed, both the team and Zulu Relay reported secondary explosions, a positive sign. It was toward the impact area that Corporal DeSaro was heading with his team when they left the previously authorized operational area. While he did not so state, it was obvious that Joey wanted to do a short poststrike assessment of the impact area before extracting when the morning missions began.

What he was doing was dangerous, but it also appeared reasonable. I did not feel any need to remind DeSaro about security when he moved into the area where the NVA had supposedly been sitting when the bombs landed. As the early morning hours dragged by, I watched the markers at the map station plotting the reported movement of the team. First, they ventured slowly into the road-net area on the valley floor. Then, the plot shifted westward toward the scheduled extraction site. All we could do in the COC was wonder what Corporal DeSaro had found. His submissions to us did not shift from short position reports; any intelligence data would come in with the team upon extraction.

Our job was to get the morning lift of in-bound teams briefed and ready. I was flying mission command again that morning with Major James, and it was time to get ready to go to work.

Once in the air, everything seemed to go with a special smoothness. We swept into the Ashau Valley with the helicopters swirling the mists at treetop level. Our flight would offer the NVA nothing to shoot at other than a flash of reflected light as the Cobras and UH-1H aircraft dashed past openings in the jungle canopy, the sound of their rotors reflected and re-reflected off the small hills until it seemed to come from everywhere.

Some officers criticized Major James for this sort of flying, but he and I both preferred to be down in among the trees as opposed to lumbering along at four thousand feet where the antiaircraft guns that we occasionally encountered could knock a helicopter out of the sky. On this particular day everything worked to perfection. Our teams were inserted without receiving any fire, and both scheduled extractions went flawlessly. Within a short time we were back on an easterly heading, the morning tasks completed. Major James came up on the intercom and told me that the pilot lifting Corporal DeSaro's team reported that they had a "surprise package" for me.

Back in Phu Bai, when I turned to head toward the COC, I found a grinning team of reconnaissance Marines standing at attention in front of me. Directly centered in front of the group was an item on the ground, covered with a poncho. Joey the Cool saluted and said, "Boss, we brought you something. Maybe you can pass it on to someone who would appreciate it. We thought you could use it to get those assholes to understand that there are trucks in the Ashau!"

With that, one of the Marines knelt beside the object and ceremoniously uncovered a front wheel and tire assembly from a Russian-made GAZ-37 truck. Attached to the assembly were some bits and pieces of the brakes, a foot or so of hydraulic line, and a short chunk of steering system tie rod. Obviously, this junk had been forcibly blown from the GAZ-37 during the A-6 offset bombing the night before. By God, there had been trucks in the Ashau Valley—just like we said there were.

Corporal DeSaro and his team had willingly, with a clear understanding of the dangers, risked their lives to do two things. First, they had accomplished a valid military mission to determine the effect of the bombing strike. That was a commendable act, worthy of praise. Second, they had chosen to stake their very survival against poor odds to vindicate themselves and their company. I fell upon the team, alternately laughing with them at what was to come and hugging them wordlessly. Taking a moment to be absolutely formal, I looked at Joey and his team and said, "Thank you! You know that this is important to us all."

After sending the team off to get debriefed, cleaned up, and fed, I made ready to go see Colonel Patton. Several of the men from the Third Force who could see what was afoot volunteered to come along, but I suggested that this was my show. Tossing the wheel with its fragment-riddled tire into my Jeep, I told Corporal Arguello we had a delivery to make.

When we arrived at the headquarters area, Colonel Patton was not physically present. I was forced to deal with a subordinate, but he was pretty close to the flagpole in the pecking order of that particular staff. The officer who accepted the GAZ-37 parts as a token of our esteem was a dull, pompous, and slow-witted lieutenant colonel who was assigned to work for the deputy chief of staff for intelligence. He was not thrilled to see me, nor did he seem to be appreciative of our gift to his leader.

I plopped the dirty mess down on his desk, carefully pointed out the freshly shattered metal that showed absolutely no rust, and quietly suggested that he deliver the item to his boss in exactly the same state as it was when I delivered it. In as measured a tone as I could muster I stated, "Colonel, my Marines do not lie. Tell that to your boss when you present this wheel to him with the compliments of Third Force Reconnaissance Company. Tell him also that there are trucks in the Ashau Valley: this is part of one that was in the valley last night. If he wants the rest of this one, we can take him to get it at his convenience."

Since the officer seemed so utterly nonplussed at this entire turn of events, I decided to leave him that way. I gave him as sharp a salute as I had in my bag of tricks and returned to the company feeling profoundly pleased and so proud of my Marines that I could hardly refrain from shouting out loud.

Knowing full well that winning in one of these petty personal battles with arrogant seniors is always costly, I got Colonel Polakoff on the covered circuit as soon as I got back to the company area. He was in a magnificent mood when he came on the line, laughing as he told me that he had already heard from the XXIV Corps staff. The Commissar told me to keep on doing what I was doing while he took care of the garbage details in the rear.

Later I learned from Maj. Hugh Scott of the SRC that Polakoff had gone to the mat with Colonel Patton, telling him to get off his dead rear end and show the tire and wheel to General Zais, without any further whining about Third Force. I was gratified at the support and passed on Colonel Polakoff's most sincere expression of pride in a job well done to Corporal DeSaro and to his team.

Two weeks later Corporal DeSaro asked for a private moment of my time. I asked him to come into my living area in the rear of the COC where we could talk. Once seated, Joey the Cool solemnly opened a box and removed a small plastic toy truck with a carefully hand-lettered note attached to the front axle. It read, "For the Commissar. There are trucks in the Ashau. Here is one of them."

Almost reverently he handed the small toy to me and asked that I take it or send it to Da Nang for Colonel Polakoff to put on his desk. "Boss," intoned Joey, "we heard how much crap the Commissar took over the reports of trucks in the Ashau, and how he took on the Army for Third Force when that guy bad-mouthed us. This truck has been to the Ashau in my pack. We want him to have it so he can tell any more of those shitheads that come along that there are trucks in the Ashau, and that this is one of them."

Corporal DeSaro was as serious as death as he presented the toy to me, and I took his offering with every bit of the respect that it merited. I gave Corporal DeSaro my word that his wishes would be observed to the letter.

I borrowed an aircraft and a crew from Colonel Bindrup of the 2d Squadron of the 17th Air Cavalry the next morning and flew to Da Nang. In the SRC I carefully explained the wishes of Corporal DeSaro and the Marines of his team to Colonel Polakoff. Gerry Polakoff was a deeply caring man who was not ashamed to let his emotions show. He held the tears back, but just barely. We talked quietly for a few minutes about duty, honor, and the love we had for the young Marines who would rather chance death than accept the slurs of someone unfit to walk in their shadows.

It was an emotionally difficult time, for both the Commissar and I knew that our days of service for General Nickerson, who understood Marines like Corporal DeSaro, were numbered. We knew that neither of us had the rank needed to protect my Marines from those who had no respect for their abilities or their willingness to accept the challenges of assignment to Third Force Reconnaissance Company. We parted that day with feelings of great pride and aching sorrow.

Colonel Polakoff loved his truck. He kept it with him for the rest of his tour in Vietnam, and it went home with him to duty in the United States. He displayed it proudly to his classmates at the Naval War College, and it again graced his desk when he served another tour in the development center at Quantico, Virginia. Upon his retirement from the Marine Corps, the Commissar took his truck to California, where it sat on his desk so the light would fall upon it every time he turned on his desk lamp.

Col. Gerald H. Polakoff died an untimely death in 1980. That toy truck, enshrined in a custom-designed glass case, with the original note from Joey the Cool still attached to it, lay centered upon the flag that covered the coffin of our Commissar on the day we laid him to rest in grave M-100 in the cemetery on Point Loma that overlooks the Pacific Ocean near San Diego Bay.

NVA trucks rolled through the Ashau Valley in 1970, and Third Force Reconnaissance Company was there to report their movements. We did not lie, and we shall never forgive, nor shall we ever forget, being branded as liars while we risked our lives to report the truth. One should never permit such a thing to pass unremembered into history. Honor must be preserved.

22

THE FIRE DIES

In the unusual world of special operations of any kind, everything hinges on the nature of the man who makes the final decisions. That was clearly proven after the death of President Kennedy in November 1963, when our lives in Weapons Planning Group came under the direct influence of Lyndon Johnson. It was no less true in Third Force Reconnaissance Company when General Nickerson was rotated home on March 9, 1970, to duty at Marine Corps headquarters in Washington. The new general, Lt. Gen. Keith B. McCutcheon, did not know us and was not interested in us. It did not take long to find out how the new command situation was going to affect Third Force.

When General Nickerson, our leader, our ally, and our mentor, went home, our lives shifted steadily toward the kind of operational nightmare that we had dreaded. We could easily anticipate Third Force being controlled by several masters, all of whom might have conflicting views on what we should be doing at any given time. In fact, that was exactly what began to happen the day after the change of command at the III Marine Amphibious Force headquarters in Da Nang.

With our nation's commitment to winning gone for political reasons, things were going to be terminated for us all in the dying Republic of Vietnam. For Third Force Reconnaissance Company the end came in bits and pieces—all accompanied by an unwarranted hostility from those whom my Marines had served so well.

The newly arrived commanding general of III MAF was a fine and well-regarded officer with a long record of exceptional service to the Marine Corps and the country. He was an aviator who may well have known all manner of things aeronautical, but he was not interested in matters relating to special operations and the units who performed that type of mission. I was never permitted to meet the man, nor was there any opportunity to brief him on the role that Third Force Reconnaissance Company had been performing for his predecessor.

As one would candidly expect, the general played vigorously and with good effect to his strong suit—aviation—and leaned away from things about which he knew little or nothing. He arrived, listened to the advice given by his intelligence staff, and shifted everything that had to do with Third Force Reconnaissance Company—including operational control—to that staff for action.

We no longer worked for the man in command; we now worked for something that resembled a committee on that amorphous staff, none of whom had ever seen any of us up close. We did have continued direct access to Colonel Polakoff's SRC, but only on a reporting basis: the link between Third Force and the SRC was almost severed. Third Force was no longer the tip of anyone's spear, nor did we enjoy any sort of access to the general at all. It was time to make us humble—for our past sins of hard work under Nickerson's leadership—and the staff weenies made sure I knew that it was payback time.

While I expected to get shoved around a bit, I hardly expected the animosity to extend beyond me to every one of my Marines and corpsmen. Perhaps I should have guessed that such men would make war on those far down the pecking order, but the idea was so far-fetched that I initially dismissed it from my mind.

My first lesson was administered within just a few days when a telephone call at 0900 to the COC contained an abrupt order to report to Da Nang immediately to confer with the assistant chief of staff for intelligence, Colonel Canton, who was unhappy. I couldn't respond immediately to that direct order because I was in the cockpit of a UH-1H some fifty to sixty miles west, in the Ashau Valley, trying to oversee the extraction of a team that was in trouble. Captain Hisler took the heat about my lack of immediate response.

When I finally returned and learned of the need to go to Da

Nang, I acquired, through my good relationship with the Army, the use of a UH-1H for three or four hours. When we arrived overhead at the III MAF compound, several CH-46 helicopters were parked on the pad for regular visitors, so I directed my pilot to drop me at the empty VIP pad that lay nearer the general's headquarters. The landing was textbook perfect; the results were amusing. Little worried-faced men scurried out to see who was on their sacred landing ground. I bade my pilot farewell and told him to fly to the Army's Viking compound to fuel the aircraft, eat something, and return to the III MAF regular pad in two hours.

As the dust from the lifting UH-1H was still filtering down on us all, I was verbally assaulted by a red-faced major of Marines. He called me most of the profane names that I had learned in the third grade and a few that I had come across later in life.

In response, I explained quietly that on my body at that moment I happened to have two knives, four hand grenades, a number of flares, a real five-shot getaway pistol of last resort, and a loaded M-16 with twenty-one short magazines and a thirty-round magazine. I suggested that I was now ready to employ any and all of these items to his personal detriment. I further pointed out that I too was a major who was there on official business and that if he had the stupidity to open his mouth again, he would go home in a bag. While looking into the muzzle of my M-16 he appeared to be listening, so I left him to gape at my back and departed from the landing pad to meander through the headquarters rabbit warren to find the office of the Colonel Canton who had sent for me.

When I arrived at the proper office I was informed that a telephone call had preceded me, one that accused me of threatening an officer of the U.S. Marine Corps with death. Agreeing that that was exactly what had happened, I pointed out that time was being wasted and that I had come to answer whatever questions the assistant chief of staff might have. A blank stare was all I got in return, and the officer who had snarled at me as I first entered the door went inside to receive his instructions.

Before long I was whisked into the inner sanctum, and Colonel Canton and I got down to the meat of the matter. He demanded to know in the most angry fashion just who in the hell

I thought I was when it came to putting teams into and taking them out of various operational areas.

It seems that that morning I had ordered an extraction—and personally participated in it—of a team that had been under pressure from pursuing NVA troops for three days and nights. The assistant chief of staff had been informed by the SRC as part of the normal routine, otherwise he would never have even known about the action taking place seventy-five miles or so from his comfortable office. I had not cleared that decision with him personally before taking the Army helicopters into the Ashau Valley to see if I could save the lives of my men. It was his contention that I needed his permission for every insertion into an AO that was not ordered from his office and for every extraction that was made earlier than scheduled or was the result of enemy action.

Needless to say, we were not on the same wavelength during this discussion. He had never been out to see the Ashau—or Phu Bai for that matter—and I felt that he was demanding something that was operationally impossible.

Remaining deathly calm, I explained quietly that as the commanding officer, who was also officer-in-tactical-command on the scene and under fire at the time, I felt that I was the best person to reach a correct decision with regard to the lives of the men of Third Force. I offered the view that there was not a single person in the headquarters, with the possible exception of Colonel Polakoff, who was current enough on the NVA and their capabilities in the Ashau Valley to make informed and rational decisions.

This commonsense approach evoked a vile and bitterly hostile response. I was told that I was just a "lousy major" who had no concept of where operational decisions should be made or by whom. Later in his diatribe the staff officer threatened that he was going to have me relieved from command for ignoring my responsibility to obtain his permission for extracting the team. While this was hardly the first time I had been subjected to a one-sided conversation like this in III MAF headquarters, this was the first time I had no hope whatsoever of winning the fight.

Believing that attacking is far superior to defending, I became very aggressive. I told the assistant chief of staff that this same sort of ill-conceived demand had been made some months earlier by another colonel who had held the intelligence staff billet. It had not worked then, and it would not work now. I pointed out that we had better get to the new general quickly to effect a resolution. This appeared to shake his basic confidence a bit, and he began to make a slow retreat from the arrogance of before. He could see that destroying me in front of the general might be a bit harder than he had originally thought. Even the new general might well side with a combat commander, and the colonel was not willing to take that chance.

After an hour of pointless wrangling, during which the tone of things began to shift from hostile to coldly polite, I was dismissed with roughly a zillion admonitions to amend my ways. The demand to clear *all* extractions had not been resurrected, and I was not about to seek clarification. I did not have the slightest intention of forcing anyone in Third Force to sit under the NVA's guns while waiting for the distant colonel to decide whether or not the team could be extracted.

The second lesson in humility that was administered to Third Force came in the form of an immediate reduction in the quantity and quality of all forms of external support. Prior to the departure of General Nickerson, we had always had the kind of direct access to our boss that permitted us to discuss problems that he, and he alone, could solve. The situation changed because I no longer had any access to the man who was our boss.

When we worked for General Nickerson, clearing away various difficulties took only the simple act of the general affixing his green "N" on the routing slip. Now that he was gone, everyone had the option of thumbing their nose at our requests with relative impunity. Consequently, Third Force began to increase our reliance on other means. We could employ chicanery, do without, or seek help from the U.S. Army.

Our third lesson came in the form of a summons to speak with the chief of staff. I arrived at the designated time, as ordered, and found that several senior officers had been assembled to deal with Third Force Reconnaissance Company's reputation for being too close to the Army. I was astonished and severely depressed to learn that my pleasant and professionally rewarding relationship with the 101st Airborne Division and General

Wright was considered a threat by some of my seniors in the Marine Corps. Somehow we could not put aside our professional jealousies long enough to fight a war together.

It was disgusting to waste time on this subject, but I had no choice. I was forced to justify my preference for use of the 2d Squadron of the 17th Air Cavalry's UH-1H helicopters over the Marine CH-46 and of Army Cobra gunships over Marine fixed-wing aircraft for strikes against NVA forces attacking my teams. Only one officer, an aviator, seemed swayed by my explanations with regard to aircraft size, lift capability, and the time it took to get fixed-wing aircraft from the hot pad at Da Nang to the teams in the DMZ or the Ashau. None of the operational considerations seemed to matter, only that we kept evidencing some sort of anti-Marine sentiments that the senior officers could not live with.

As the meeting wound down, I agreed to make more use of Marine aviation and to tone down the rhetoric of Third Force troops on the subject of what fine support we were getting from Army sources. (Certain vocal team leaders, for example, had responded to the arrival of Marine Cobras with such comments as "Hey, who sent for you? We want the Cav!" or "We prefer to go brown" [that is, to fly with the Army's Commancheros].) Naturally, we would continue to seek support from whatever source we thought most responsive, regardless of service affiliation, but these senior officers all wanted me to say it, so I said it, and it made them happy.

Third Force was also subjected to a spate of pointless missions. Most of these directed the company to patrol and conduct surveillance in areas where we already knew the NVA was located in semipermanent garrisons. Thus, most teams were either taken under fire on landing or became engaged shortly thereafter.

One mission of this type directed us to return to the area to the west of Khe Sanh in order to determine whether or not the NVA was using National Route 9 to bring supplies and personnel into the Republic of Vietnam. Since we already knew, and the aerial observers were also reporting, that trucks were using that road every day, it seemed pointless for us to insert a team directly into that hornet's nest. No matter, Third Force was directed go there without delay—in fact, without so much as an overflight, which was characterized as being "too costly." The team went in, listened to trucks all night, and withdrew, on my order, to the south where we extracted them successfully three days later.

This particular extraction was even more difficult than the norm because of the extended range involved and the presence of numerous NVA 12.7mm weapons nearby. As a matter of fact, they nearly bagged the mission command helicopter with me in it! In keeping with my promise to use more Marine air, we had gone for the team with two CH-46 helicopters, two Cobra gunships, and a UH-1E from the Marine Observation Squadron out of Da Nang. The pilots of the UH-1E were two first lieutenants whom I had never met before. Neither had ever flown with a reconnaissance package.

Despite their boyish good looks and breezy attitudes, they seemed willing and capable of carrying out the mission, so I was comfortable with them as part of the operation. The Igor conducted his usual thorough briefing and eased up to the two lieutenants as they left to threaten them with death-most-cruel if they were thinking about losing his boss in the weeds. We all laughed and went off to war.

The flight to the west went according to plan, with the gunships leading and setting their course in such a way that the portion of eastern Laos that projected into Vietnam—called, for lack of a better name, the Salient—was bypassed with room to spare. Once north of the Salient we turned to the west, alerted the team for extraction, and collected it without incident.

At that point things began to unravel, but I didn't immediately recognize it. The two CH-46s were detached, and they headed east around the end of the Salient, heading back to Phu Bai. My UH-1E and the two Cobras proceeded north and west to examine the Khe Sanh area from the air before turning for home. While we were looking over the old combat base, one of the lieutenants up front called to the Cobra leader that the UH-1E was at the fuel state for return, and we were heading back. The boss of the Cobras, who happened to be a lieutenant colonel, merely acknowledged the message and went on to the northwest along National Route 9, looking for targets. The Cobras, known as scarface guns, were going hunting and we were heading back to Phu Bai.

As the young pilots turned the UH-1E eastward, we climbed to an approximate altitude of four thousand feet, and the crew chief closed the sliding doors to keep out the wet and the chill. Because I was tired and wrapped in my own thoughts, a few minutes had passed before I sensed the danger posed by the reality that the sun was in the wrong place. We were heading south, not east! I jumped up and slammed the sliding door to the rear so I could see the terrain below. There I saw what I did not want to see— cultivated ground.

There was no agriculture in that area of the Republic of Vietnam: all the farmers had fled the war and the depredations by both sides. That meant we were inside Laos, where the NVA maintained garden plots for the troops so they could grow vegetables to supplement their diet. In addition, the presence of gardens might mean the presence of antiaircraft guns. This was not a good place to be.

The lieutenant in command of the aircraft began to shout over the intercom that my opening the door had had a bad effect on the helicopter's stability. His raspy little voice was overpowered when I roared at him, "Down! Get down. Break left and down. Ack ack is all over this place. Break left and down. Now!"

The two of them dropped the UH-1E like a stone and cranked it hard left at the same time. Just as we left our straight and level course for a corkscrewing ride down toward the deck, the first burst of a high-explosive antiaircraft projectile appeared roughly fifty meters away to our right. Dozens more followed, but they all were now above us and well away to the south of our new course, which was almost due east. Though totally unprepared for the event, the young pilots reacted magnificently. NVA units were in Laos with their 23mm, 57mm and ever-so-much-larger weaponry to interdict any U.S. Air Force aircraft that were transiting from Thailand to take part in the bombing campaigns. Our single UH-1E was not a prime target, but the NVA gunners nonetheless seemed quite happy to spray the sky trying to kill us.

As the two pilots were handling treetop dodging, I took over the role of navigator for the wild ride. Kneeling on the deck just aft of the console between the pilots, I recommended course changes and pointed out areas that appeared to be inhabited.

As we closed in on the border, the pilots selected a stream to follow, and I urged them to cross one of the ridges instead. Both pilots preferred the stream line, and the NVA got another chance to shoot at us. They sent us on our way west with streams of 12.7mm tracer fire as we flew right between two of those hard-hitting weapons. Not one round hit the helicopter, though, nor did one piece of shrapnel find its mark. The aircrew and I were deeply gratified to find that despite a grave error in judgment—one that was compounded by all of us—we were still alive. I never again flew with those two lieutenants and will always wonder how they tell the story of their one exposure to reconnaissance work in Vietnam.

Early in April 1970 Third Force Reconnaissance Company was ordered to cease operations and to begin preparations to be placed into a cadre status. We were finished with our missions to the DMZ, the Ashau Valley, and the rest of Northern I Corps. Even though we had known that the order was coming someday, we all felt a certain sense of betrayal when it arrived. It was hard to see the value of chopping 160 U.S. Marine Corps personnel spaces out of the total authorized in-country strength by eliminating a prime intelligence-collection entity and retaining all those billets in the various staffs. Regardless, we had our orders and the stand-down began.

Humility was imposed on the company with a vengeance. Those who were so short that they had less than three months left on their tour in combat were ordered to leave for home. Those who possessed the badges and formal reconnaissance-related school certificates in their record books were sent to First Force Recon and the 1st Reconnaissance Battalion of the 1st Marine Division—both of which were located in Da Nang. Regrettably, the teams were split up, despite desperate pleas on my part asking that the personnel people remember the value of unit integrity. This decision resulted in the shattering of professional relationships that had been forged in blood, an unneeded stupidity. About thirty members of Third Force remained on the roll as cadre—ostensibly to manage the matériel assets of the unit and to train members of the Korean Marines.

Worst of all, the Marines and corpsmen who had some time left on their tour of duty, but who did not possess badges and special-school training, were sent into the personnel mixmaster for assignment anywhere they were needed. These men had amassed a great amount of specialized combat experience while serving in Third Force—some were team leaders—yet the personnel staff took no notice. It was insulting and demeaning to them. They were embittered to find that, once again, they were mere ciphers on some printout, not fighting men of dignity and proven ability. I was able to track a few of them and to make their new leaders aware, at least partially, of their abilities. Sadly, many just vanished into the system and were swallowed up in units all over the Vietnamese landscape, units where they were nothing more than slot fillers.

Despite our violently hostile feelings, we executed the standdown orders as we received them. The adjutant, Lieutenant Morris, issued orders; Lieutenant Coffman worked ungodly hours to carefully craft the final command chronology submissions that would be the historical record of Third Force Recon's operations; Lieutenant Robertson developed a complete briefing package on our operations for presentation to the III MAF commanding general and his staff. We had been asked by Colonel Polakoff to be prepared to educate them on what we had been doing and how our efforts had been melded into the larger scheme of things at the MAF level.

Within a few days the men had begun departing, reports were ready, and the briefing had been refined to a clean forty minutes of well-organized information. Third Force had become a unit in cadre status, not a fighting unit.

When directed by Colonel Polakoff, Robertson and I flew to Da Nang. The Commissar took us to a headquarters briefing room where we set up our maps and charts. Shortly thereafter, about forty-five officers of various ranks filtered into the room and took their seats. The general could not make it to the presentation, and only three or four colonels were present. On cue, we began to explain the conversion of Third Force into an independent entity and its relationship with the MAF commanding general of the time—General Nickerson—and the subsequent operations. Very few of the officers seemed willing to give either me or Lieutenant Robertson the courtesy of their full attention. Several side conversations were going on, and some officers either took their leave or dozed quietly in their chairs. I cut Lieutenant Robertson off at a convenient point, and we excused ourselves from further contact with that group.

Colonel Polakoff was utterly shamed by the unprofessional turn of events, and he was totally sincere in his apology for our being humiliated for no reason. Nothing he could do or say, however, could ease the devastation that Robertson and I were feeling. The men in that room flatly did not care to learn anything at all about Third Force: they had been forced to come to that room, but nobody was going to make them pay attention.

Taking pride in our efforts, Robertson and I went back to Phu Bai to gather whatever personal gear we had prior to executing our own orders. We tried to skirt the issue of what had happened at the briefing, but Coffman was quick to sense that we were deeply troubled, and we told him the truth. Buck pointed out that at least we had the command chronologies going forward up the chain; the operations of Third Force would be added to the long history of our corps. Alas, that too was frustrated, and we learned years later that some of the command chronologies were trashed by someone who considered our operations to be no more than a mere sideshow. They never made it to the historical branch at headquarters in Washington—ever.

I left Third Force for duty with the 1st Division's Headquarters Battalion, where I became the operations officer in the G-4 section. When I got there I found that they had two or three officers for every billet, and there was little challenging work for me to do in a slot that had three majors in it already. This was a short-lived experiment, however.

Late one night, after only three weeks and a few days, I was ordered to the quarters of the G-1, where I encountered four colonels with a problem. They put it to me bluntly: one of the real comers of the Marine Corps was in deep professional trouble as a battalion commander, and he needed an operations officer who could get him out of it. Would I take the job? I replied that I would be happy to be operations officer for the devil himself if it got me out of the headquarters.

I left in the morning for duty with an infantry battalion where I was treated shabbily by a man who obviously hated me for being sent to pull him out of his predicament, but I was busy doing something productive again.

While I was in Da Nang a few of the Third Force Marines had

a party on the beach as a goodbye gesture. We drank too much, I was tossed into the surf many times, and we cried a little together. I was given a small plaque on which some Vietnamese had been contracted to inscribe the entire score of "Impossible Dream" from *The Man of La Mancha*. Until it was lost in a fire in 1989, that small battered plaque was one of my most treasured possessions.

23

REFLECTIONS

He is indeed alive and so alone that I must show him
through this dismal valley.

Dante's *Inferno*, Canto XII

Any man who has ever commanded a fighting unit during combat
operations needs to look back, years later, at his performance. He
should do so with as much honesty as his personal introspection
permits. He should reflect deeply on what he did and how his
actions affected those who served under his leadership. If you
take the time to be honest with yourself, you will find that it is
possible to learn a great deal from this trying process. I have
looked back over the twenty-five years that have passed since I
commanded Third Force Reconnaissance Company. I have
reflected and learned. It has not been easy.

Looking back was difficult for a number of reasons. The effort
was hampered because of an internalized anger about our treatment after the Vietnam War that continues to this day. It was emotionally painful because those men were family to me, and I miss
them. Last, it was agonizingly sorrowful because in 1969/70,
Third Force Reconnaissance Company was asked to attempt the
impossible, against great odds, for a nation that had given up any
pretense of trying to win the war that we were busily fighting. It
was a lost cause. My Marines and corpsmen knew it, my officers
knew it, and the hardworking Army and Marine pilots who flew
us daily into the gravest danger also knew it. It made everyone
bitter. Yet, bitterness aside, the Third Force Reconnaissance Com-

pany did everything they were ever asked to do with a willing spirit, a cooperative unity, and a level of dedication that was, as they say, "in the finest tradition."

My entire adult life was devoted to the study of military leadership and the underlying philosophy of the warrior breed. I tried hard to be a student of my profession. That study, and all of my early years of training as a Marine officer, made it clear to me that the commander is logically and *always* responsible for all failures, and the men who do the work are responsible for all the successes enjoyed by the organization he commands. With specific regard to the combat operations of Third Force Recon in 1969/70, this was, and still is, my interpretation: I accept the failures as mine, and the successes rightly belong to the young men of the company who did the job.

I will leave this life believing in the absolute and utter responsibility of command. Marines and corpsmen were sorely wounded, and a number of them died, serving in Third Force Reconnaissance Company. Their injuries and their deaths came at my hand; the responsibility was entirely mine. They went where I sent them, under the leaders that I selected, and died on missions that I had accepted as valid or on missions that I had generated from my personal analysis of the situation. While I was in command, no other person in the company made those decisions, and no other person in the company was ever expected to do so.

In many ways we faced life as the condemned man on death row must face his daily existence; it was not a matter of if one got hit, only when. The men of Third Force were realists, and every one of them knew that sooner or later the law of averages and the professional skills of the enemy could result in his death or maiming. We also knew that sometime we would stand the company down from combat operations as part of the withdrawal of U.S. forces from the Republic of Vietnam. While we did not know when that might happen, we did know it would be coming, and we might well have chosen to coast in order to maximize survivability.

That dishonorable course of action was unacceptable to the men of the company. They were unable to ignore their duty and coast because they had come to understand that for them, duty with the company was a unique experience wherein the exercise of professional responsibility under great duress surpassed all other considerations. As the fighting men of old expressed it, they had "taken the king's shilling," now it was time to "do the king's bidding." They chose to do so, no matter what.

Our losses were relatively few in number, but each loss had an enormous impact on our lives. We grew closer on a personal level than most brothers do, and the loss of anyone cut deeply into our souls. Some deaths were more shocking than others, either because of the nature of the fight or because of an unusual circumstance that surrounded the death. It was essential that we get the grief out into the open as quickly as possible.

To do that we conducted a memorial service where religious beliefs, personal relationships, and history were conjoined. For each lost fighting man we asked his closest friends to stand and speak out for him in keeping with an ancient Asian philosophy, attributed to no less a figure than the great Genghis Khan, that, "No man dies without merit who has one friend who will stand and speak for him." We mourned in precisely the same way that we fought—together.

In August 1969 Third Force lost a Marine who was new to the company in a tragic action in the DMZ. The Marine died because he needed to relieve himself after spending several hours staring at possible enemy routes of movement from an observation post. Instead of slipping into the dense brush as we had trained him to do, he stood and walked upright to an opening in the undergrowth. An observant NVA regular spotted him and shot him through the heart. I accepted, and still accept, personal responsibility for his death. Had I ensured that the training was more explicit, emphasizing that this was a twenty-four-hour-per-day war in which bodily functions did not permit a time-out, he might well have lived.

One of the most important aspects about our patrolling deep in NVA-dominated terrain was an absolutely rock-hard proscription against use of any of the many trails that the teams located in their search. Anyone who was even suspected of placing his foot on an NVA trail was scorched with an ass-chewing that we hoped he would remember for the rest of his life. These trails belonged totally to the North Vietnamese Army, and only bad things would ever come to those of us who made the error of walking on one.

Despite this well-known and strongly enforced guidance, in February 1970 we lost three men of Team Snaky. It happened when a freshly inserted team, led by a competent, experienced sergeant, left the landing zone and turned to walk boldly down a well-used NVA trail. The sergeant ordered the point man to walk right down the trail. The sergeant followed immediately behind the point himself, and the remaining men of the team followed him. The result was exactly what one might expect. The team ran directly into a strong NVA force—probably a hundred men or more—who initiated a hasty ambush and shot Team Snaky to ribbons.

After a brutal fight and an extraction effort of enormous further expense in men and matériel, including the loss of an OH-6A helicopter and the wounding of several soldiers of the 101st Airborne Division, we recovered our wounded and our dead. When we began the sad task of collecting the personal effects of the dead Marines, we found that the sergeant had already prepared his effects for shipment home. It was evident that he had expected to die on this mission and that he might well have accelerated his own death by choosing to make an operational blunder that was certain to result in disaster.

As we examined matters further we learned that the sergeant, who was a veteran of more than twenty-five long-range patrols and who had taken the initiative to extend his tour of combat duty, had been growing steadily more morose and withdrawn in the final month of his life. He was evidently no longer capable of living the stressful life of a Third Force Marine, but I had missed that fact completely.

With great personal lament I accept responsibility for the action that the sergeant took that day and will always feel that I somehow failed the men of Team Snaky who went on that terrible mission. We did not have in place any mechanism to spot the mental problems of team leaders, or anyone else for that matter, who might be beginning to crumble under the pressure. Captain Hisler, Lieutenant Coffman, and I had often discussed our lack of skills to fully evaluate the psychological state of the men of Third Force.

Occasionally, we noted individuals who had to be removed from further combat stress, but it was always a difficult determination to make. We could rely only on our own mental resources and personal feelings about the various individuals when we looked at the problem of their mental state on any given day. The days were long and the tension unremitting, but I accept the fact that somehow I should have noted the steady deterioration of that sergeant's ability to exercise judgment under pressure. He should not have been made to suffer alone and in silence, and he should not have remained a team leader after his attitude and resolve began to weaken.

Third Force lost men on another operation when a team leader made a carefully considered choice not to engage in a firefight. The entire firefight would have been resolved in a far different manner, with the team initiating the battle, if I had found a way to include training in the Vietnamese language for the men of the company.

While it may sound odd, this was true because the NVA infantrymen were famous for chattering as they moved on the trails, and we often heard them at great distances. None of us was capable of understanding just what was being said. In the case in point, the team was moving across an open area above an oft-used trail and had just stopped when they heard many voices, and an NVA unit appeared. The team was halted, with good camouflage and a heavy tree line to their backs. The team leader had two choices: either to start a battle with a superior force who might not know he was there, or to go to ground and hope that his team had not been spotted. He chose the latter, and it was a fatal choice. Obviously, the NVA soldiers were not engaged in idle chatter. They were saying something akin to, "Look, there are those damn Marines."

The team members had no way of knowing that they were about to be taken under fire because I had never found a way or the training time to provide them with the language tools needed for such an occasion. I had to accept in my own heart that I had failed those men. By not finding a way to give them any language training I had taken away their chance to be first on the trigger that hot, stinking afternoon in the jungle.

Reflection on my performance during 1969/70 as the commanding officer of Third Force Reconnaissance Company also brings pain from smaller failings. I was bitterly unable to brook the seemingly insolent disdain for my unit expressed by some of the staff officers in Da Nang, and I may have taken some actions in error. I often relied on my own force of personality in my dealings with such people. Perhaps I should have taken the time to seek the exercise of the commanding general's power for the good of my men. Instead of winning a skirmish, I might well have terminated the career of some who spent much time, in the words of the troops, "screwing us over."

On the other hand, I was also well known for my aggressive nature and my own disdain for certain seniors who appeared, to me, to be shirking their sworn responsibility to be supportive. Perhaps I might have been more circumspect and less challenging with these personnel, but it would have been difficult. I was often angry and confrontational when it might have been more effective to be conciliatory. It might have been more effective on some occasions, but I will never know because it was utterly impossible for me to be conciliatory at the time. In my heart I was convinced that my men were getting the short end of every stick, and the anger was so deep that it overwhelmed any sense of the value of getting along with those with whom we quarreled so contentiously.

I also could have done more in the area of securing recognition for the Marines and corpsmen who served in Third Force. When the men were scattered out to various units on our stand-down, I should have found a means to follow up on their awards and decorations status. I did not find a way, and many who served with honor and dignity far above the norm went home without so much as a piece of ribbon beyond that given to the "I was there" group that included those who answered the telephones in headquarters in Southeast Asia.

The Marines who served this nation as members of the Third Force Reconnaissance Company in the Republic of Vietnam in 1969/70 were decent, resourceful men who accepted great challenges as the order of the day. Those men deserved leadership of the highest order. My long reflections have convinced me that in many ways I failed them. I gave everything I had within me but still feel, to this day, that it was not enough.

The people of the United States of America also failed those gallant men, and many thousands like them, by permitting them to be vilified upon their return home. Those who served in Vietnam were characterized as personifications of evil, and the nation ignored the honor, the dignity under pressure, and the bravery that they exhibited in a war that was not to be won. The men of Third Force Reconnaissance Company were a diverse group of men who came together from every corner of this great land. They did their duty as they saw it at the time—holding back nothing. They have now passed on into history, unremarked and unremembered by a nation that should not be allowed to forget that some men willingly go forth to risk both their lives and their honor when the bugles call.

AFTERWORD

Organized opposition to the concept of specialized units generally takes two basic themes. First, there are those who pooh-pooh the need for any sort of elite, special units, be they reconnaissance or any other kind. They argue: "You can't have any kind of an elite within an elite. All Marines are members of an elite force, and any Marine should be able to do the mission set out for a force reconnaissance company." These people also fight furiously against the loss of any of their "superior" talent to these special units, finding ways to subvert the desires of both the headquarters—which seeks to get the units staffed and running—and any individual Marines who seek the challenge of being part of a unit with a complex and difficult mission.

The other opposition team cannot accept at face value the idea that a small unit like a force reconnaissance company needs equipment that is expensive, different, and frequently not available from within the Department of Defense supply sources. They protest against high-cost training, extensive temporary additional duty expenses, parachute pay, and any other expenses that they can use to illustrate the expensive nature of specialized units. Sadly, despite the passage of more than thirty-five years since General Nickerson got the whole thing off dead center, little has changed. There are still those who hate the force reconnaissance Marines for being "elitist" and those who constantly harp on the dollars that they would like to reprogram to some other use within the Marine Corps.

It is interesting to note that in more recent times, the post-

Kuwait view of matters organizational and the resurfacing of a serious need to address cost reduction have caused yet another reorganization of intelligence-gathering assets. This time things are different. Force reconnaissance has become part of a larger element, the Surveillance, Reconnaissance, Intelligence Group, SRIG for short. The force-level commanders will retain an ability to seek information with assets that report directly to them and an ability to establish in one entity a coordination center for intelligence matters. This time it is the division commanders who are being shortchanged, for the division reconnaissance battalions have been removed from the organization of the Corps, making intelligence gathering more difficult at that level.

A force reconnaissance company is *not* a simple unit to staff, train, and operate. The Marines who are needed must be bright, capable, independent thinkers who also possess superior infantry skills. The psychological stress involved in force reconnaissance operations differs greatly from that encountered in the infantry, where Marines take part in combat as part of much larger forces—forces that are not frequently required to operate alone in terrain dominated by the enemy. Success requires a resolute and stable Marine who has the fortitude to weather uncertainty.

Training one of these units is complex and never ending. Each Marine needs to complete a series of schools in order to master all the entry skills, and he needs considerable field experience before he even approaches being fully ready for active operations.

This need for extensive training suggests a parallel need for longer tours of duty in the reconnaissance field. Of course, that idea flies in the face of normal transfer policies set forth by rear-echelon personnel staff sections, the members of which see no reason why men are not interchangeable pieces to their personnel jigsaw puzzles. Maintaining a true operational capability is made difficult as Marines rotate in and out, training deployments continue, the enlistments of Marines end, and cost caps are imposed that serve to reduce overall readiness. Fund limitations mean fewer operational deployments for training, and fewer deployments translates immediately to a lower level of operational readiness. Preparing a force reconnaissance company for war is *not* a simple matter of ordering in some men and some gear for a mission. Long-range reconnaissance work cannot be assigned to just "any" line unit from the infantry.

INDEX

Find out the whole story about
'Nam—from the swamp warrior
who served five tours in hell.

Death reigned as king in the
jungles of Vietnam. Gary R. Smith
and his teammates gave each other
the courage to attain the unattainable.

DEATH IN THE JUNGLE
Diary of a Navy SEAL

by Gary R. Smith and
Alan Maki

Published by Ivy Books.
Available in bookstores everywhere.

Follow the riveting, true-to-life account of survival and death in one of the most highly skilled units in Vietnam.

FORCE RECON DIARY, 1969

by
Bruce H. Norton

Published by Ivy Books.
Available in your local bookstore.

It began as a war to win—
and ended as a battle to survive.

VIETNAM, 1969–1970
A Company Commander's Journal

by Michael Lee Lanning

At twenty-three, Lanning was made company commander in Vietnam. One hundred men counted on him for their survival.

But lying ahead there would be blood, death, exhaustion, and, finally...pride.

VIETMAN, 1969–1970
A Company Commander's Journal
by Michael Lee Lanning

Published by Ivy Books.
Available in your local bookstore.

*They were the eyes and ears of the
1st Marine Division.*

FIRST RECON— SECOND TO NONE

A Marine Reconnaissance Battalion in Vietnam, 1967–68

by Paul R. Young

Paul Young was a schoolteacher and former enlisted
Marine whose only Recon experience had been as an
unenthusiastic enlisted man in the late 1950s at Camp
Pendleton. When the war in Vietnam heated up, he joined
the Marines, earned a commission, and volunteered for
duty in Vietnam as a grunt. But the day he got to
Vietnam, 1st Recon Battalion was hit badly, and what
the Marines needed was a Recon platoon leader. . . .

FIRST RECON—SECOND TO NONE

by Paul R. Young

Published by Ivy Books.
Available in bookstores everywhere.